THE   BEST   OF
Ad Campaigns!

THE BEST OF
Ad Campaigns!

Steve Blount and Lisa Walker

ROCKPORT PUBLISHERS

Distributed to the book trade
and art trade in the U.S.
and Canada by:
North Light, an imprint of
Writer's Digest Books
1507 Dana Avenue
Cincinnati, Ohio 45207
Telephone: (513) 984-0717

Distributed to the book trade
and art trade throughout the
rest of the world by:
Hearst Books International
105 Madison Avenue
New York, New York 10016
Telephone: (212) 481-0355

Other distribution by:
Rockport Publishers
5 Smith Street
Rockport, Massachusetts 01966
Telephone: (617) 546-9590
Telex: 5106019284
FAX: (617) 546-7141

ISBN 0-935603-09-3

Copyright © 1988 by Rockport
Publishers, Inc. All rights
reserved. No part of this book
may be reproduced in any form
whatsoever without the express
written permission of the
copyright owner:
Rockport Publishers, Inc
P.O. Box 396
5 Smith Street
Rockport, Massachusetts 01966

The Best of Ad Campaigns was
produced and prepared by
Blount & Company
12-A Station Road
Cranbury, New Jersey 08512

Jacket design by
Alton Cook
Freelance Ink
Tampa, Florida

The Best of Ad Campaigns!
was designed, pages
composed and type set on an
Apple MacIntosh ™ publishing
system. The type was output
via Allied Linotronic 100 by
Press Graphics/TW Inc. of
Montgomeryville, Pennsylvania.

PRINTED IN HONG KONG
10 9 8 7 6 5 4 3 2 1

CONTENTS

FOREWORD

Len Matthews

We hear a lot of criticism these days: that advertising is all technique and no talent, that there are no practitioners of the stature of an Ogilvy or a Bernbach, that there is little in the advertising world that is good. *Ad Campaigns!* tackles those criticisms head-on.

Ask ten people on the street what good advertising is and they may say that good advertising is entertaining or informative.

Ask ten advertising professionals to define good advertising and they'll likely talk about achieving a breakthrough and fulfilling creative potential.

Ask ten marketers about advertising and you'll hear one message: Good advertising sells.

Who's right? All of them, of course. At its best, advertising informs, entertains *and* sells. It achieves awareness for the client. It persuades. And occasionally, it goes beyond these definitions and touches a deeper, emotional chord.

By any of these definitions, there is plenty of good advertising being done today. This book captures some of the more notable examples. Much of what makes advertising "good" is arbitrary and depends on personal tastes and interests, so the selections in this book are necessarily arbitrary. However, they were chosen with the advice of the Creative Committee of the American Association of Advertising Agencies, a group whose members are among the very best the profession has to offer.

The advertising of today does differ in one significant respect from the work done back in what the critics call the "golden age"—it reflects a very different society with different goals, ambitions and attitudes. Like literature, art and music, advertising changes as its audience changes. It adapts to its environment. The work chosen for *Ad Campaigns!* is right because it is right for the client and right for its time. Carefully studied, these efforts offer a fortune of insight into what our age thinks is important and what motivates people to act. I hope they inspire you as much as they inspired me.

Len Matthews
President
American Association
of Advertising Agencies

A.A.A.A. Creative Committee 1987-1988

Burt Manning
J. Walter Thompson

Rich Badami
Phillips-Ramsey Inc.

Mike Becker
BBDO International Inc.

Fred Brownfeld
Patchen Brownfeld Inc.

Jeffrey W. Buntin
Buntin Advertising Inc.

Patrick J. Cunningham
N W Ayer Inc.

Frank DeVito
Lintas: New York

Gene Federico
Lord, Geller, Federico, Einstein, Inc.

Sean Kevin Fitzpatrick
Lintas: Campbell-Ewald

F. William Free
Laurence, Charles, Free

Amil Gargano
Ally & Gargano, Inc.

Marvin Honig
FCB/Leber Katz Partners

Richard Karp
Grey Advertising Inc.

John M. Keil
DFS Dorland Worldwide

Richard Levenson
D'Arcy Masium Benton & Bowles

Roger Livingston
Livingston & Company

John Neiman
McCann-Erickson USA

Kevin O'Keefe
The Sandler Group

James B. Patterson
J. Walter Thompson

Frazier Purdy
Young & Rubicam Inc.

Ronald M. Rosenfeld
Rosenfeld, Sirowitz & Humphrey Inc.

Charles F. Ruhr
Ruhr/Paragon Inc.

John J. Smith
Leo Burnett Company Inc.

Jay Schulberg
Ogilvy & Mather Worldwide, Inc.

Kurt Willinger
Saatchi & Saatchi Compton, Inc.

Bernard Ryan, Jr.
Secretary for A.A.A.A.

INTRODUCTION

For better or worse, advertising has become the predominant source of information. In the United States, the promotional budget of the biggest advertiser—Procter & Gamble—is larger than the combined budgets of the most influential news organizations—ABC, CBS and NBC—by a factor of better than three to one. Granted P&G has to pay to distribute its communications while network news budgets don't include the cost of the air time they consume. Still, the amount of money and energy brought to bear on advertising dwarfs that spent to create "informational" media: A senior copywriter is paid two to three times what a good newspaper desk editor makes. And the desk editor churns out hundreds of words for every syllable that trickles from the copywriter's word processor. In the contest for the public ear, traditional media are outmanned, outspent and outgunned by advertisers.

Responsibilities to the client—who foots the bill—aside, everyone in the business of advertising should aspire to create better communciations; if for no other reason than the fact that one day all of us will be old and the world will be left to the care of those who have grown up swimming in this vast sea of commercial messages. Their values, expectations and perceptions will be deeply affected by the world as viewed through the—properly—prejudiced eye of the commercial sponsor.

Ad Campaigns! is about people, clients and agencies who have aspired and about the success of their advertising.

Despite the moans of critics who lament the passing of what they call the profession's Golden Age, this moment is the most challenging in its history. True, there are few new symbols that compare in stature with the Marlboro Man or Commander Schweppes, but in this age of sixty-second celebrities the public may be too jaded, too media-wise to feel a lasting affinity for one-dimensional icons. Despite the kaleidoscopic profusion of products and messages, advertising has become less shrill, less demanding, more compelling and more entertaining. Examples of bad or at least mediocre advertising still abound, but the general quality of broadcast and print ads is slowly improving.

The direction of advertising appeals, the forms and messages that can persuade, have been shaped by this proliferation of product and media choices. There are few monopolies of goods or services. If the buyer isn't attracted by the *personality* of the product as portrayed through advertising, he buys from the competition. If network television or its advertising aren't to the consumer's taste, there are a welter of magazines and books, radio, cable, music videos and of course the videocassette recorder as alternatives. In this environment of choice, you score not by screaming, but by entertaining.

For an audience force-fed on the one-minute kitchen dramas of the 1960s, the three-x dramatic exposition of product attributes has no charm. It's dated, predictable and therefore boring. The appeals that persuade are subtle and they play to the senses: Sense of pride, sense of place and time, sense of nostalgia, sense of mystery; to the eye, the ear and the heart rather than to the head alone.

That demands a keen understanding of the audience's psychology and a high level of visual and verbal craftsmanship. Happily for advertisers and the health of the economy, the advertising profession is equal to that challenge.

None of the campaigns profiled here ask consumers to buy simply because the product is great. While some of the most powerful ideas as still simple ones, the execution of those ideas is as subtle, varied and complex as the people they address.

Surprisingly, less than half of the pieces included were produced in New York. California, both north and south, is well represented. But the regional leader in inventing and exploiting new forms of emotional appeal is the Midwest. The reason offered by Susan Gillette, executive vice president of DDB Needham in Chicago and creator of the current Michelob campaign, is that the area is not only America's heartland but the "gut" land as well. Midwesterners are a little more settled. They know what makes them feel good. And as a consequence, they can make the rest of us feel good too. More and more, they are learning to do it with pictures, music and allusions rather than with dialogue.

Humor has become the tool of choice for a large number of marketers. As writer/comedian/director David Steinberg explains in his interview (page 12), humor can give products great warmth if it's done right. There are plenty of examples of how good humor can equal good sales in six of the featured campaigns.

This book would not have been possible without the help and guidance of the American Association of Advertising Agencies, the members of its Creative Committee and in particular of its vice president, Bernie Ryan, and president, Len Matthews.

The visual materials, information and time generously donated by the advertisers and agencies represented here were extended graciously and with no motive other than to help further the craft of advertising.

Thanks are due to Jeff Williamson of BBDO New York for his great patience with numerous bothersome requests and especially for his substantial intellectual contributions to the tone and content of the commentary in this book.

Good books do not happen without the active involvement and dedication of good publishers. The staff of Rockport Publishers—Don Traynor, Stan Patey, Janet Traynor, Doris Patey and Marie Foss—played a major role in bringing this book into being.

To the editor who put *Ad Campaigns!* to bed, Lisa Walker, goes my greatest appreciation for saving me from the pitfalls of prepositional phrases and other sundry treacheries of the English language.

I hope you find the efforts of these good people worthwhile.

STEINBERG

A Funny Thing Happened
On The Way To The Marketplace

An epidemic of mirth has swept the airwaves in America. Humor, once considered a distraction in advertising, is now widely regarded as the most effective way to sell many products. One of its foremost proponents—and practitioners—is David Steinberg.

Steinberg is probably best known as the irreverent stand-up comedian whose sketches prompted CBS to cancel the *Smothers Brothers Show* in 1970. He had come to the show by way of the University of Chicago, the Hebrew Theological School and the Second City improvisational comedy group, which launched the careers of such artists as Mike Nichols, Elaine May, Alan Arkin, Joan Rivers and John Belushi. Steinberg won a Grammy for his comedy album *Booga Booga,* has been a frequent guest host on *The Tonight Show,* is a successful concert act, played several roles on Broadway and has directed two feature films (*Paternity* starring Burt Reynolds and *Going Berserk*). He's developing a new television series for Fox called *Duet,* and has directed a slew of other network shows including episodes of *Designing Women, The Golden Girls* and *The Bob Newhart Show*. David Steinberg knows from humor. He also knows advertising: Since 1985, he has directed television commercials for products including Miller Lite beer, NCR computers, ZipLock bags, Pizza Hut, Jell-O and Meisterbrau beer.

Why is humor an effective way to sell?

If humor is done properly it can foster all the things you want to do with a product through advertising. It can create warmth, make people like a product and it can be memorable.

Humor is the means by which Ronald Reagan—not a very, very bright man—manages to remain buoyant as president. He has charm and he has humor. His style is perception of strength, when in fact we don't know if he has any. Or a perception of wisdom where we don't know he has any. I'm a firm believer in the power of humor.

Some clients get nervous about putting up big money for a shoot when they're not sure the humor is right. Unfortunately, humor depends on individual taste. Even if the client likes a spot, he might be unsure of how the audience will react. How do you get around that?

You get around it with trust. It's hard for the client to trust the agency. And it's hard for the agency to trust the director. The thing I rail against most in advertising is research. Once you start to hedge by using research to formulate humorous concepts the humor instantly suffers because you're going to make a decision based on a committee's view of what's funny.

These compromises or hedges on

trust weaken the overall concept of a spot. Unfortunately, the nature of advertising is that it gives a lot of say to the clients, who don't know much about this sort of thing. How a director eases the client into the humor and eases them into having confidence in what he's doing with a spot is really as much a part of the artistry as the act of creativity itself. Research has its place, but not in the actual act of creativity. If it did, none of us would be working.

I don't like presenting this point of view because people on the other side of the argument say, "Well of course he feels that way. He's a comedian." But when I'm writing or directing a spot, I have to make it work. It has to be memorable and it has to make its point.

Clients worry that if a spot is truly funny the audience will remember the gag and not the product.

That only happens if the humor isn't handled right. If it's done well, they'll remember both.

There are so many products on the market that it's harder for people to remember your spot than ever before. That's a general problem and it's a shame to blame humor for the fact that the marketplace is crowded.

It's very hard to differentiate between a good product and a bad product, yet people have an uncanny ability to know

certain things. For the life of me, I can't figure out why Hyundai cars have been such a big success. There was some sort of underground word. How did people know instantly to stay away from Woody Allen's movie *September*?

There's a perception among advertising folks that if they could just make the leap to Hollywood, they wouldn't have to kowtow to the client and they could do terrific work. You work in both worlds. Are they right?

In the 1950s, there was a cartoon that showed two trains crossing in the Midwest; one is headed from Los Angeles to New York and the other from New York to Los Angeles. There's an actor on each train leaning out the window shouting to the other "Go back!" That's my feeling about advertising and show business.

The self-loathing advertising people feel comes from their perception that they aren't doing creative work, that they're being held back by all these limitations. You're always going to feel the pressure of limitations whether you're working on a feature film or a commercial.

The self-loathing seems odd to me because advertising doesn't feel less creative than any of the other things I do. I'm still offered features to direct. Shooting three-camera film is very complicated, very mathematical, because you're cutting the footage in your head as you direct. But when I'm directing commercials, it often feels more creative rather than less creative. The fact that you're selling a product in thirty seconds makes you simplify. Your choices have to be *exactly* right.

Is there an American style of humor?

What is generic to America that doesn't exist anywhere else is stand-up comedy. It's a pure American form, very much like jazz. When I was a kid, everyone wanted to grow up to be a rock star. Today, kids want to be stand-up comedians. I see that influence in a lot of commercials. They're in the *Saturday Night Live* smart-ass comedian style. And too often it isn't right for the character.

To be effective, that kind of humor has to come out of the personality of the comedian. Instead, the writers are translating that attitude into a character.

The Second City style of comedy, where *Saturday Night Live* came from, was never broad. When you played a broad character, you never played him broadly—you played him from the inside out. Bill Murray is not a broad comedian; he's sort of interior in a way. The writers don't do that when they script the commercials. If they want to do a Bill Murray character, he'll be drawn too archly—he'll be the lounge lizard that you've seen too much of.

Mark Twain had all the qualities of a stand-up comedian when he did his traveling lecture series. He was irreverent and edgy. People went to his performances to be titillated, to be shocked a little, and of course to be moved upward by his intellect.

I'm a strong believer in how much you can communicate with humor and how much you can communicate by *not* underestimating the intelligence of the audience. I think H.L. Mencken would be wrong today. People know a lot more than we give them credit for.

What strikes me about stand-up comedy is how intelligent it has to be—not elitist, but just how smart on any level it has to be—to engage an audience.

Joey Lewis was the first of the lounge comedians to do stand-up comedy. Every night he'd go to the Blue Angel or one of the other clubs that flourished in New York in the late 1940s. When his separation from his wife or his gambling were in the news, he'd talk about it on stage. He was the first comedian to do that, and people flocked to see him. But the word on him in the entertainment industry was that he was "too smart for the room," you couldn't play him outside of New York. They didn't trust the intelligence of the rest of the country. Of course, when he began playing outside of New York, he had his biggest success. The truth is that, if something is funny, it will work everywhere.

The other style of American humor is exemplified by Joe Seidelmeyer. Curiously, he has a more European style, he likes grotesqueries. That's not something I can do. I like my characters more than he does. That doesn't mean he's less funny in any way. That's just the way he paints, and it's brilliant and quite funny.

More often, though, I see the *Saturday Night Live* stand-up comedian influence coming out in advertising.

Unfortunately, it crops up in some very inappropriate places.

Yes, they haven't organized it yet. They haven't used it as a springboard to go to the next plane. The most important part of humor is appropriateness. The difference between someone who is professionally funny and an amateur who's quite funny is the appropriateness of their humor. Where you use a line and how you use it is the selectivity that amateurs lack.

I think the next level for advertising writers is to throw away the comedy a bit more, not lean on it so much. They can allow a phrase to penetrate the marketplace without having to lean on it. The mind set in advertising is that if you say it once it's good, but if you say it three times it's better. I feel that if it's good, say it a *half* of one time, give it enough focus in the commercial and repeat the spot enough. That might be the next level for advertising humor.

The Jell-O commercials I've been doing for Young & Rubicam are more subtle than anything I've done before. Bill Cosby's new commercials on the air are subtle. They're almost a bit vague and whimsical. I think they're very successful. You can watch them again and again and see different things in them. One of the reasons Cosby has been so successful as a product

spokesman is that he's one of the best stand-up comedians. He's able to translate himself onto video in all these McLuhanistic ways. And he's used to directing an immediate contact with the audience. When you put him in front of a camera, he connects. He just knows how to do it.

Doug Kenney, the former editor of National Lampoon, *once said that humor that's any good is going to offend someone. Are there limits on the use of humor?*

Any artistic point of view is going to exclude someone; humor is always going to offend someone. If you have a responsibility to a product, you should try to stay away from things that will offend *a lot* of people.

Charlie Chaplin wasn't offensive and he was very funny. But when he made *Modern Times,* suddenly he was parodying his audience and that got him into trouble.

I've collected a group of commercials that I think use humor the wrong way. I have some spots for a hotel chain which focus on the negative aspects of the opposing chain. There are no benefits to that kind of advertising whatsoever. By being negative, you only create negative imagery. That's not the right way to use humor. You don't want to be nasty.

You can work with anger though. The ability to sublimate anger is what most humor is all about. Cary Grant was one of the best light comedians of all time. In his movies, when he's angry, you never feel that the anger is going to erupt into visible anger. It's anger with a kind of protective shield around it. Cybill Shepard does that. When she plays anger it's humorous.

That's how you play things that otherwise might be perceived as nasty. When Jackie Gleason says, "I'm going to send you to the moon, Alice," you never feel for one second that woman is a battered wife. Not even when he makes a fist. But a lot of advertisers wouldn't use a Jackie Gleason if he came into their office as Ralph Kramden. They'd feel he was too nasty. That underestimates the audience's capacity for humor.

There is a difference between humor and satire, however. With satire, you presume that you and your audience hate the same things, and that's a dangerous assumption when you're doing advertising or any other form that has to play to a mass audience. If you want to do it in late-night television and you're willing to take a select audience it can work well.

Look at what's happened to the original cast of *Saturday Night Live*. They're very satirical and intelligent in the framework of *SNL*, but not one of them has done a movie that's really memorable. The movies that made them wealthy have nothing to do with anything intelligent. If they were satirical in their movies, it would alienate too many people.

The way to reach a mass audience is through general humor—to take the familiar and make it look just a little off-beat. Make the audience think, "Gee, I know what he means by that. I've had that thought. I'm that person," or "I've seen that person." Just that little bit of

recognition is the way you can make a spot indelible.

There are ways to broaden humor too. Like Joey Lewis, the Marx Brothers were also considered "too smart" for their audiences. *Duck Soup* and *Animal Crackers* were both very well received critically but they died in the hinterland. When the Marx Brothers moved to MGM, Irving Thalberg told them they'd made a mistake by making themselves the stars of those movies. He said to them, "You're still going to be the stars, but I'm going to have you support a love interest. We'll have Alan Jones and Kitty Carlisle and you'll make these two lovebirds come together. That's the formula audiences accept in movies." That was when their movies took off and made a fortune.

You have to be flexible. You can't say, "I think this is right because I think it's funny." Be flexible, but not because you think the audience can't get something, that they aren't smart enough. You have to determine whether they're used to a certain form and formula. If they are, fine, play off of that and sort of move them upward slowly.

You know something about pushing the limits of acceptability. Most people think your "sermonette" sketches got the Smothers Brothers cancelled in 1970. Were the Smothers Brothers too radical for network television?

They certainly wouldn't be radical by today's standards, but we were in the middle of the Vietnam War and they were making fun of Lyndon Johnson.

I feel differently about my stand-up comedy than I do about my directing. My directing is very middle class. I like contact with a large audience. But my stage wit is very acerbic. I'm satirical and very Jewish, all the things that aren't supposed to work for a mass audience—although I've defied those preconceptions throughout my career and have been accepted by a large audience. I knew that the sermon sketches were controversial, but we felt television was becoming so commonplace that if you didn't have an edge, you weren't going to penetrate. We just thought it was time to be edgy, to try it. We went ahead and I found myself on the front page of *The New York Times* one morning.

One humorous campaign in particular has upset a lot of people in the advertising business. What do you think of the Liar *spots for Isuzu?*

I think it's a good way to identify the product. Let the audience know that the people who sell this car are secure enough to have a sense of humor about their own product. That's a very subtle component of humor. You're letting them know that you don't have to compete by throwing out a lot of facts, that you have a sense of humor just like they do. The last execution they did—*Buckingham Palace*—was one I was supposed to direct and I just never got around to it. I thought it was done beautifully—David Leisure's delivery was wonderful.

What will the next breakthrough in advertising humor be?

The next level of humor won't be dumb humor; it will be smart. If the people it depicts aren't smart, then the concept has to be smart. You can see that kind of humor in shows like *Frank's Place*. They're getting more subtle, they're willing to trust the audience more. They're taking Woody Allen's formula from *Annie Hall*.

The thing they do with Levi's 401 jeans, that long-lens master shot without a close-up, you could do that same thing with comedy. You don't have to be so *close* to everything. A spot can be amusing without being jokey.

I imagine there will be a form of subtle salesmanship that will be successful. The unfortunate part of it is that when you breakthrough with quality, not everyone falls into line and does quality commercials. They almost regard these breakthrough successes as aberrant. But again, it's not just the advertising business. *On Golden Pond* made $90 million for Universal Studios, but they didn't do another film about people over 50 for the next eight years. Often, you're not set up for quality and you don't trust it when it works.

Despite the limitations, I like directing advertising. I get to work with tremendously talented people; the best there are, great art directors. It lets me work in the form I want to be working in. The nice thing about directing is that, like acting or writing, if you're doing a lot of it, you're getting better at it.

CAMPAIGNS

TBWA Creates An Absolut Success For Carillon

Client: Carillon Importers Ltd. USA
Agency: TBWA, Inc. New York

ABSOLUT

If there was ever a case to be made for the power of excellent print advertising, Absolut Vodka must be the archetypal example. The power part is easy to define: In 1979 Absolut was a struggling new imported vodka selling about 54,000 cases annually. In 1987, it was the number one imported vodka selling 1.6 million cases annually. While imported vodkas (Finlandia, Stolichnaya and Absolut at the head of the pack) have made dramatic gains against well-established American brands such as Smirnoff, imports are still only 5% of the total U.S. vodka market. But in those eight years, Absolut has grown more than 1750%, far outpacing the growth of the category and its competitors.

The second operative condition in this story is "excellent." Everyone agrees that the Absolut print ads, created by the New York office of agency TBWA, are excellent. But where does the seemingly endless fountain of new ideas originate?

According to the client, Michel Roux, president of Carillon Importers, the ideas come from a variety of people—Geoff Hayes, senior vice president of TBWA and the art director for the campaign, from Dick Costello, the agency's chief operating officer, from Roux himself and even from complete outsiders.

The credit for the very first ad, though, clearly goes to Geoff Hayes and copywriter Graham Turner. It was 1981, and TBWA had just inherited the account. The agency also inherited a campaign that wasn't working. Their solution, making the bottle the hero of the campaign by depicting it with props to form a visual pun, is certainly one near and dear to the hearts of many a brand manager. But it flew in the face of conventional wisdom about Absolut's position in the U.S. market. Even if the ad hadn't been terrific (it was), that fact alone probably would have convinced Roux to play along.

"We didn't have a big marketing department when we started," Roux explains. "We were 'streetwise' marketers. But we did spend $65,000 on a market study. The research showed that the name was all wrong, too gimmicky. The bottle was wrong, it was getting lost on the shelves in bars and liquor stores. The country of origin was wrong because consumers didn't think of Sweden as a producer of fine vodka. The researcher's conclusion was that we shouldn't even try to sell

ABSOLUT BRAVO.

ABSOLUT CLARITY.

Making the product the hero of a campaign is like saying you're in favor of motherhood. That TBWA was able to do it in such a compelling and creative way—not once but over and over again—is a powerful testimony to what can be done with single page magazine ads if you put your mind to it. The bottle was an unlikely hero, at best. Before the campaign was created, a researcher told client Carillon that the bottle was "invisible" on the shelves of bars and liquor stores. TBWA's ads have made it, and the accompanying visual puns, one of the best-recognized brand images in the U.S.

Of course, print ads are not made with photos alone. Carillon president Michel Roux commissioned Andy Warhol to create the painting opposite. Although the assignment made both Roux's own marketing people and the agency nervous, the piece was a stunning success. Not only visually but also through the implied endorsement of cult-figure Warhol, it successfully links Absolut with the sophisticated, high-fashion world of the avant garde artist.

Absolut in the U.S. We did just the contrary. We thought that, if everything was so bad, maybe we had a chance to do something with the brand."

The "invisible bottle" issue was on Hayes' desk when he proposed using the anonymous glass container to promote brand awareness. As he puts it, what he sold Carillon was brand registration and whimsy.

It is the whimsy—and the remarkable consistency of the campaign—that Roux bought.

"Although all of the ads are very different, all of them give the same message: That Absolut is a symbol," Roux says. "We are sending a message of smartness and sophistication. The consumer associates himself or herself with that symbol.

"In a subtle way, we tell consumers 'Absolut is something you need to be associated with if you are somebody in life.'

"The U.S. is a country of aspiration. People want to have a better life. Vodka has the same qualities as fine cognac. Of course, it takes longer to make fine cognac, but the quality of the craftsmanship is the same. That craftsmanship and the image we project give consumers self-confidence. They feel comfortable with the product; they feel good looking at it and they feel good consuming it."

Roux gives TBWA credit for creating the sensual look of the ads. The texture of the bottle, revealed and highlighted by the dramatic lighting, is central to the power of the images. Hayes, in turn, says that photographer Steve Bronstein has been the biggest contributor to the perfection evidenced in the print ads. While having a stark, almost severe simplicity, the photographs are very carefully and deliberately crafted still lifes.

The pieces Bronstein has created—from the falling roses for *Absolut Bravo* to the floating fish for *Absolut Treasure*—are master works of studio photography. The falling roses, you see, weren't actually falling. The blurring

effect was created in the camera. And the fish weren't really fish. They were models of fish carefully hung from the most evanescent of cord so that no matting would be required in the final chrome.

Such perfection costs money; lots of it. Reportedly, TBWA has spent up to $40,000 to create a single execution. That kind of budget requires trust. And evidently, there's quite a bit of trust and even something of a love affair between TBWA and Carillon because they say such nice things about each other.

"Many times an agency will try to impose things on a client, but TBWA doesn't do that," Roux says. "They come in with their ideas, and they really believe in what they're bringing us, but at the same time, they listen. They accept our constructive criticism very well. Sometimes they work to perfect our ideas, sometimes we help perfect theirs. We have a middle ground where we both try to come to a positive conclusion. So far, we haven't had a crisis where we've had complete disagreement."

It was Roux's brainstorm, for example, to extend the campaign beyond photographs and into the world of fine art by commissioning a painting by the late avant garde artist Andy Warhol. Not everyone involved thought it was a good idea.

"My marketing department thought it was risky and the agency thought it was risky, but I didn't think it was too risky," Roux chuckles. "We are projecting an image that is stylish and fashionable. I had known Andy Warhol for some time, and he was setting trends in fashion. I felt that whatever he did, it might be controversial, but it would be recognized as sophisticated. It did work, and the rest is history."

The "history" Roux refers to is the series of fine art commissions that followed the appearance of *Absolut Warhol* ads illustrated by Keith Haring and Kenny Scharf.

"There are many ways to be innovative. Some are more risky

ABSOLUT WARHOL.

than others. For another of our products, I had photographer Helmut Newton shoot a scene in Paris. Two women are in a room drinking the product. It was a very provocative picture, *very* ambiguous. We had a lot of people who reacted to that. I think that was risky, an example of something I wouldn't have tried with Absolut."

Despite moving from a position where the brand had nothing to lose by being outrageous to being the category leader, Roux says he doesn't want to forget the "wild and reckless" ways that put the brand on the map. With $17 million to play with over the next year, TBWA should be able to accommodate him. A lot of clients say they want to be a leader. The difference with Carillon, the agency says, is that Roux "puts his money where his mouth is," and is willing to experiment with new techniques and new vehicles.

Absolut was the first liquor advertiser to appear in *Spy*, *Details* and *Elle*. The magazines have even had a hand in dreaming up new executions. A 1988 issue of *Spy*, for example, will carry a spread that includes a set of watercolors at the bottom of the right page. Readers will be encouraged to grab a paintbrush and complete the ad themselves.

Roux says they're also looking at crystal designers. "Why not an *Absolut Lalique*, or even an *Absolut Steuben* if it was possible?"

Along with proving that print ads can, in fact, push sales, this campaign proves another old saw: Clients get the advertising—and perhaps the advertising agency —they deserve. Michel Roux (or Michael Rocks as linguistically unsophisticated Americans sometimes call him) is a self-assured, street-wise client; Geoff Hayes is a transplanted South African with the bushy red hair, wild eyes and mustache of a proper English eccentric. As the fruit of their efforts prove, these two are a marriage made in heaven. Absolut heaven, no doubt.

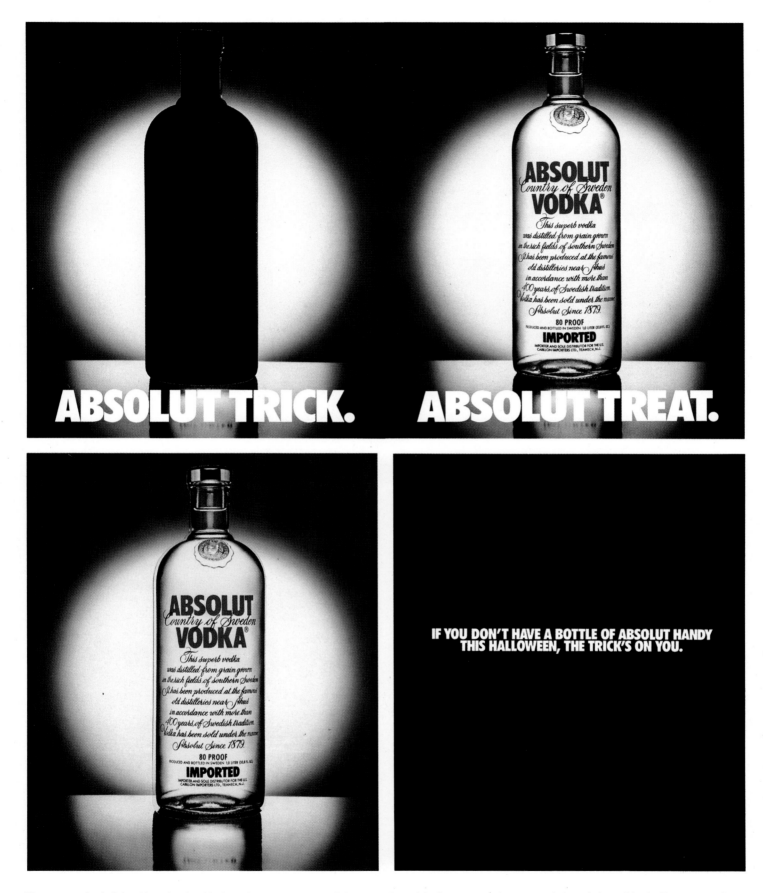

The once-invisible Absolut bottle has become so well-known that this four-page insert makes a joke of it. A die-cut on the front panel allows readers to see the bottle, which is printed on page three. When opened, the visual suggests that if the viewer is missing Absolut, he's missing it all.

Call them gimmicks if you will, but the Absolut archives are filled with more tricks than a magician's trousseau. For *Absolut Treasure*, model maker Ray Mendez fabricated a school of tropical fish. Photographer Steve Bronstein required the models because he felt that shooting the ad in an aquarium would diffuse the sharp image of the bottle. An exception to Bronstein's penchant for getting difficult shots on a single piece of film is *Absolut Masterpiece*. The trick was to make it appear that the painter's hand is rendering a finished bottle with a single stroke. The effect was created by matting together images of the hand holding the brush against a white canvas, an image of black brushstrokes on a white background and finally the bottle. Such forays into the world of illusion aren't cheap; one execution, an image of the bottle embossed on white paper, cost $40,000 to produce.

Whatever your taste in art, the money spent on Kenny Scharf (opposite) was well worth it. Scharf doesn't thrill us with the technique of a Picasso, but he doesn't need to. The point is in the humor of his illustration. Check out his interpretation of the portrait embossed on the neck of the bottle and of the wording on the label. Carillon offered lithos of Scharf's painting at $150 per copy. When you can hire someone to illustrate your product and then sell the illustrations for $150 a pop, you know you're doing something right.

ABSOLUT SCHARF.

The trick to *Absolut Rainbow* was a physical one. The agency left room for magazines to print editorial between the two images, giving the effect of a rainbow crossing over the top of a page and down onto the other side of the spread. There's no trick to artist Keith Haring's rendering of Absolut (opposite). Haring, a New York City street artist who became a celebrity, is another example of Absolut's approach to being a category leader. If style is your territory, it must pay to have a French client. Roux has also suggested using trendy fashion designers, such as David Cameron, in the campaign. Everyone who has ever worked for a client who thought Norman Rockwell was the crown prince of contemporary American art can begin eating their hearts out now.

ABSOLUT HARING.

Keye/Donna/ Pearlstein's Spreads Reposition The Californias

CALIFORNIA

Client: California Department of Commerce
Agency: Keye/Donna/Pearlstein

What happens when you give a party and nobody comes? If you're the California Department of Commerce and the party is the Olympics, you rethink your advertising strategy. That led the Department to another question: What do you do when you go to review your advertising and find that you have none? Quick, somebody hire an agency. Enter Paul Keye and Keye/Donna/Pearlstein.

"At the time we picked up the assignment they really weren't advertising," Paul Keye explains. "They thought 1984, the year the Olympics were held in Los Angeles, would be a huge year for tourism but it turned out to be quite ordinary. That's when they realized they had this problem. The state had always viewed tourism as its birthright, but it had gotten quite flat. People have so many choices of places to travel and there are many other entities competing for the same travel dollars."

And travel dollars, like petro-dollars, are something every state lusts after in its heart. Tourism employs the least employable. It's a cash business. It doesn't tax government services; tourists don't use a lot of hospitals or jails. It generally doesn't degrade the environment. Most tourists want a place to look like it did before they got there. Some of them will actually make an effort to pick up after themselves.

There are a number of problems you can have when you pick up an account. The product may be totally unknown because it hasn't been advertised. That's bad because you have find a way to make enough noise so people will notice you. It's good, though, if you have an interesting story. It's new information, and people will stop a bit and listen. The obverse problem occurs when the product is very well known. That's good because you start from a high base of awareness. It's also bad because it's hard to get people to pay attention—they think they already know the product.

Or you could have a third problem, which may be the worst of all possible worlds: A well-known product that hasn't been advertised,

"Toto, I've got a feeling we're not in Kansas anymore."

It's a theme park—a seven hundred and eighty-six square mile theme park—and the theme is "you can have anything you want."

It's the most California-looking of all the Californias: the most like the movies, the most like the stories, the most like the dream.

Orange County is Tomorrowland and Frontierland, merged and inseparable. 18th century mission. 1930s art colony. 1980s corporate headquarters.

There's history everywhere: navigators, conquistadors, padres, rancheros, prospectors, wildcatters. But there's so much Now, the Then is hard to find. The houses are new. The cars are new. The stores, the streets, the schools, the city halls—even the land and the ocean themselves look new.

The temperature today will be in the low 80's. There's a slight offshore breeze. Another just-like-yesterday day in paradise.

Come to Orange County. It's no place like home.

When the swallows come back to Capistrano it will be Saint Joseph's Day, 19th of March. At least it always has been.

If you were born to shop, welcome to heaven. We're talking world class shopping here, folks.

They come from the ends of the earth to surf this coast: Huntington. State Park. Trestles. The Wedge. Newport Pier. Awesome.

Pacific Coast Highway
Buena Park
Anaheim
Huntington Beach
Newport Beach
Laguna Beach
Dana Point
San Clemente

Orange County: One of The Californias.

How began the boysenberry? Scholars, men of science vary. (Rasp and black and logan blending. Pie for Sunday dinner ending.) Most would credit Walter Knott for making Boysen's berry hot.

This isn't the only place where you keep your boat in the backyard. But here the backyard goes to Tahiti.

Californias, here I come!
Now there's a free pocket guide that takes a fresh look at California—divides it into a dozen different regions, each with its own special surprises.
Call toll-free 1-800-CALIF-85 Ext. 637, or write for yours today.
California Office of Tourism, P.O. Box 9278, Dept. T6-37, Van Nuys, CA 91409

THE CALIFORNIAS

Name _____
Address _____
City _____ State _____ Zip _____

which was the situation facing Keye/Donna/Pearlstein.

"There aren't many products as well known as California," Keye says. "Gillette razors. Coca-Cola. Chevrolet and Ford. So if you say to someone, 'let me tell you about California,' you could be in the Congo or in Cleveland but they're going to say the same thing: 'I know all about California.' That's because we've had seventy years of movies and almost fifty years of television about California."

According to Keye, the publicity began a lot earlier.

"The name California came from a 16th century Spanish novel, a potboiler, about a mythical place named California. When the Spanish hit the west coast of North America in 1510, they called this place California. It has that kind of magic, which is enhanced by the weather, all the things we know about the Gold Rush, Western movies and so on."

Sounds like the underpinnings of a pretty good campaign, right? Unfortunately, Keye says, most of those things had been reduced to

"a set of repeatable icons: swimming pools, beaches, the Golden Gate Bridge, Hollywood." So what's wrong with that? If you've got a product with that recognizable imagery going for it, what's the problem? As Keye saw it, there were two.

First, California has just about everything a tourist could want, so a lot of other states have usurped those icons for their own advertising. By being everybody's image of California, the ads would end up looking like what New Jersey might run.

Second, like most symbols, the well-understood icons grossly oversimplify the place. It's no secret that California is atypical, but have you ever pondered how different San Francisco is from San Pedro? California is an enormous place—you could fit Ohio, Illinois and Indiana inside its borders and still have enough room left over to squeeze in most of Pennsylvania. North to south it stretches from the latitude of Chicago all the way down to that of Selma, Alabama. Add the

No, California isn't Kansas. And the campaign created by Keye/Donna/Pearlstein for the California Department of Commerce isn't much like any other state tourism advertising being done. While not solely a print effort—it was kicked off with television and outdoor—copywriter Paul Keye feels the twelve spreads featured on the succeeding pages are the heart of the campaign. The basic idea was to reposition the state (no earthquake jokes, please) as a collection of destinations rather than a monolithic entity.

What's going on here, anyway?

Welcome to The Land of New.

El Pueblo de Nuestra Señora la Reina de Los Angeles. The Town of Our Lady, the Queen of the Angels. The city beyond words. Initials only, please. "L.A."

L.A. Its mother was a movie. Its father was a car.

L.A. From the people who brought you The No-Sweat Olympics, Rodeo Drive, sunshine, shades, Beach Boys, Valley Girls, Norma Jean, Lucy, Beverly Hills Cop and avocado sushi.

Ninety-five cities with a mountain range through the middle. Oz with a beach. Five world class art collections: The County, The Getty, the Norton Simon, the Huntington and the astonishing new Contemporary.

Gawk. Tan. Bike. Surf. Skate. Nosh. Splurge. Kick back. Mellow out. Get down. Lighten up.

Rock with the stars at The Bowl. Catch Ringo's star on The Boulevard. Taste a 3-star. Beachwalk under a billion stars.

Welcome to L.A. Welcome to Tomorrow. Soon to be Today in a city near you.

What if Betsy Ross had sewn television sets? See Video Flag z at the Los Angeles County Museum of Art.

Santa Barbara to Long Beach. More than a hundred miles of breakers, coves, cliffs, dunes and an occasional one-owner castle.

Concerts. Improv. Cool sounds. Hot ticket. Symphonies. Stand-up comics. Don't laugh. It could be you.

Malibu

Sunset Boulevard. Twenty-seven miles of drive-through history.

Hollywood
Sunset Strip
Westwood
Beverly Hills
Bel Air

To those of you who have said, "Dining is theatre," welcome to Front Row Center.

Sheet metal Gothic. Oedipus Wrecks. Classic. Import. Indy specs. Convertible. 4x4. Limousine. Bus. This is L.A., friend. Cars R Us.

Where were you when the cowboy flew out the window? Hollywood, of course.

Californias, here I come!
Now there's a free 144-page travel guide that takes a fresh look at California — divides it into a dozen different regions, each with its own special surprises.

Name

Address

City

State   Zip

Call toll-free 1-800-TO-CALIF, Extension 820A, or write for yours today:
California Office of Tourism, P.O. Box 9278, Dept. T8-20A, Van Nuys, CA 91409

The Californias

Los Angeles: One of The Californias.℠

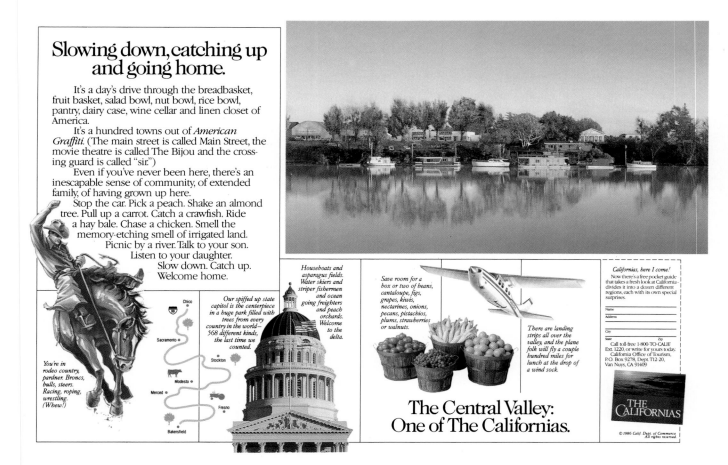

The campaign does offer some of the familiar things we've come to expect: Gorgeous four-color photos, splashy backdrops, vivid colors. It also offers something we haven't been treated to often enough: Killer copy. Read the fine print of these ads. Keye's recipe seems to be one part *Encyclopedia California*, one part tongue in cheek and one part poetry. Keye's verse is really charming. If he'd chosen a more sedate existence, he might have had quite a career as a lit professor.

variety of topography and about as many climatic zones as there are in the whole of the rest of the country and you get a feeling for the diversity. Kind of makes you wonder how they ever agree on somebody to be governor. Well, Californians did elect Ronald Reagan and Jerry Brown in the same decade.

Paul Keye saw opportunity in that diversity.

"In order to point out the enormous diversity we did what advertising agencies always want to do: We renamed the product and called it 'The Californias,'" Keye says.

"What that means to even the least curious person is 'Oh, I guess there's more than one California.' You know you have a good idea when there's a kind of closure on the idea," Keye says.

The idea of the Californias made sense for other reasons as well. Half of the tourists in California are Californians. And they don't know much more about California than people from New York or Iowa. That's because

half the people in California moved there from someplace like New York or Iowa.

"With this campaign, we tried to go past the bromides and talk about the state as if we were talking about Finland or Sri Lanka," Keye asserts.

"If you were one of the people who came through during the service, sometime between 1945 and 1970—on your way to the Pacific Theater, Korea, Vietnam— you could say, 'Yeah, I was in California.' I went to China about ten years ago. I saw Shanghai and Beijing. But I can't really say I saw China because of the enormity of the culture and the history. That was the first thing we wanted to say: 'No you probably haven't been to California.'

"To talk about multiplicity, to talk about detail and texture, we divided the state into twelve regions and wrote an ad about each. I'm a native Californian and I know a good bit about the state. The twelve regions are quite logical. Only one is a bit artificial, the one we call the Inland Empire,

I love Perris in the springtime.

The first thing you learned about California was:
"It's a place where you can ski down a mountain, dive in an ocean, tan your body in the desert sun, and dine in a fancy, big city cafe. All on the same day."
True. But you have to be in the right California. Here, in the Inland Empire. You've probably been through here. This is where most of the world came to California first: on the Spanish Trail, on the Butterfield Stage, on the Atchison, Topeka & Santa Fe, on the freeway.
And what did the folks around here do when they met you? They gave you a big smile, a helping hand and sent you on your way, right?
And all you missed was a hundred gorgeous little towns with lots of country in between. All you missed was two centuries of history, valleys full of orange groves, hillsides covered with vineyards, a dozen championship golf courses—some with as many as twenty players on them—and mountain lakes, mountain meadows and mountain folks.
If you'd like to see the California that Californians saved for themselves, come to the Inland Empire.

Perris is Southern California headquarters for thermals and updrafts—the stuff that balloon rides are made of.

You want to get into show business? Move to Hemet. Ramona, the annual springtime pageant of Early California, has openings for 350 actors.

Blessings on thee, yuppie camper. Stemware, brie and wicker hamper. Picnic mid the gourmet wine. Where Two Fifteen hits Seventy Nine.

Arrowhead
Big Bear
San Bernardino
Riverside
Redlands
Perris
Lake Elsinore
Temecula
San Diego

Discover Winter a la Carte. Spend the day at Big Bear or Lake Arrowhead. Then come on down the mountain in time for an evening swim.

Most towns around here have an elegant Victorian gingerbread house or two, built by the folks who planted the first orchards and turned orange juice into gold.

The Inland Empire: One of The Californias.

Californias, here I come!
Now there's a free pocket guide that takes a fresh look at California— divides it into a dozen different regions, each with its own special surprises.

Name
Address
City
State   Zip
Call toll free 1-800-TO-CALIF Ext. 1038, or write for yours today. California Office of Tourism, P.O. Box 9278, Dept. T10-38, Van Nuys, CA 91409

THE CALIFORNIAS

Behold. The Middle Kingdom.

It's not on the way to anywhere else. The nearest superhighway is a mountain range away. You don't drive along the central coast; you enter it.
South, out of San Francisco at the Presidio, past Half Moon Bay, through a corridor of carnations and roses and strawberries and wetlands. Past the funky towns and fancy waterholes that rim Monterey Bay.
South, past the Carmel mission, to Big Sur. (In most of the world, by some prior agreement, oceans and mountains stay away from one another. But at Big Sur they meet head on, and the first thousand feet of shore line is straight down.)
Suddenly, San Simeon. Ceilings from Italy, carpets from Persia, royalty from Hollywood. Wow.
South again, along an epilogue of easygoing beach road designed to send you on your way. Just below Morro Bay the road turns, the ocean vanishes, the land closes in behind you, and you're back in the outside world.

For a free pocket guide to all The Californias, write: Office of Tourism, P.O. Box 9278, Dept. T1-20, Van Nuys, CA 91409

Forget the map. Read Steinbeck. People will think you're a native.

Bring your sticks. Pebble Beach and Spyglass are public courses. Not free. Public. Bring money, too.

No other thistle Makes gourmets whistle Like this'll.

The Monterey Bay Aquarium is the newest, largest, spiffiest in the world. There's a kelp cathedral, a giant reef and a gang of baby otters that were raised on a waterbed.

The Hearst Castle, home of America's first media mogul. Take a day to see it; it took a lifetime to build.

They named a Festival after it. No place has jazz like Monterey has.

San Francisco
Santa Cruz
Watsonville
Monterey
Carmel
Salinas
Big Sur
San Simeon
San Luis Obispo

The Central Coast: One of The Californias.

Astonishments, contradictions and miracles.

You're chasing a little white ball across the high pile carpet of a world class golf course. Next to a cactus forest. You're floating in a swimming pool. At the foot of a snow-covered mountain.

Welcome to the California desert. You'll never see as many things as clearly.

You can see a cactus bloom across a canyon. You can see a jet trail, hanging like lace six miles above you. Everything in sight is etched, outlined. Everything is foreground.

And you'll never miss so much. Now you see it; now you don't.

There's a lost gold mine around here. Somewhere. Over that hill, maybe.

A cloudburst dropped a ton of water on the tennis court an hour ago, but now it's bone dry.

That mountainside of poppies wasn't there last week.

You're riding a bike through a grapefruit orchard. A hundred yards from a prehistoric oyster bed.

Welcome to the desert, the land of a million moments.

Everybody loves a show-off, especially a Mojave springtime field full of wild primroses.

The desert's favorite eccentric, the roadrunner. Want to guess what family he belongs to? Right. The cuckoo family.

Presidents & Other Residents: Eisenhower Place, Gerald Ford Drive, Wayne Road, Autry Trail. In Hollywood they give you a star. In the desert resorts, you can have a whole street.

BOB HOPE DR RANCHO MIRAGE

FRANK SINATRA DR RANCHO MIRAGE

If 7,435 swimming pools were lined up side by side, you'd be in Palm Springs

Californias, here I come!
Now there's a free pocket guide that takes a fresh look at California— divides it into a dozen different regions, each with its own special surprises.

Name

Address

City

State   Zip

Call toll-free 1-800-TO-CALIF Ext. 920A or write for yours today.
California Office of Tourism, P.O. Box 9278, Dept. T9-20A, Van Nuys, CA 91409

West of Needles. South of Daggett. Opal, garnet, bloodstone, agate. Grab a rock in East Newberry. See your local lapidary.

Sand dune to snow pack. Sahara to Switzerland. Up 8,500 feet, down 40 degrees, in 14 minutes. Next time, take the tram.

The Deserts:
One of The Californias.℠

THE CALIFORNIAS

the area between L.A. and the desert."

With the strategy settled, it was time for the real work—actually writing the ads. Actually, Paul Keye wrote the ads. And did it brilliantly. It didn't happen one enchanted evening.

"I think the client thought I was going to sit down one day and write the ads," he chuckles. "It took the better part of two years to finish the series with the people in the tourism department kind of grinding their teeth. I wanted each ad to have a kind of stand-alone individuality, and that ain't making sausage. That takes time."

Keye is philosophical about that. He's also philosophical about the kind of consensus-gathering that sometimes accompanies tourism accounts.

"Budgets for tourism advertising are not in and of themselves economic decisions," he explains. "They're really political decisions. There are a lot of people in this state who would be absolutely appalled if they knew we were spending the taxpayers' money to get more people out here. They can't get home on the freeways as it is. If we'd said, 'We want to take some money and spend it like this,' we'd probably have gotten a reaction like, 'Boy is that a stupid idea.'

"I think the better tourism campaigns, the ones that are memorable, happen when someone is able to collect the political will and then just goes out and does it. The *I Love New York* campaign is archetypal in that respect. After it started running it got all these owners and fathers. That's happening with this campaign.

"You wouldn't believe the number of convention bureaus there are—each supplied with its own squeaky wheel. This job was done very quickly. It was out there and the cement was dry before we could get a lot of help with it. Now that it's done, we're getting lots of help—phalanxes of help."

Although not primarily conceived as a print campaign, the print ads are by far Keye's favorite element in the mix, which includes some television executions and outdoor as well.

The television spots he calls electronic postcards. That may have something to do with his bias about video: "My feeling is that you can take thirty seconds of film about open heart surgery and make it interesting. Television is a form of communications that I don't happen to like, but it works swell."

The print insertions have been concentrated in high-demographic travel books. "As an economic matter, we don't want back-packers," Keye points out. "We just want rich folks to come out here and spend a lot of money and then leave. If they'd just mail a check, that would be okay too."

The campaign gets an added boost from co-op placements by airlines, hotel chains and travel agencies. In Seattle, the state of California advertising is actually run by Alaska Airlines. In Chicago, by United. In New York, TWA. Sometimes they buy all the media. In some cases, Keye/Donna/Pearlstein runs two weeks of television and the airlines pick up two weeks. It multiplies the several million dollars of taxpayers' money the state has put behind the campaign very nicely.

Although precise figures are hard to come by, the effort has bulked up the numbers of foreigners (those of us from the other 49 states are included in that pejorative term) pouring across the borders. That's made the Department of Commerce happy. It's even made the squeaky wheels at the convention bureaus happy.

And working on the campaign has made Paul Keye happy. Sort of a revenge factor. "I went to school in the East. I was in the service. Then I worked in New York. For years I had to listen to all that tedious B.S. about fruits and nuts [as in 'Why is California like a bowl of granola...what isn't fruits and nuts are flakes']. This gave me the chance to print a few facts about California's history and culture; something those yahoos didn't know a thing about."

Well, they know now.

The Indians won.

It's a very special corner of the world—the top, right-hand corner of California—above the valleys, past the cities, away from the crowd. Welcome to Shasta Cascade.

This is the land of the eagle and the bear, of Brewer's Spruce and Ponderosa Pine and Incense Cedar, of steelhead and salmon, ice caves and lava tubes and huge wild rivers that hide in the forests.

The only Indian war in California was fought here in 1873. Fifty-three Modoc braves took on the United States Army. And won. (It wasn't a victory they enjoyed for long, progress being what it was in those days. But they won. You can look it up.)

There are enormous man-made water skiing–bass fishing–houseboating lakes here. There's a shrine the Chinese built a century ago. And rock paintings that someone made a thousand years ago. But, most of all, there is the land as it was.

If you've ever wondered what the world would be like if the Indians had won, come to Shasta Cascade.

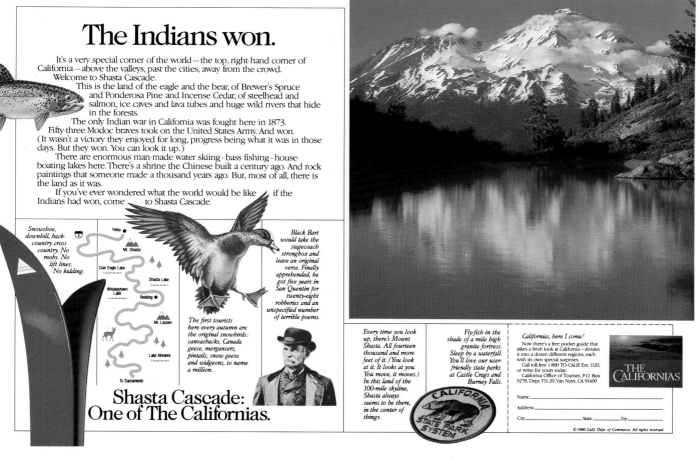

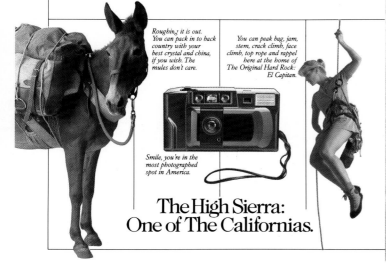

Snowshoe, downhill, back-country cross country. No mobs. No lift lines. No kidding.

Yreka
Mt. Shasta
Clair Engle Lake
Shasta Lake
Whiskeytown Lake
Redding
Mt. Lassen
Lake Almanor
To Sacramento

The first tourists here every autumn are the original snowbirds: canvasbacks, Canada geese, mergansers, pintails, snow geese and widgeons, to name a million.

Black Bart would take the stagecoach strongbox and leave an original verse. Finally apprehended, he got five years in San Quentin for twenty-eight robberies and an unspecified number of terrible poems.

Shasta Cascade: One of The Californias.

Every time you look up, there's Mount Shasta. All fourteen thousand and more feet of it. (You look at it. It looks at you. You move, it moves.) In this land of the 100-mile skyline, Shasta always seems to be there, in the center of things.

Fly-fish in the shade of a mile high granite fortress. Sleep by a waterfall. You'll love our user-friendly state parks at Castle Crags and Burney Falls.

CALIFORNIA STATE PARK SYSTEM

Californias, here I come!
Now there's a free pocket guide that takes a fresh look at California—divides it into a dozen different regions, each with its own special surprises.
Call toll-free 1-800-TO-CALIF Ext. 1120, or write for yours today:
California Office of Tourism, P.O. Box 9278, Dept. T11-20, Van Nuys, CA 91409

THE CALIFORNIAS

Name _____
Address _____
City _____ State _____ Zip _____

Don't just sit there. Do something!

Ski a thousand miles of powder. Fly down a river. Walk on a cloud. Ride a horse. Catch a trout. Sleep in the sky. Go jump in a lake.

Come to the High Sierra, the big island in the sky.

Four hundred miles long. One mile high. Or higher. Three national parks, eight national forests, five national wildernesses, a thousand lakes.

Rediscover your nose. You know. That whatchamacallit in the middle of your face. Your nose. You could learn to tell the difference between pine and cedar and redwood with your eyes closed.

Camp out. Pack in. Sail, schuss, soak. Yell down a mountain. Hear your heart. Memorize a million stars.

Read John Muir. "God always seems to be doing His best here."

Mammoth Lakes and Tahoe and Central Sierra. And downhill and cross country. Two hundred and twelve ski lifts and tows.

Lake Tahoe
Yosemite National Park
Mammoth Lakes
Kings Canyon National Park
Sequoia National Park
Owens Lake
Mt. Whitney

The 212 miles of the Pacific Crest Trail from Yosemite to Mount Whitney is called the John Muir Trail. Nice name.

Californias, here I come!
Now there's a free pocket guide that takes a fresh look at California—divides it into a dozen different regions, each with its own special surprises.

Name _____
Address _____
City _____
State _____ Zip _____
Call toll-free 1-800-CALIF-85 Ext. 819, or write for yours today.
California Office of Tourism, P.O. Box 9278, Dept. T8-19, Van Nuys, CA 91409

THE CALIFORNIAS

Roughing it is out. You can pack in to back country with your best crystal and china, if you wish. The mules don't care.

You can peak bag, jam, stem, crack climb, face climb, top rope and rappel here at the home of The Original Hard Rock: El Capitan.

Smile, you're in the most photographed spot in America.

The High Sierra: One of The Californias.

The Russians were here! The Russians were here!

Have you ever made the only footprints on a beach? Have you ever stood in a forest, in the middle of a thousand square miles of silence?

Come to the North Coast. It's not another part of California. It's another time.

Breakfast is steak and three eggs. Sun tans stop at the wrist. Boats are wood. Experience counts. Work is outside: timber, fishing, dairy farming, ranching. Inside is for fireplaces and talk with that new couple who moved here twelve years ago.

The Russians came in 1812 and stayed for about thirty years. But when the sea otter and the fur seal began to disappear, they picked up their samovars and went home.

Did you ever fight a twelve pound steelhead? Would you like to meet the artist whose painting you just bought?

Come to the North Coast. And bring a friend.

For a free pocket guide to all The Californias, write: Office of Tourism, P.O. Box 9278, Dept. T3-22, Van Nuys, CA 91409

The New Englanders took one look at this coastline, and knew they were home. (Except that the sun ran backwards.)

Fort Ross. The commandant's wife was a princess. Really. Princess Helena Gargarin Kuskov. She brought a grand piano and left a rose garden.

What has eight legs and a huge smile? Your family and a table full of Dungeness crab.

Bed & Breakfast & More Breakfast. Wood fire. Kerosene lamp. Down pillow. Were we going somewhere today?

One of the original residents, the Sequoia Sempervirens. Been here since the dinosaurs.

The North Coast: One of The Californias.

Skinny roads, fat skies and ghosts.

The roads are wider than the first wagon trails, wider than the old railroad rights of way. But not by much.

The big highways are the original ones: the Tuolumne, Merced, American and Stanislaus rivers that tumble out of the Sierra toward the Pacific.

In 1848, four hundred settlers came here, to farm, to trap. In 1849, ninety thousand showed up. They'd heard about gold.

No people on earth left a better written history than the Forty-Niners. It's all there in the names of the gold towns:

Rough & Ready. Confidence. Snow Tent. Poison Lake. Poverty Hill. French Corral, Chinese Camp, Spanish Dry Diggings. Dutch Flats.

Have you ever panned for gold? Or walked into a saloonful of Tiffany glass? Or slept in a hundred year old bed?

Have you ever wondered about Californians — about their exasperating optimism?

Come see where it all began.

For a free pocket guide to all The Californias, write: Office of Tourism, P.O. Box 9278, T2-20, Van Nuys, CA 91409

Follow the tracks to Sacramento and see the best railroad museum in the world.

It's right up the road from Red Dog, You Bet, Poker Flat, Port Wine, Brandy Hill, Drytown, Hangtown and Priest Hill.

FIDDLETOWN
POP. 150   ELEV. 1687

The first miners were mostly just a flash in the pan. Then the pros moved in—hard rock miners from Wales and Cornwall and Ireland.

The Celebrated Jumping Frog, resting between celebrations at his estate in Calaveras.

Classic, classy and kitsch. Don't throw anything away around here. You'll hit an antique store.

Whitewater rafting comes in three delicious flavors: Nice, Scary and Insane.

The Gold Country: One of The Californias.

If it's Tuesday, this must be Tiburon.

Chinatown. Russian Hill. Japanese Tea Center. Ghirardelli Square. Treasure Island. Golden Gate. Baghdad by the bay.

Come to The City and see the world.

Talk to a chimpanzee. Eat some dim sum. Hang out in an all-paperback bookstore. Wave to an ocean liner. Buy a balloon and give it back to the sky.

Side trip to the Russian River. Overnight in the wine country. Day trip down the peninsula to the redwoods.

Concert in Stern Grove. Murals in Coit Tower. Sundown at Seal Rocks. Cable car to Fisherman's Wharf. Jazz at the pier. Bogart movie. Street mimes. Espresso and gelato in North Beach. Dancing. Sunrise breakfast on Powell Street.

Don't stop. You'll miss something.
You can sleep when you get home.

Our most regular visitors come by twice a year. (Just mom and dad in the Winter; the whole family in the Spring.)

If (for some weird and inexplicable reason) you don't like French bakeries, you'll have to choose among German, Greek, Italian, Russian or Mexican bakeries.

Use a ticket, go to prison. Boats leave from Pier 41 for the infamous Alcatraz Island.

You'll never be closer to London. Jack London. *The Sea Wolf, The Call of the Wild, Martin Eden.* He grew up right over there, in Oakland.

You haven't heard about the Garlic Festival in Gilroy? It's...well... it's breathtaking.

If you're tired of walking, try running. You'll never find a nicer place to pull a muscle than Golden Gate Park.

All roads lead to the wine countries—Napa, Sonoma, Santa Clara Valley, Lake County, Mendocino. Salute!

Golf Course (9 holes) · Golden Gate Park Stadium · Spreckels Lake · DeYoung Museum · Murphy's Windmill · Strawberry Hill · Hall of Flowers · Conservatory · Steinhart Aquarium · Kezar Stadium

Californias, here I come!
Now there's a free 144-page travel guide that takes a fresh look at California—divides it into a dozen different regions, each with its own special surprises.

Name
Address
City
State   Zip
Call toll-free 1-800-TO-CALIF yours today:
California Office of Tourism, P.O. Box 9278, Dept. T15-22A, Van Nuys, CA 91409

San Francisco: One of The Californias.™

The near Down Under.

It's as Southern as California gets. It's where the last of the Great American Desert touches the first of the Pacific.

Welcome to San Diego, the little town that grew up beautiful.

Hit the beach. Wrestle a marlin. Fill a spinnaker. Empty an oyster bucket. Sun till you're done. Shop till you drop.

Your first time in San Diego, they tell you there's a park in the middle of the city. Which is true enough. But when you've been here a while you figure it out: San Diego is a city in the middle of a park.

Harbor cruise. Mid-day snooze. Tee up. Chowder down. Avocado trees. Coronado breeze. Stare at a Goya. Buy out La Jolla. Horse race. Jazz place. Tijuana trolley to the Big Tamale.

But how do you tell the out-of-towners from the locals?

Easy. The locals are the tourists that live here.

When you're floating a hundred feet above the cliffs at Torrey Pines, "hanging out" has a whole new meaning.

Koalas. Sssnakes. (And their spouses.) Thriller whales. Penguin houses. Lions, tigers, animal park. All the folks from Noah's Ark.

Spain won the 16th Century Economy Run from Europe to the Pacific and back, averaging better than 25,000 miles to the galleon.

Old Globe Theatre · Balboa Park · Museum of Man · Zoo · Botanical Building · Museum of Art · Casa de Balboa · Natural History Museum · Space Theatre and Science Center

Point Loma is often called "California's Plymouth Rock," ignoring the fact that it was discovered a half-century before Plymouth Rock.

Mexico's not even a short drive away. More like a putt.

The America's Cup was known briefly as "The Australia's Cup," but the name didn't stick.

Californias, here I come!
Now there's a free 144-page travel guide that takes a fresh look at California—divides it into a dozen different regions, each with its own special surprises.

Name
Address
City
State   Zip
Call toll-free 1-800-TO-CALIF Extension 1621A, or write for yours today:
California Office of Tourism, P.O. Box 9278, Dept. T16-21A, Van Nuys, CA 91409

San Diego: One of The Californias.™

FCB's California Raisins "Heard" Loud And Clear

Client: California Raisin Advisory Board
Agency: Foote Cone & Belding, San Francisco

Let's face it. There are a lot of things raisins don't have. They don't have the smooth lines of a sports car. They aren't as intimate as an after shave. In the cosmic scheme of things, raisins rank somewhere between finding out what really happened to Amelia Earhart and deciding whether to wear the blue suit or the gray suit to your least favorite brother-in-law's wedding. And they aren't sexy. Definitely not sexy. Raisins are an intellectual product, right? Nutritious. Healthy. Taste good. But nobody gets excited about raisins; at least not anyone who has all their dogs on one leash.

How do you advertise raisins? Obviously, you tell people they taste good. Show lots of agile, healthy young people munching raisins on top of the Rockies. Have them make "mmm good" facial expressions directly into the camera. Hire Barry Manilow to write an upbeat jingle.

So how come the 1986 campaign created for the California Raisin Advisory Board (CALRAB) by the San Francisco office of Foote Cone & Belding (FCB) has no young people, no glistening fruit and no mountains?

Partly it's because of their past success positioning raisins as a healthy, nutritious food.

CALRAB is a marketing board established by the state of California. Although the board isn't run by the state, membership is mandatory. If you pack raisins in California, you belong to CALRAB. In reality, all commercial raisin growers in the U.S. belong to CALRAB; by an accident of geography, California's San Joaquin Valley is the only place in the country with precisely the right climate for raisins. The heights of the Pinnacles National Monument to the east and King's Canyon National Park to the west hold in the heat, turning the Valley into a four-million-acre oven and baking the dark purple goodness of the local grapes into wizened little shelf-stable nuggets.

When the board began advertising in 1973, it asked FCB to let people know that raisins are a great food. But it didn't want to spend a lot of money telling them.

"We had a budget of about $1 million that year," says Bob Phinney, director of advertising and public relations for CALRAB. With relatively small budgets and very wide targets, Phinney says the board has always relied on television to give it a broad reach. Airy, light spots featuring young mothers cheerily spooning out raisins for their children trickled across the airwaves. Both sales of raisins and the advertising budget climbed; the latter to a high of about $8.5 million in 1986. Phinney credits that advertising with gradually building the sales of CALRAB growers to more than 300,000 tons of raisins annually. At a 1987 wholesale price of $890 a ton, that makes raisins a quarter-billion dollar agri-business, all of it conducted within 75 miles of Fresno. All around this was solid, if unspectacular, success.

Then came a day when CALRAB realized it had trouble. Trouble right at home in Fresno.

"The snack market seemed to peak out in the early 1980s," Phinney explains. "We began

promoting other uses in our advertising—raisins as an easy addition to other foods, what we called spontaneous use. But the emphasis was still on using them because they're natural. It was a rational appeal."

Sales plateaued and began to slip ever so slightly. Total tonnage subsided at the rate of 1% a year in 1983, 1984 and into 1985. So what do careful clients do when the going gets tough? Of course. They call in the statisticians. Focus groups were conducted. Surveys filled out. The computers whirred.

"Consumers told us they understood the rational appeal we'd been using. If our advertising told them raisins were healthy, we weren't telling them anything new or particularly motivating," Phinney says. "We also found that, while our target groups knew the rational benefits and understood they were desirable, they had a neutral to negative emotional image of raisins."

Aha. People said they were eating fewer raisins because raisins were *boring*. "They felt

Raisins getting down to the strains of *I Heard It Through The Grapevine?* Get serious. These wrinkled little guys have done some serious selling for the California Raisin Advisory Board. The frolicking fruits reversed a three-year slide in raisin sales, single handedly rescuing Fresno, California, from a potential innundation of surplus raisins. They transformed the humble raisin from a boring, black-brown has-been to a cult figure that outscored even the techno-chic Max Headroom in the annual Video Storyboard recall tests.

(MUSIC UP)

(SFX: Finger snaps)

SINGERS: *Ooo, Ooo*

I heard it through the grapevine.

Raised in the California sunshine.

ANNCR (VO): California Raisins from the California Vineyards.

SINGERS: *Don't ya know*

I heard it through the grapevine.

ANNCR (VO): Sounds grape, doesn't it?
(MUSIC OUT)

Late Show was the first of two executions which ran in periodic flights from September 1986 to March 1987. A young couple watching late-night television is treated to a rhumba line of raisins Motowning their way across an end table. This spot ended the year at number three on the Video Storyboard Tests' list of the ten most remembered television commercials of 1986.

raisins were out of it, wimpy, not a fruit of the times," Phinney says. "We also did some research in Great Britain. A consumer there summarized the raisin as 'a faintly ridiculous but endearing little fruit.' "

It is an article of capitalist faith that one of the things that makes the Free World great is its choice of snack foods. However, we're undeniably jaded. Not only must the snacks taste good and be convenient, they have to be fashionable and intriguing. Somehow a raisin lacks the chic of a Dove bar or a crudite dripping with yogurt-jalapeno dip.

Here was some research the agency could get its teeth into. CALRAB needed a campaign that would improve the emotional image of raisins.

Talk about faintly ridiculous. How would you feel about responding to the "what are you doing now" question with, "I'm creating a new image for raisins."

Fortunately for CALRAB there are those among us who can take such assignments seriously—at least as seriously as they deserve to be taken. Even more fortunately, several of these serious-minded types were working in the San Francisco office of FCB. Copywriter Seth Werner was one of them. Werner saw his duty toward these raisins clearly: Make 'em funky.

"People didn't think raisins were hip enough to eat; they were commonplace, has-beens,"

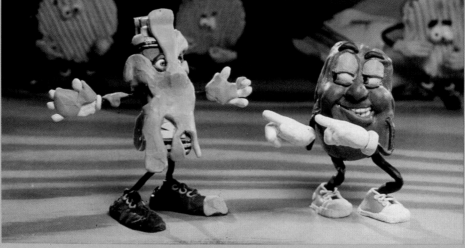

Werner says. "You know, 'they could have been somebody, they could've been wine.' Dexter Fedor and I were up in my office trying out silly ideas on each other. Of course, the song *I Heard It Through The Grapevine* came up. Afterwards, we just tried to make sense of it. It could have turned into a really silly ad, so we worked hard to keep it from coming out that way."

Obviously, using 60s songs as a backdrop isn't even close to being an original idea. Bob Phinney says CALRAB's spots work because the interest isn't borrowed. "When you hear an old song being used for a brand-new product you think, 'they borrowed that song.' But *Grapevine* fits the product."

Werner's explanation is less cerebral: "We tried to keep it simple. Don't change the music because it's wonderful. Try not to change the lyrics too much. Keep it cool. Cool is hard for me to explain, but I know it when I see it. We tried to show raisins as these funky little beans. Looking at music videos, my favorites are the ones with people dancing to the music as opposed to doing surrealistic things. So we decided we wanted to show raisins dancing to *I Heard It Through The Grapevine*."

Werner and art director Fedor had the unenviable task of taking their raisin show to Fresno for a presentation to Phinney and his staff.

Although CALRAB raisins face no domestic competitors and very little competition from imported raisins, as a snack food they go head-to-head with the likes of Doritos and Fiddle-Faddle. *Late Show* cleverly shows the raisins zapping nerdy-looking snack foods as part of their dance routine. They make the point that raisins are a healthier, hipper snack without using any words at all. The only dialogue in the whole spot is at the very end when the narrator asks, "Sounds grape, doesn't it?"

"The things we wanted to say about raisins couldn't be put into words," says copywriter Seth Werner. "There wasn't a need for a lot of dialogue, so we left it out."

Lunchbox was the second execution. It features three construction workers. One of them opens his lunchbox and instead of a quiet, well-behaved Twinkie finds the California Raisins crooning their now-famous theme. Again, there are very few words spoken, the only dialogue being a comment from one of the other workers who says, "Sounds better than what I got."

(MUSIC IN)

(MUSIC OUT)

(MUSIC IN)

(MUSIC IN)

(MUSIC IN)

SOLO RAISIN SINGER: *Ooh, ooh, I heard it through the grapevine…*

RAISIN SINGERS: *Ooh*

SOLO RAISIN SINGER: *Raised in the California sunshine.*

ANNCR: California raisins

from the California vineyards.

RAISIN SINGERS: *Don't ya know that I heard it through the grapevine.*

CONSTRUCTION WORKER: Sounds better than what I got. (MUSIC OUT)

The CALRAB reaction? "We liked it," Phinney says. But the troupe had one more critical audition to survive: The 40-odd raisins growers invested with the responsibility of ensuring that the contributions of the 500 CALRAB members are spent prudently. Werner's funky little beans were convincing.

Colossal Pictures of San Francisco was commissioned to design the raisins and they did a limited animation under the watchful eyes of the team at FCB, which included Werner, Fedor, creative director Tim Price and producer Flo Babbit. The animation looked good. It proved to FCB and CALRAB that the concept would work. But not as a traditional animation. One crucial element was still missing: The Claymation technique of Will Vinton Studios in Portland, Oregon.

"We wanted the viewers to buy into the idea of these dancing raisins as fully as possible," Werner says, "and Claymation seemed like the best way to do that. It was a technique which I didn't think had been overdone yet. Also, there's a three-dimensional aspect to Claymation that you don't get with standard animation. Claymation was more believable than people dressed in raisin costumes and more realistic than standard animation would have been."

In Will Vinton's studio, raisin figurines were sculpted out of clay and then painstakingly photographed in stop-motion animation, frame by frame, one movement at a time.

At this critical juncture, the agency and the client entered into a conspiracy that both felt was vital to the success of the spots. They conspired to leave Vinton alone and let him do his work.

"We worked with Will on the choreography, but the most productive thing we did was to leave him alone and let him do it," Werner says.

Phinney believes the results justify Werner's confidence in

In addition to supervising the Claymation process, Will Vinton also directed both *Late Show* and *Lunchbox.* The agency team worked with Vinton closely to choreograph the dance routine. Both CALRAB and FCB say they were careful to keep the steps archetypically Motown and avoid letting the raisins slip into unconscious racial caricature.

What lessons should we draw from the success of *Lunchbox* and *Late Show*? "If I could tell marketing people one thing, it would be this: If you have good people, let them do the job," says Werner. "The people at CALRAB were great. They let us do our jobs. And we let Will Vinton do his job." The results speak for themselves.

Vinton. "The raisins immediately took on a character that's almost human," he says. "I've seen those spots hundreds of times, but each time I look at them I see something new. Partly that's the technique and partly that's Will Vinton."

Phinney was looking for a slow climb back to ground zero, perhaps a two- to three-year journey to regain the sales that had been lost between 1984 and 1986. In that expectation he was very much disappointed.

The spots broke in September of 1986. Almost immediately, FCB began getting telephone calls from viewers. The people out there in Nielson-land liked the raisins. This was good news.

By October, sales had increased 1%. That wasn't going to appreciably fatten the purses of Fresno's raisin brokers, but it was the first monthly increase in almost three years. November sales were up 5% over the previous year. And December sales were up more than 6%. Now this was *really* good news.

The increases came at a time when in-store support for the category at the retail level was down 25%. "We weren't getting the displays or promotions," Phinney says. "The retailers liked the spots, but there was nothing for them to tie into."

If the retailers liked the spots, the public loved them. Video Storyboard Tests reported that the first execution, *Late Show*, scored higher than any other spot in its survey of television commercials run during the fourth quarter of 1986. Up to 70 letters a day were arriving at CALRAB and FCB painting paeans to the raisins.

The agency hadn't just created a commercial; they'd created a fad. The raisins were an overnight sensation. Werner says his father, who has taught school in an all-black neighborhood in New York for 20 years, became a mini-celebrity when it became known that Seth was behind the spots. Television producers approached

FCB and CALRAB, jockeying for the rights to produce an animated cartoon series.

In the summer of 1987, the raisins led the American contingent at the Cannes Film Festival, dancing off with a silver award from what has in recent years been a very tough, almost anti-American jury.

So what's the future of the "has-been" beans? A third television execution broke in September of 1987. To increase retail support, a unique promotion was scheduled. The scheme capitalized on two of the most fortuitous results of the initial efforts: First the creative team had managed to give each of the raisins a distinct character.

Second, the raisins had evoked an enormous outpouring of consumer empathy. The promotion, which was kicked off with print ads in *USA Today*'s weekend edition, *TV Guide* magazine and the comics sections of major metropolitan newspapers, invited shoppers to write in to name the raisins. The winners received a trip to "Hollywood and Vine;" that is, a vacation to Los Angeles with a side-trip to the vineyards of Fresno. Also, after being briefly derailed by a lawsuit, the raisin characters have been licensed in a wide range of product categories. Raisin lunch boxes and plush toys were scheduled to show up in

stores in time for the Christmas 1987 buying season.

How long can this show go on? "I have a feeling it's not as susceptible to wear out as some other snack spots because CALRAB just doesn't have the budget to run it a lot," predicts Werner, who has moved on to a senior creative post at The Bloom Agency in Dallas. "Part of the magic of the spots in the first year was that they just weren't on enough. People didn't have a chance to get tired of them. If you can couple that with fresh spots released periodically, there's no end to it."

The CALRAB growers are betting their farms he's right.

CHEVY

Campbell-Ewald's Heartbeat Sells America For Chevrolet

Client: Chevrolet Passenger Cars
Agency: Campbell-Ewald

Chevrolet's *Heartbeat of America* campaign is a benchmark—and a radical departure from the norm—in American automotive advertising. So you expect something a little different when you talk to the creative director behind it. What you get is someone who's *a lot* different; different in ways that preordained Chevy's advertising to break new ground.

The first things you learn about Sean Fitzpatrick, creative director of Campbell-Ewald, are that he says what he thinks and that he's provocative. Not Muhammed Ali-running-off-at-the-mouth provocative. More like lightbulb-going-on provocative; I-can't-believe-he's-saying-this provocative. Some Fitzpatrickisms:

"Elvis Presley was more important to the reformation of America than John Kennedy."

"Advertising hates ambiguity. Most of the research done by advertisers is used to emasculate advertising from having any meaning other than the exact one that was intended."

"The last place you'll find automobile lovers are in the car companies. Car companies are filled with guys who might just as well be selling toothpaste."

That's not the kind of talk journalists have come to expect from people who hold positions of great responsibility in advertising—a world where "evanescent" is a better adjective to link with "job" than is the more common euphemism "mobility." The guys in the suits will shoot you if you go around giving interviews like that.

None of the above seems to bother Fitzpatrick, who certainly qualifies as a target of opportunity for the suits.

The third thing you realize when you talk to Fitzpatrick is that just maybe a whole bunch of what you thought you knew about advertising is wrong. Dated. Obsolete. Non-op.

Heartbeat was universally praised when it broke in 1986. The

advertising press raved. Then, as Fitzpatrick made the rounds picking up awards and spelling out his philosophy, the scribes began to recant. What is all this stuff, they asked. Who is this guy, and if he's such a hot property, how come *Heartbeat* isn't selling cars?

Fitzpatrick has an answer: "When you phrase it that way, it's like asking someone when he stopped beating his wife. Who says the campaign isn't selling cars? And what makes you think you know what you're talking about anyway?"

What makes this dust-up worth examining is that *Heartbeat is* selling cars. In fact, it has stabilized and actually turned around Chevy's market share trendline, which had been heading south since before the Gulf of Tonkin Resolution doomed LBJ's Great Society to schism and strife.

According to Chevrolet's own figures, in 1962 Chevy sold 2.13 million cars and had 31.5% of the

U.S. auto market. By February 1983 that share had dropped to just 13.8%. Imports were picking off more of Chevrolet's traditional customers every year, and the angle of declivity of the trendline was "steeper than a ski slope," Fitzpatrick says.

Chevrolet isn't bashful about its troubles either. Listen to Danielle Colliver, advertising manager for General Motors' Chevrolet Passenger Cars: "Chevrolet was in big trouble. The Chevette had been in the market for nine years. And while it was cheap, customers didn't love it. The X-car was destined to go to court. Cavaliers and Celebrities were so undistinguished that no one could remember their names. The median age of buyers of Caprice was over 60, and the agency came in with a campaign saying 'Caprice—Your last car, make it a good one.' We didn't have a Corvette and people who bought Camaros tried to hide the fact that they were Chevys."

What happened? What

Chevrolet dropped nearly 18 share points in as many years before *Heartbeat*, launched in 1986, stabilized its position.

"A few years ago some of the big hitters in the auto industry were saying there would be a shake out and we'd be left with four or five auto makers," says Sean Fitzpatrick, creative director of Campbell-Ewald. "Well, they were wrong. Auto makers are crawling all over the place. The reason is that if anybody produces a car that runs well and has some distinctiveness, someone will be willing to buy it."

happened to seeing the USA in your Chevrolet? What happened to "What's good for General Motors is good for America"?

"When I first started working on this business in 1983, I set out to discover why people weren't buying Chevrolets," Fitzpatrick says. "When I went to focus groups I found absolute anger against Chevrolet. People recognized that this was the brand that had stood for America. Somehow it had let them down by having products that were not very exciting and didn't work all that well."

In response, Fitzpatrick and Colliver—along with folks like writer Dennis Plansker and Bob Berger, who is general manager of the Chevrolet division—created *Heartbeat*, which is at least part of the solution to this disaster. In the process, they defied the rules that have circumscribed automobile advertising in America.

What's their secret? If you believe Fitzpatrick, it's nothing more than a bit of Greek

philosophy and a song. That's it.

The chestnut is from Socrates: Know thyself.

Besides traveling all over the country to talk to consumers, Fitzpatrick also talked to Chevrolet about who and what Chevrolet was.

"No matter who I talked to at Chevy, I got a different answer. Bob Berger called in a few of us from the agency and four or five people from Chevrolet. We sat down and created a vision statement for who Chevrolet should be. We did it without regard to where we were. Instead, we focused on where we *should be* in the marketplace," Fitzpatrick says.

The group went back to basics. "Historically, Chevrolet has not been the absolute cheapest transportation," Fitzpatrick says. "At its best, Chevy has always offered consumers a little more than the competition. We phrased that as 'more than you expect to get for the price.' You might pay $100 more for a Chevrolet than a

Ford, but you got more. Chevrolet had six-cylinder engines when Ford only offered fours. Buyers got an automatic transmission when they couldn't get one on a Ford. There's a history of Chevrolet having something a little bit better but maybe costing a little more."

The group distilled Chevrolet's mission into a single paragraph: "To be America's leading source for a full line of distinctive cars and trucks, products known for up-market features at low prices. Products that stir the imagination and reward the buyer with more than expected."

After defining what had made Chevrolet great over the years, the group acknowledged that Chevy was no longer doing that. Then they analyzed the positions of the other car makers.

"It was a frightening moment," Fitzpatrick recalls. "We all just looked at each other and said, 'Oh you dummies!'

"The companies that were doing what Chevy had done for

Chevrolet had to recreate its historic association with the American way of life and with young people in particular.

Ironically, Campbell-Ewald turned to a cadre of foreigners to purvey its message: Not one of the directors of the first four spots was an American.

"We were looking for unpolluted vision," Fitzpatrick says. "But once we had a vision of who we were, it became easier to work with any good director. We worked with a lot of expensive, top-level directors in our first year, and we're still working with some of them, but we're also trying to incorporate new young talent. We're cutting costs while getting the fresher visions of guys on the cutting edge."

Young and fresh fit the needs of the campaign: Its first target is 18-to-34 year olds, the second target is women and the third target is first-time buyers.

"The first target was young people because that's where Chevy was dead," Fitzpatrick explains. "We lost a whole generation, maybe ten or fifteen years of young adults who will never buy an American car."

so many years were Toyota, Honda and Nissan. In the last two decades Chevy lost seventeen share points. And guess how much share the imports had picked up? There is no magic to the Japanese system of management or the Japanese system of building of cars. The Japanese supplied the vehicles that Chevrolet stopped supplying and they got the market share that Chevrolet lost."

Ouch. But hold on. It gets worse.

While Chevrolet has always sold to a broad cross section of middle-America, historically, many Chevy buyers were young people. Chevy was Nova SuperSports, Camaro convertibles and Chinese-red Corvettes. A Chevy was more than just transportation, and backseats were for more than just carrying extra passengers. But the company had let that franchise get away from them.

"Young people in particular were angry at Chevrolet because they felt the company had let them down," Fitzpatrick says. "They told us Chevy made cars for their grandfathers and fathers, but not for them.

"The young people had a clear idea of what Chevrolet was, and it wasn't good. The most famous Chevy words of all—baseball, hot dogs and apple pie—were actually a curse because they reminded these young people that Chevy used to be hot and no longer was. There may be nothing worse than being a has-been.

"No amount of factual evidence could turn them around. We could show them a Z-28 or a Corvette and say 'See, Chevy's just as hot as your imported sports car.' Their answer, while not logical, was emphatic: 'Those cars aren't really Chevys.'

"We had to reestablish a relationship between Chevrolet and Young America and we had to do it fast. We had new products coming down the pipeline, but a significant number of young people wouldn't even walk into a

DISCOVER A NEW SPECIES
BERETTA

BERETTA.
It has evolved. Not just a new car, but a new species. An unusually roomy sport coupe with a natural instinct for the road.
A DISTINCTIVE NEW SHAPE.
From nose to tail, the stylish contours of Beretta make a unique impression. Angular hood. Flush, pillar-mounted door handles. Lots of glass.

Aggressive stance. And a bold tail lamp. See it on the road and you won't soon forget. Drive it, and you never will.
QUICK 2.8 LITER MULTI-PORT V6.
With the optional 2.8 Liter V6, Beretta can move from 0 to 60 in less than 10 seconds.* This refined Multi-Port Fuel Injection engine features a computer-controlled coil

ignition for accurate spark performance and an electronic control module with brand-new microprocessor technology that can handle

600,000 commands per second. Beretta's sport suspension and a smooth-shifting, high-torque 5-speed transaxle turn that raw power into inspired performance.
A NEW LEVEL OF INTERIOR COMFORT.
The Beretta cockpit. A world of aesthetic design. Both front bucket seats have their own suspension systems to help tune out road vibrations. Watch

Beretta's vital signs come to light as you turn on the optional electronic instrumentation. With a touch of your finger, you can even check your gas mileage or the temperature outside.

Make the road your natural habitat: put yourself in the unforgettable shape of Beretta. A new species.
*Performance figures compiled by a professional driver on a GM test track.
Let's get it together... buckle up.

THE *Heartbeat* **OF AMERICA** — **TODAY'S CHEVROLET**

Fitzpatrick is fond of quoting Wordsworth's *A Few Lines Above Tintern Abbey*, in which the poet posits that a waterfall is not a poetic experience until the poet sees it. Coleridge took the argument even further, theorizing that a poem doesn't exist until the reader reads it. In Fitzpatrick's view, advertising should be ambiguous, to leave room for the viewer to finish the image in terms that mean something to them on a personal level. Even though the Beretta ads were purposefully vague, Fitzpatrick says that consumers who'd seen them consistently "played back" all of the car's essential selling points: That it had front-wheel drive, was a high-performance sedan. Ironically, he says, the advertising for the new Corsica—which was filled with facts instead of suggestions—didn't communicate as well.

Chevy dealership to see them!"

While the team at Campbell-Ewald and its counterpart at Chevrolet could see the target, hitting it was problematic. Fitzpatrick had found the focus group participants totally unpersuaded by logical arguments. No matter how many reams of cleverly-written copy, how many mouth-watering photos, how many reels of artfully-produced film Chevy threw at them, logic wasn't going to change their opinion. That's a tough hand, but it had been dealt to the right player.

Fitzpatrick doesn't believe that logical arguments sell products.

"People don't make decisions with facts. They *support* decisions with facts.

"I've been following the work of psychologists in the area of racial prejudice—studying why racial prejudice can't be eradicated even among well-educated human beings. The researchers theorize that people don't carry around with them a total understanding of events, ideas or even other human beings. What they carry around in their heads are silhouette images of a thought—a very thin representation. For example, when you think of a person, you tend to isolate a couple of points about that person; key impressions rather than a list of specifics.

"The same thing is true of brands. People don't read all the catalogs, packaging, instructions and ingredients before they buy. What they do carry around with them is all of the 'evidence' they've accumulated about a brand. That can start with childhood relationships, how their parents viewed the brand, how they saw it growing up, how their peers see it and, finally, the experience they've had with the brand themselves. Ninety percent of that evidence is *emotional*.

"The mind compresses all that into what I call a Q-bias. It's somewhere between the head and the heart; not logical and not entirely emotional. But evidence that conflicts with that bias is often rejected. For example, if you believe that Englishmen are cold and aloof, when you meet an outgoing Englishman, you think 'He's an exception' or 'He had too much to drink.'

"You develop a bias for or against a brand. You're either for Chevrolet or against it. Or you're for Ford or against it; for imports or against them. You made up your mind based on your Q-bias, not pure logic.

"You probably picked your best friend, your mate, your favorite teacher or employee without words. Somebody walked into a room. They wore their hair in a certain way, dressed just so, noticed you or didn't. And you made a decision. Finally, they spoke. The tone of voice most probably was more important than the words. You touched hands; warm or cold. And you married them or didn't, or did and shouldn't have. Most of this occurred without or in spite of logical arguments. Why should a consumer's choice of soap, beer, clothes or an automobile be different?

"Through advertising we can provide cues that help change a negative brand Q-bias or reinforce a positive Q-bias."

Fitzpatrick commissioned Phase One of Los Angeles to study all of the automobile advertising then running. A majority of the spots featured telephoto shots of autos running down a two-lane road with an authoritative announcer shouting the virtues of the car over heavy, Wagnerian music in the background. When people appeared, it was likely to be a man in a tuxedo or a woman draped over the hood.

"There was a tremendous void in the marketplace for human-oriented advertising. I think we were lucky to encounter that void and leap into it," Fitzpatrick says.

"Americans don't relate to automobiles the way the Japanese or Germans do. To Americans, a

THE *Heartbeat* OF AMERICA

TODAY'S CHEVROLET

Heart and Soul. It's your pride and joy, the car you've dreamed about since you were a kid. We understand. That's why we bring you cars that make you proud. Cars born out of a racing heritage, like Camaro IROC-Z. Cars like Cavalier Z24 that have the performance built in, not just painted on. Fun small cars that give you something a little unexpected when you put your foot down, like new Turbo Sprint. Our drive to be Number One in everything we do is the reason we can bring you a world-class champion: Corvette. We're bringing you cars with the latest technology and most advanced engineering—and we're making them affordable. Your Chevy dealer has cars that drive strong and feel like winners. Cars that are the heart and soul of performance.

Today's Chevrolet is keeping a commitment we made 75 years ago, to give you the kinds of cars you want. So when you get behind the wheel, listen to your heartbeat: That's Today's Chevrolet. The Heartbeat of America.

1987 Chevrolet Corvet

Let's get it together...buckle u

The two keys to *Heartbeat* are the music and the emotional relationship it shows between cars and people.

"The images we've chosen to show, virtually every single one of them has been thought out, even in those quick-cut commercials that look like random cutting. They were carefully designed to show individual human beings relating to their cars, and somehow their lives are a little better because of that car. I think that's the secret of its appeal."

The keystone spot (above) was one in which a young man in a small rural town visualizes himself driving a brilliant red Corvette.

car is more than a way to get from point A to point B. It's part of their lifestyle. For young people who can no longer afford to live very well—maybe they live at home with their parents—the inside of their car is what they decorate.

"We committed ourselves to a focused emotional advertising campaign that featured the customer and would be designed to stand out in the category—to stir the imagination of the customer and build a new relationship between Chevrolet and the customer."

But where was the point of connection between Chevrolet and these customers? Chevy had had some problems with themes for a while—like the last twenty years. During the long period of share decline the company hadn't had a theme line that had lasted for more than a year. What was the slogan that could revitalize the brand's image?

Sometimes you make your own luck. Bob Berger and Fitzpatrick were attending a stock car race. Berger saw "Heartbeat of America" painted on racer Dale Earnhart's race trailer.

"Berger said he wished we could use that for our theme and I told him we could," Fitzpatrick

chuckles. Fitzpatrick knew the agency had written that line. "The Heartbeat of America" had been used as a theme in a Chevy performance catalog several years before.

To hear Fitzpatrick tell the story, it was all downhill from there. "Our eureka moment came when one of our young writers, who was a poet in his spare time, came through my door with the idea for a commercial about a young boy living in a 19th-century town. He's walking down a dusty road when he sees a brand new Corvette—all red and glorious—roaring down the road. As it passes, he sees himself behind the wheel. We all realized at that moment that we weren't just selling cars. We were selling aspirations. The aspirations of a young boy or the aspirations of a smart consumer who wants the best value for the money.

"Aspirations and being a part of the American life experience is what *The Heartbeat of America* campaign is all about. What we intended to do was to create imagery that allows consumers to rewrite that imagery in terms of their own lives."

But how do you talk to consumers about that in a way that's going to be received?

Simple. You put it in a song.

Remember what Fitzpatrick said about Elvis Presley being more important than John Kennedy?

"Of all the cues people receive, music is the greatest. Music is the single most important thing in our lives," Fitzpatrick says. "I saw a study once, I believe it was done some years ago at the University of San Diego. Asked to rank the ten most important things in their lives, women rated music number one and sex about number six. Men rated music second and sex first. The researchers concluded that the men were lying.

"Music transcends our jobs and our relationships; virtually every period of our lives is shaped by the music we listen to. Our personalities are developed and reshaped by the kind of music we have; you can tell a lot about a person by the kind of music they listen to.

"If you only buy 10% of that, ask yourself how much good the car companies did themselves by running old-fashioned, Stentorian music behind their ads. Basically it said, 'These cars are boring.'"

Fitzpatrick and crew went to work on lyrics for a song that would tell Young America "Hey,

ATTENTION: SHARP OBJECT.

SPECTRUM.
A sharp car has to do more than look good. It has to *act* sharp, with intelligent design and function backing up the good looks. That's a terrific combination. It's also the philosophy behind Chevy Spectrum.

ADVANCED GEOMETRY.
Spectrum's dual purpose take shape up front, with the ne look of flush-mounted headligh

THE

 OF AMERICA

TODAY'S
CHEVROLET

and streamlined aircraft-style doors that open into the roof line. While these smooth contours contribute to a great look, they also make Spectrum a champion of aerodynamics.

CLASS ROOM.
The layout of the Spectrum interior performs as good as it looks—with reclining front bucket seats and a roomy rear seat that give you and three passengers a way to get comfortable. And the instrument pod offers information and controls within a fingertip's reach of the steering wheel.

HONORS IN ENGINEERING.
Spectrum has the substance to meet real-world challenges—and have fun in the process. With standard features like a 1.5-liter overhead cam engine, computer controlled for changing elevations and driving conditions. Front drive and MacPherson-strut

front suspension for great footing and accurate cornering. And a slick-shifting manual five-speed gearbox that puts you in complete command. Chevy Spectrum: hot new styling, roomy comfort, superb engineering. All told, it's one sharp object.

Let's get it together...buckle up. GM

S P E C T R U M

YOUR WORST NIGHTMARE.

FEEL THE POWER.
Standard 5.0 Liter 4-Bbl. V8 and 5-speed.
Optional 5.0 Liter V8 with Tuned-Port Fuel Injection. Available for the first time, with a 5-speed manual transmission. Zero to 60 in 7.0 seconds.* A 4-speed automatic overdrive is optional.

EXPERIENCE THE HANDLING.
A modified MacPherson-strut front suspension provides increased caster for precise steering. A beefy front stabilizer bar is standard.
At the rear, a torque-arm suspension with Delco/Bilstein gas-pressure shocks and available 4-wheel disc brakes.
Standard P245/VR50-16 Goodyear Eagle GT unidirectional high-performance tires on 16" aluminum wheels help IROC Z28 achieve .88g of lateral acceleration on the skidpad.*

TAKE CONTROL.
Special instrumentation with tachometer, temperature gage, oil pressure gage, voltmeter and trip odometer.
Thick leather-wrapped

steering wheel and shift lever await your commands.
New optional leather seating surfaces give your IROC-Z that glove-soft feel of luxury.
Optional high-output Delco-Bose stereo system delivers superb high-performance sound.
*Performance figures compiled by a professional driver on a GM test track.

Let's get it together ...buckle up.

THE Heartbeat OF AMERICA TODAY'S CHEVROLET

CAMARO IROC-Z

---

it's okay to have a Chevy, and here are some nifty ones for you to have."

Fitzpatrick meanwhile had one more mission. He was afraid to break cover with *Heartbeat* until he could be sure that it wouldn't go the way of the 30 or 40 themes Chevy had used over the past two decades.

"*Heartbeat* was incorporated into our racing advertising within a month after Bob Berger saw it on Dale Earnhart's trailer, but we held it out of the mass market for almost two years," he explains. "I was afraid that *Heartbeat* would be just another six-month theme line, so I wasn't willing to reveal our trump card until I felt I had the ammunition to keep it in place for five years."

The only way to do that was to get everyone at Chevy to buy into the mission statement and the notion that it takes more than a good logical argument to sell cars in America.

Campbell-Ewald and Chevrolet set up an image conference and invited the company's top 100 thinkers to evaluate the one-paragraph statement of purpose that had been developed earlier. The result? The group spent about 18 months writing and rewriting the one paragraph into nearly a thousand pages of analysis of the automotive market. But in the end, the engineers, designers and sales people bought the image of the "new Chevrolet," which of course was an updated reincarnation of the "old Chevrolet."

"That was the hard work,"

Fitzpatrick says. "Usually you write five campaigns to sell one. I went in with one campaign and sold it in an hour."

Having spent almost two years developing his "trump card," Fitzpatrick wasn't about to play it carelessly. A media blitz was carefully orchestrated. Its construction fully reflects Fitzpatrick's prejudices: Chevrolet, the fourth largest television advertiser in the U.S., broke *Heartbeat* on the radio, running it for four weeks before unveiling the keystone Corvette spot on network TV. Sort of a softening up of the airwaves before sending in the troops.

"The purpose of breaking on radio was to get everyone singing our theme and to drive Lee Iacocca and Chrysler out of the

While Fitzpatrick talks a lot about visual imagery and emotional appeal, the Chevy spots are backed with compelling, fact-filled print ads which spell out the details and provide the logical reasons consumers use to justify decisions.

position they'd staked out in the 'America' category," Fitzpatrick says.

Calls poured into Chevrolet asking for recordings of the theme. Campbell-Ewald released the TV spots and followed quickly with hard-hitting newspaper and magazine ads supplying facts and logical arguments to bolster *Heartbeat*'s claim on America's heart.

Did it work?

"The Radio Advertising Bureau recently sent me a Bruskin Report showing we had 60% unaided recall among young consumers and about 45% unaided recall overall," Fitzpatrick says. "ASI reported recently that one of our Celebrity commercials broke every existing record for a thirty-second automotive spot."

Scores aside, more important is the fact that *Heartbeat* is in fact selling cars.

September, October and November of 1986 were "lousy," Fitzpatrick says, coming on the heels of the company's traditional fall sell-off, which clears a lot of potential buyers out of the market.

Since January of 1987 they've been running 15.5% of the market. And there's every reason to believe that as the Beretta and Corsica come onstream in full production Chevy will be up to 16.5% to 17% of the market by the end of 1988.

"Mark Twain once said that by the time you need a good reputation it's too late to get one. We're attempting to restore Chevrolet's reputation. We've taken a decline

and turned it around and now we're headed up. The question is, how do we get it to go up faster?

"I think it all has to do with dog food. If the dogs don't like the dog food, it doesn't matter how good the advertising is. But if the dogs like the dog food, then the advertising works with the taste of the dog food. Pretty soon the word gets around and all the dogs on the street are eating the same dog food. I think that's what we're starting to see, that the dogs are liking the dog food again."

Despite all of Fitzpatrick's unfamiliar talk about Q-bias, music and half-perceived messages, in the end he's talking about product quality and forceful presentation.

Perhaps Sean Fitzpatrick isn't such a radical after all.

Lintas: New York Fills Citizen's "Hand"some Menagerie

Client: Citizen Watch Co. USA
Agency: Lintas: New York

CITIZEN

The business journals look at Japan and marvel. Why not? The Economic Miracle represents the greatest accumulation of national wealth since the Pope gave Spain leave to pillage the New World. And haven't the Big Two (Toyota, Nissan) done a dandy job of internationalizing the U.S. auto market? But there's still a good deal of market smarts on this side of the Pacific. And Japanese companies are among the first to admire, emulate and improve on American marketing ideas that work.

Citizen Watch Company's introduction of Noblia, for example, is a rousing reaffirmation that the General Motors vertical marketing strategy has been right all along. The Chevy-Buick-Pontiac-Cadillac pyramid was a good idea in 1950 and it's a good idea today.

Citizen is a major power in the lower end of the world watch market. But increasing affluence has created an increasing demand for watches that not only tell time, but that also tell other people something about the wearer.

"Income is growing, there are more dual-salary households. The baby boomers, many with advanced college degrees, are entering their peak earning years," says Bruce Kravetz, vice president of Lintas: New York and account director for the Citizen business. It's a point of human nature that folks who have more want more. Mere wealth is not enough. They need *trappings.* Designer suits. Designer warm-up clothes. Designer baby booties. Designer coffins (by Bill Blass, no less). And designer watches.

"You can walk down the street today and see more Movados, more Concordes, more $500 to $1,000 watches than ever before," Kravetz notes. "People are investing not only in the basics—fashionable suits, as a real accessory to fashion and personal style. Citizen wanted to take

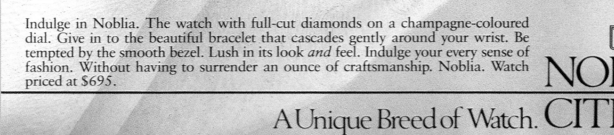

As Exotic As a Parrot.

Indulge in Noblia. The watch with full-cut diamonds on a champagne-coloured dial. Give in to the beautiful bracelet that cascades gently around your wrist. Be tempted by the smooth bezel. Lush in its look *and* feel. Indulge your every sense of fashion. Without having to surrender an ounce of craftsmanship. Noblia. Watch priced at $695.

NOBLIA®
CITIZEN®

A Unique Breed of Watch.

For brochure, send $2 to Citizen, 1200 Wall Street West, Lyndhurst, N.J. 07071

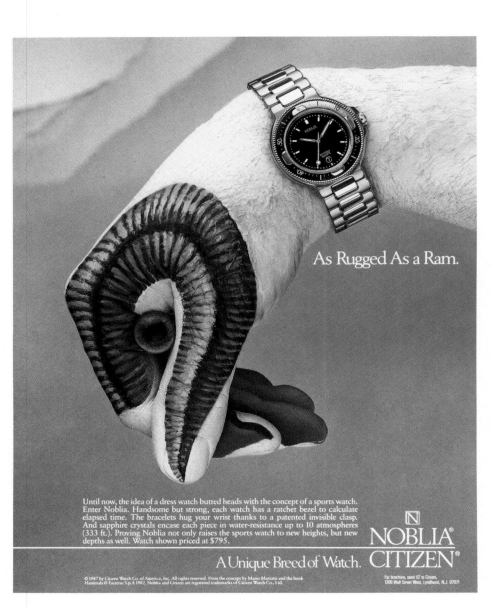

As Rugged As a Ram.

Until now, the idea of a dress watch butted heads with the concept of a sports watch. Enter Noblia. Handsome but strong, each watch has a ratchet bezel to calculate elapsed time. The bracelets hug your wrist thanks to a patented invisible clasp. And sapphire crystals encase each piece in water-resistance up to 10 atmospheres (333 ft.). Proving Noblia not only raises the sports watch to new heights, but new depths as well. Watch shown priced at $795.

N NOBLIA® CITIZEN®

A Unique Breed of Watch.

The first "hanimals," created by Florentine artist Mario Mariotti, were just quick sketches, without much detail. To match the exquisite detail of the Noblia line, Lintas: New York art director Bruce Arendash spent as much as three hours working with the hand model and make-up artist for each shot. The results were well worth the wait.

Hiro photographed the first batch of "hanimals," including the ducks and giraffes opposite.

advantage of that trend and develop a strategy to upgrade the image of its entire line."

Upgrade is probably not the right word; research done by Lintas: New York showed that although it was moving enough watches to equip a couple of battalions of hydra-armed Shivas, Citizen had no distinctive image in the U.S. The significance of that opportunity was not lost on Lintas. Taking a page from the Chevrolet playbook (a playbook partially written by Lintas' new sister agency, Campbell-Ewald), what was put up on the chalkboard was a variation on the Corvette deep-threat option play. Noblia for the status- and style-conscious opinion leaders, Citizen for the masses.

"Introducing Noblia gave Citizen a way to bracket the market," Kravetz says. "Noblia isn't a high-volume entry, but it does offer a high profit per unit. The bulk of the Citizen line is under $100, with a relatively low profit per unit. But they move a lot of units."

Citizen knew that they wouldn't get by with mere imitation. Noblia needed more. What they did was pair European design with their own ultra-thin movements. "The Noblia casings and bracelets are for the most part European, actually designed and manufactured in Switzerland," Kravetz explains. "While there are pieces in the line that list for $1,500, they are generally priced slightly under Concorde. It gave them a beachhead with terrific styling and quartz reliability at a lower price point."

While Citizen had a strategy and the right watch to make it work, they didn't have a lot of money for promotion. They weren't going to take that beachhead by sinking Movato, Concorde et. al. under a barrage of sheer media throw weight. They needed what every client wants: Smart, breakthrough advertising.

What they got was a trip to the zoo. Mike Jordan, the copywriter assigned to the business, had a

Anyone can see the fashion inherent in Noblia. Full-cut diamonds, stately gold-tone
bezels and art deco design. But equally impressive is what you can't see. Like
water-resistance to 3 atmospheres (99 ft.). Or the ultrathin quartz movement that is accurate
to within seconds per annum. The invisible deployment clasp that fits the bracelet
neatly to your wrist. Even the clear sapphire crystal that is far more scratch-proof than
ordinary glass. Noblia. Watches shown priced from $475.

A Unique Breed of Watch.

As Splashy As an Alligator.

NOBLIA®
CITIZEN®

book of "hand sculptures" which had been created by an Italian artist, Mario Mariotti. Mariotti's technique was to take someone's hand, quickly daub it with paint to resemble some kind of animal, then photograph it. Arendash felt that, if the concept could be refined, "hanimals" would be a terrific way to show off Noblia.

"It took a brave group to walk into the conference room with that campaign," admits Kravetz. "It was so different it even made us nervous. But our president, Frank DeVito, has a motto: If it makes you itch, it's the right thing to do. The 'hanimals' certainly made us itch.

"We were afraid of creating some kind of advertising vampire, that the concept would overpower the product. But our research convinced us that while the concept was very arresting, it was also going to sell watches. We were fortunate enough to have clients—Larry Grunstein, president of Citizen Watch in the U.S., and Mr. Itoh, the chairman—who understood the need for us to be innovative in order to break through the clutter of advertising in the high-grade watch business."

Despite an initial uneasiness on both sides of the table, the very bizarreness of the concept had something important going for it.

"Noblia is a brand-new marque, so initially we needed to reach people who aren't motivated by labels," Kravetz says. "Those people, the early adopters and innovators in any market, aren't motivated by brand acceptance. We felt that if the look was right, the styling was right, they would buy it."

These are people whose self-image depends on staying slightly ahead of the crowd. With twenty-twenty hindsight, it's easy to see how well the "hanimals" execution fit that need. Responding to the standard buzzwords "different," "unique" and "breakthrough" could have resulted in jerky *cinema verite* footage of London street punks

passing up a Movato in favor of mugging someone wearing a Noblia. Stranger things are running on network television right now.

Working with Mariotti's idea of the hand as an animal, Bruce Arendash and creative director Lynn Giordano began putting the pieces together. They hired Hiro, the famed Japanese photographer. Matching product attributes to animal characters, they came up with a duck, a swan, a giraffe and a zebra. The headlines pointed up the similarities: "Waterproof as a duck," "Elegant as a swan," "Thin as a giraffe," "Bold as a zebra."

A few hundred cubic feet of compressed air and many hours of airbrushing later, both client and agency agreed: The ads were stunning.

At this stage in many television campaigns, the team would kick back while the media mavens dumped a couple of spots into the Super Bowl line-up, maybe reserved some time on the Breeder's Cup telecast and started talking PGA Tour. The client would sweat a bit over the number of zeros on the checks, but it would all work out when the awareness tracking studies came in.

While they could emulate GM's product pyramid marketing strategy on the product side, Citizen wasn't about to go into television with a line that might do $15 million at retail. And they weren't going to blanket the newsweeklies and hope that sheer volume of exposure would translate into sales.

For one thing, Citizen didn't have the right distribution to get Noblia into glass cases in fine jewelry stores. Because its business had been in the under-$100 segment, Citizen was amply represented in discount or modestly-priced outlets, but had very little penetration in high-line department and jewelry stores.

"If we were going to sell Noblia, we had to get into Tourneau Corner, Bailey Banks & Biddle, Carson-Pirie-Scott, Saks, Bloomingdale's," Kravetz

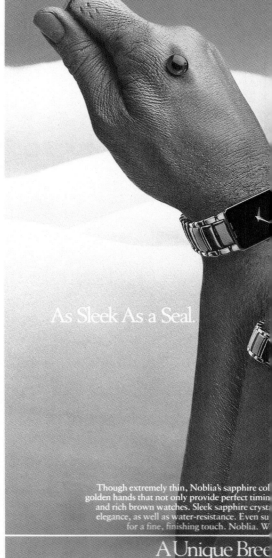

As Sleek As a Seal.

Though extremely thin, Noblia's sapphire col
golden hands that not only provide perfect timin
and rich brown watches. Sleek sapphire cryst
elegance, as well as water-resistance. Even su
for a fine, finishing touch. Noblia. W

A Unique Bree

explains. "Fortunoff might cherry-pick a few items, but they never carried the nuts and bolts of the line. We had to open up those stores for Noblia."

The consumer print schedule was one way to do that.

"The print schedule was almost as important as any other aspect. We really needed to set an image. The 'hanimals' did a good job of that from an advertising point of view, but *where* the ads appeared was just as important," Kravetz continues. Lintas bought heavily in the fashion list: *GQ, Harper's Bazaar, Vogue* and *Esquire.* It also bought *Town & Country,* a key play in the jewelry industry.

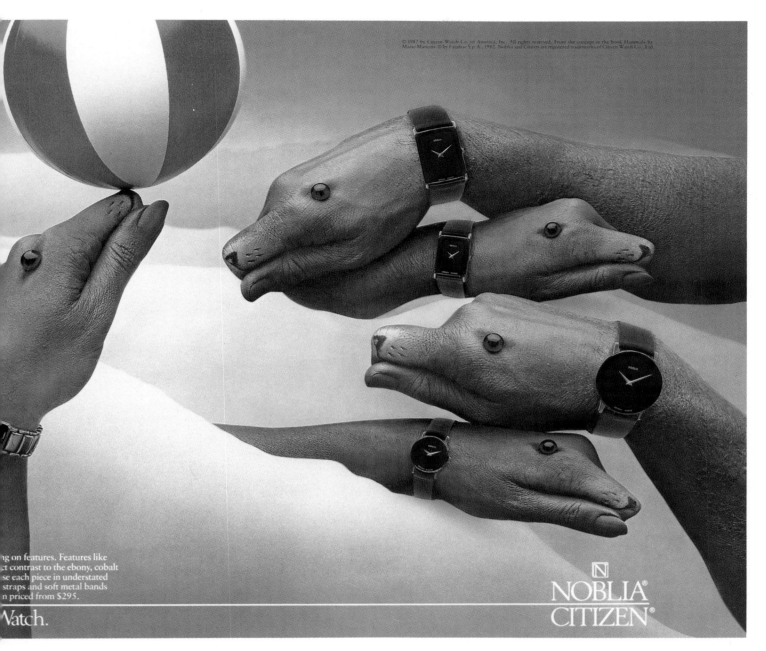

ng on features. Features like
ct contrast to the ebony, cobalt
se each piece in understated
straps and soft metal bands
n priced from $295.

Watch.

NOBLIA®
CITIZEN®

"*Town & Country* is a pivotal book. It carries more high-grade watch advertising than any other U.S. magazine," Kravetz says. "Partly that's because of its audience but it's also due to the fact that so many influential retailers read it."

The "hanimals" were unleashed in Fall 1986, to coincide with the second half of the 1986 buying season. Citizen put about $2 million behind the effort, and a bit more than that for 1987. For their money, they got a series of spreads and a special twelve-page insert in jewelery trade magazines. For the consumer books, Lintas preprinted four-

page inserts. To help build reach and frequency, single-page units—cleverly cutdown versions of the spread ads—were sprinkled into men's audience magazines.

The results surprised even the optimists at Lintas. In 1986, Citizen shipped 35,000 Noblias. Of those, Kravetz estimates two-thirds sold through at retail.

"That left us with about a third of the initial inventory to supply orders made in spring 1987," he says. "But the reorders were way beyond anything we had predicted going in. We're going into the fourth quarter and it looks like the 1987 orders will be 50% over the 1986 orders. It's so

"Everyone has their own personal favorites," says copywriter Mike Jordan. "Personally, I like the first group of executions photographed by Hiro, although the second batch is very good as well."

It was Jordan who initially suggested using Mariotti's "hanimal" concept to introduce Noblia. As for the headlines, Jordan says they just tried to find words that described the various animals and also made a statement about fashion.

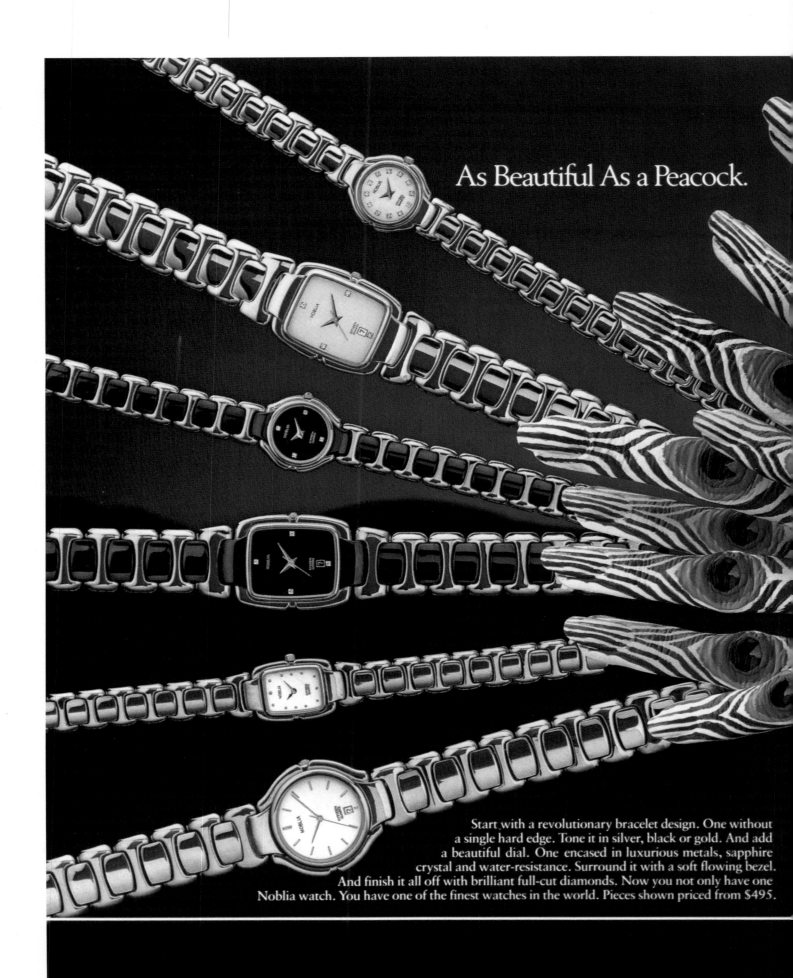

As Beautiful As a Peacock.

Start with a revolutionary bracelet design. One without a single hard edge. Tone it in silver, black or gold. And add a beautiful dial. One encased in luxurious metals, sapphire crystal and water-resistance. Surround it with a soft flowing bezel. And finish it all off with brilliant full-cut diamonds. Now you not only have one Noblia watch. You have one of the finest watches in the world. Pieces shown priced from $495.

To extend reach and frequency without doing terminal damage to Citizen's budget, Lintas cleverly designed the spreads so that they could be run effectively as single pages. These were placed in magazines with upscale male readers.

far above the projections that Citizen has had some difficulty keeping up with the demand. They've also expanded the line significantly. In the spring of 1987 we were selling approximately 100 SKUs [stock-keeping units]. In the fall of 1987, we had doubled the line to 200 SKUs."

The spectacular sales and subsequent line expansion were in no small measure due to Noblia's acceptance in the retail trade. Within a short time, venues that Citizen had been trying to crack for a decade were hounding them for more product.

"Right now the significance of this business can be measured by the fact that the major retailers in the high-grade segment want to be associated with us," Kravetz beams. "We're tagging our advertising with the majors in markets all over the country: Mayer's in Florida, Fortunoff in New York, Marshall Fields in Chicago, Carson-Pirie-Scott in the Midwest. There are eighteen or so chain jewelers—Kay and J.B. Robinson—which are tagging our ads and running them locally."

Fortunoff went one step further. It asked the company if it would be okay to reproduce the "hanimals" in three dimensional displays in the windows of its Fifth Avenue store. That's like asking a manufacturer if he'd like a billboard on the fifty yard line at the Super Bowl.

"It's fabulous," Kravetz says. People line up in front of the windows and stare at these tableaux. Sometimes it's like trying to get a peek at Lord & Taylor's Christmas windows, a New York tradition only slightly less claustrophobic than riding the subway at rush hour.

Lintas thought it was such a good idea that it began designing its own dioramas, planning to send them to major retailers as point of purchase displays.

Success seems to linger quite sweetly on the tongues of the group at Lintas, but Kravetz is a modest guy: "We knew we had a nice concept; we entered a lot of competitions and racked up quite a few awards with this campaign. But none of this would have worked if Citizen didn't have the product to back it up. You have to give them credit for producing a line of watches that backs us up every step of the way."

As Bold As a Zebra.

Feel the richly textured bracelets of the Noblia tissé. Each one moves with amazing grace because every link is so finely aligned. Even the dials—in gold or ivory—complement this interwoven elegance. What's more, Citizen has interwoven technology with all this style. So Noblia not only looks beautiful. It keeps beautiful time. Watch shown priced at $395.

NOBLIA®
CITIZEN®

A Unique Breed of Watch.

For brochure, send $2 to Citizen, 1200 Wall Street West, Lyndhurst, N.J. 07071

Lintas:New York Takes Diet Coke For A Walk On The Wild Side

Client: Coca-Cola Company
Agency: Lintas: New York

DIET COKE

For the first two decades of their existence, advertising diet colas was a bit like advertising a funeral home: defensive and a little bit apologetic. The reason was simple. While they had a significant product benefit—far fewer calories than sugar colas— diet soft drinks just didn't taste very good. Remember "Taste, the aftertaste is gone"? Then there was that cyclamate thing and the ongoing saccharin controversy.

Ironically, throughout this period sales of diet soft drinks were growing three to four times faster than their sugar counterparts. Despite the limitations, despite the impression that diet drinks were an inferior substitute for "the real thing," they had one critical thing going for them: Demography. Slim was in with the baby boom generation, which constituted an ever rising percentage of the population.

This was the world as we knew it prior to 1982. Diet Pepsi and Pepsi Light (which at various times was a mid-calorie drink, a cola/lemon drink, a diet drink for men and so on) together held the largest share of the diet segment. Tab, the Coca-Cola Company's entry, was just behind their combined sales but was number one in total sales for a single brand; in fact it was the largest-selling diet product of any kind in the world.

Despite Tab's impressive sales, Coca-Cola just wasn't happy being number two in a segment it felt would eventually represent a majority of the soft drink business. And while Tab hadn't been able to out-muscle Pepsi's collective diet brands, Coca-Cola had two big guns in the drawer.

One was the Coke trademark. Coca-Cola had never felt comfortable putting the Coke brand mark on Tab. You can understand their reluctance to risk sullying what is one of the top trademarks of all time by using it on a product that didn't taste as good as the original Coca-Cola. Gun number two was that, in the late 1970s, the guys in the lab in Atlanta had come up with a diet concoction that, wonder of wonders, actually tasted good.

The company had been sitting on this formula because it tasted very

different from Tab. Consumers might object to a new formulation. In hindsight, they were probably right. No one was quite ready to throw the Coke trademark into the pot, so the product stayed in the lab.

In 1982, there was a new mood at Coca-Cola, not to mention new management at the top. The time was right to draw down on Pepsi. The company decided to market its new diet formulation as Diet Coke.

"Another soft drink certainly wasn't on everybody's wish list for Christmas," says Mike Beindorff, group director for cola brands. The shelves were already overflowing with product. Another entry meant yet one more stock keeping unit for grocers, one more spigot for restaurants to maintain. "We had to have a unique position for Diet Coke. It had to be damn good and it had to stand for something special. We felt that if we played our cards right, we might eventually obtain a 5% share of the market."

Boy were they wrong.

In the first half of 1987, Diet Coke had a 33% share of the diet segment. Add in sales of Tab, still the number three diet drink behind Diet Coke and Diet Pepsi, and the Coca-Cola Company's diet products are garnering about 16% of the total soft drink market. That's 16% of $40 billion.

"Five years ago, diet colas were between four and five share points total, so we have no complaints about the performance of Diet Coke," Beindorff chuckles.

What determines who wins and loses in this business is the distribution system—the muscle—and the image of the product. "The fundamental strategy for Diet Coke has never changed. I'm from the school of thought that you create a position for the product and then you hammer it and hammer it and hammer it. Our feeling is that every year we stay on our campaign, every year we push the same positioning, we're building equity," says Beindorff.

"Probably the most important factor in the Diet Coke success has been its positioning. We'd love to take credit for it here, but the credit really goes to Lintas: New

When Lintas: New York originally proposed *Island*, a spot eventually reworked to showcase the Pointer Sisters, it looked a little fishy to the people at Diet Coke. The fanciful duo above characterize the hip, outrageous and un-Coke-like execution. Released in 1987, it became one of the most popular of the recent executions. It makes Diet Coke fun; one of the premiere hot buttons of the relatively broad target audience.

This slender California-look blonde is the archetype of the traditional diet soda drinker: a female aged 18-35. But as the Baby Boom bulge has aged, the market for diet sodas has gotten grayer and considerably longer of tooth. As a result, Diet Coke has aired appeals directed at men and at both older, and younger, targets as well.

Opposite, Sumo wrestlers, Marvelous Marvin Hagler and the Chicago Bears (then Super Bowl champs) plump for Diet Coke. The object, says Coke's Mike Beindorff, is to give the impression that "everyone's drinking it."

York. It was their idea to position Diet Coke against the mainstream attribute of taste. No one had ever done that."

By some standards, Lintas: New York had just painted itself into a corner. The positioning was brilliant, but how do you convince consumers that it's for real?

"This is going to sound a little like a cliche, but we had the product," Beindorff asserts. "We knew Diet Coke was clearly superior to other diet soft drinks. We had to create a promise that would live up to the product, not the other way around. Of course we were concerned about how people would react. We tested it thoroughly, and all of our research told us the product was so good relative to other diet soft drinks that we could make the statement 'you're going to drink it just for the taste of it.' "

This was a totally new message for consumers. No apologies. Just a straightforward pitch: Try it, you'll like it. But what pitchman could pull it off?

"Our job was to convince the world that everyone was drinking Diet Coke, to create the sense that this was much bigger than just the 32-year-old housewife who has switched to Diet Coke from Tab or Diet Pepsi. One way to do that was to use celebrities in our advertising."

Beindorff actually used it; the "c" word. Although he doesn't let on, celebrities must have been a bit of a sore point around the shop in Atlanta, what with superstars like Michael Jackson and Lionel Ritchie thumping the tub for Pepsi. Beindorff is careful to draw a distinction between the strategies of Pepsi and Coke: "We were willing to spend for celebrity talent, but every time we talked to somebody, the first thing they'd ask was, 'Gee, I guess you're going to want to pay me $5 million.' And we weren't. We've never paid anything approaching a million. That's directly opposed to what our competition is doing."

Beindorff says that's because the company didn't want the

celebrities to upstage the product. The celebrities always sing the Diet Coke jingle, never their own material, never even adaptations of their material with Diet Coke lyrics.

"We're always looking for celebrities with a very broad appeal, people like Whitney Houston and the Pointer Sisters. We don't care if they're male, female, white, black or green as long as they have that appeal."

If you're not going to spend $5 million, it's hard to find one personality and make one spot that can appeal to a segment as broad as the buyers of diet soft drinks. So Diet Coke doesn't try. Instead, it uses the pool approach, crafting a series of spots that, in sum, will cover the bases. Commercials featuring the Pointer Sisters, Manhattan Transfer and Pierce Brosnan are the nucleus of Diet Coke's 1987 effort; a nucleus strengthened by a group of supporting spots and turbocharged by an absolute fluke that is now known simply as *Penguins*.

The Brosnan spot is straight ahead product talk: Diet Coke tastes great and it has only one calorie. The tall, dark, handsome actor is definitely a lady's man, but, according to Beindorff, he's also a man's man, a suave but tough guy. A Casablanca-like setting supplies plenty of romance for the ladies, the traditional users of diet sodas, and the Ninja assassins the danger that pulls in male viewers as well. "We made that spot to help us talk to men, which tend to be an under-developed segment when it comes to diet soft drinks," he explains.

The Manhattan Transfer spot is completely different. It was filmed in the Palladium in Los Angeles and features views of the well-known jazz band bebopping on stage through a backlit veil of steamy atmosphere. Meanwhile, on the dance floor, the crowd gets into the mood with a variety of daring pas de deux, peregrinations and bumps and grinds. It's light and it's fun and it has a lot of

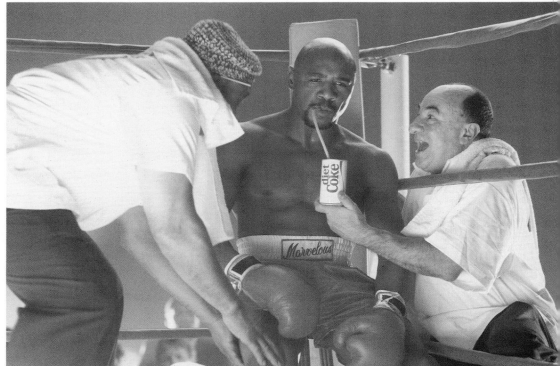

Covering the spectrum of tastes and predilections was never so delightful as when Diet Coke shot this spot featuring the Manhattan Transfer. Their fans tend to be a little older and more sophisticated than your average heavy-metal listener.

energy. Great stuff for a cola spot.

"Manhattan Transfer has been around a long time and their primary appeal is to people over the age of 25. They can effectively talk to someone who's 47 or 48 years old. They're classy and sophisticated," Beindorff says.

That leaves the Pointer Sisters. What can you say about this energetic trio? They're irresistible; probably on everyone's list of folks you'd most like to invite to a party. A "parr-tay" that is, not one of those dry affairs where lit professors from the local community college trade allusions over a bowl of mixed nuts.

But what to do with them? The girls are sassy, hip, funny and totally outrageous. Not the type of thing we've come to expect from the safe-and-sane crowd on Peachtree Street. So where did *Island* come from?

"About 80% of that storyboard was first presented in late 1984," Beindorff says. "Lintas: New York showed it to us as a mainstream commercial. It was so off the wall—penguins coming down the beach serving people Diet Coke; cans parachuting in from nowhere; people appearing from out of nowhere and walking on water. At the time we thought it could be a pretty effective commercial, but it was risky. We could spend a lot of money and if things didn't go just right, it would be a very expensive fiasco. Plus, the idea of penguins serving Diet Coke didn't appeal to everyone here.

"The board was shelved. Then, after we signed the Pointer Sisters, we were looking for an idea that was a bit different. This was it."

Lintas: New York got the—presumably good—news, and a bit of a shock. Beindorff can laugh about the ensuing mix-up, now. "When we told them we wanted to shoot the board, they said, 'Of course you know we have to animate this; you can't use real penguins.' We had presented the board at Coke saying we were going to use real penguins, so we told Lintas: New York that if we

The Manhattan Transfer spot was filmed in the Palladium in Los Angeles. Lots of smoke, undulating bodies and 40s fashions make this a sizzling visual and aural delight. Whether listeners are getting into jazz for the first time or whether they remember it from the days when Tommy Dorsey was the closest thing we had to a superstar, Manhattan Transfer is able to pull viewers into a bebopping time warp.

A Casablanca-like setting proved the perfect vehicle for the ever-cool heartthrob Pierce Brosnan. Co-star of the *Remington Steele* TV series, Brosnan has also made a host of TV movies and appeals to both men and women, according to Beindorff. The spot features Brosnan being shadowed by a hapless Ninja assassin. Every time the assassin strikes, fate intervenes, as when the throwing star he hurls at Brosnan strikes the waiter's service tray instead (opposite). By the end of the spot, the mysterious woman is his, with, of course, the proper enticement of a Diet Coke.

were going to do it, it would be with live penguins."

To get the vibrant, surreal color called for in the board, the commercial had to be shot indoors. The only sound stage available that could handle the props—an ocean, an island, a 15-foot tall can of Diet Coke—was Shepherd Studios in England. Lintas: New York booked the studio and found a European bird trainer, Mr. Penguin, to supply the penguins.

There are several species of penguins, and the crew had Mr. Penguin train three kinds of birds for the spot. Of the three, the emperor penguins are the only ones that really look like penguins. Unfortunately, they're also the dumbest of the three. While agency, client and talent counted down the days to the shoot, Mr. Penguin was trying to find a harness for his birds that would support the serving trays holding Diet Coke while the penguins strolled about the set. Always ready with a Plan B, the agency spent $13,000 to create four penguin costumes for child actors in case the birds balked.

"When we got to the shoot, we had two different kinds of penguins. We had these costumes and kids ready in case they didn't work. Literally, we didn't know until the cameras rolled whether we were going to get it," Beindorff says. "The morning we shot the penguins it was 32° in the studio. The penguins can't work in heat. Also, they get nervous around people, so we had to screen them off so we could only see them on the monitors. And we couldn't feed them. As soon as you feed a penguin it immediately stands up and goes to sleep. So there we were on this ridiculously expensive sound stage, with a full crew, hungry penguins and it was cold as hell. We really weren't in the mood to spend two days shooting penguins. What we hoped for was to get just enough footage—three or four seconds—of the penguins carrying the trays down the walkway, which looked like an Atlantic City-type boardwalk. Well, the first bird went out of the gate and we all held our breath. He walked. And he walked. And he walked. The camera kept

The spot features Brosnan being shadowed by a hapless Ninja assassin. Every time the assassin strikes, fate intervenes, as when the throwing star he hurls at Brosnan strikes the waiter's service tray instead. By the end of the spot, the mysterious woman is his, with, of course, the proper enticement of a Diet Coke.

Island, a tropical fantasy starring the Pointer Sisters, is as brash, flashy and sassy as the girls themselves. Ironically, the storyboard sat on the shelf for several years before being okayed because Coca-Cola wasn't completely comfortable with it. After signing the Pointer Sisters, it became the perfect vehicle for their outrageous style.

rolling until we had 40 seconds! We were huddled around the monitors trying to keep warm and going bananas. We replayed it immediately and everyone started talking at once about how we could make a whole spot out of the penguins and won't it be fabulous. During the course of that morning we shot the penguins doing two or three different things. The writers were literally writing these silly penguin spots on the set."

The spots, which included the Pointer Sisters' *Island* and three more, were all created in the editing room from footage shot that morning. Coke put the commercials through its in-house research mill and had day-after recall measured as well. They "broke the bank," in both tests, Beindorff says.

"Penguins are like puppies. They're very lovable characters. When we brought them to life, giving them a human voice via voice-over, it was funny and very appealing."

All of this brings us right back to where we started, the due caution with which Coca-Cola

treats the Coke trademark: The most successful Diet Coke spots so far are those which are most unlike Coca-Cola's traditional, tradition-laden advertising. What effect might this have on Coca-Cola Classic?

"Diet Coke's audience is not as broad as Classic's," Beindorff explains. "In 1985, if we didn't already know it, consumers told us that Classic is something pretty unique. It's more than a soft drink, it's also a symbol. When we tried to change the product, consumers said, 'Excuse me, this belongs to us. Give it back now.'

"It also said to us that Classic has an ingrained image. The product has become such a part of the culture that we don't have the license to suddenly do totally new, unique, off-the-wall things with it.

"Diet Coke gave us the license to compete with the Coke trademark in an important segment of the business. Over the long term, it gives us the ability to enhance the image of the Coke trademark in a way we couldn't with Classic, or which would take much longer to accomplish.

As the Bard says, there's many a slip 'twixt lip and cup. There was a bit of a mix-up in communications over *Islands*. Lintas: New York had conceived the spot as animation. After deciding to move ahead, Coke insisted the execution be done all-live on film. The ensuing scramble apparently made for an interesting couple of weeks for both client and agency. The result was well worth the effort. *Islands* was an instant success.

The girls' silhouettes appear out on the ocean. As the front lighting comes up, you see they are standing on top of the water. A giant can of Diet Coke comes up behind them while normal-sized cans parachute down to a crowd of appropriately-bronzed beachgoers.

Although the Pointer Sisters were the recognized stars of *Island*, the penguin waiters were the unexpected heroes, waddling off with the show. Before the shoot—done in an abysmally cold London studio—no one was sure whether they could get the penguins to carry Diet Coke. Although they never got as far as learning the Bunny Dip, the penguins surprised the crew by strolling up and down the set almost interminably. The agency folks got so excited, they wrote two executions for the penguins on the spot.

"I look at Diet Coke as Coca-Cola without the calories and without a hundred years of tradition. It's the Coke of the future.

"Sugar soft drinks continue to grow, but not at the rate that diet drinks are growing. In the first half of 1987, sales of sugar soft drinks were up a few percentage points; diet drinks were up 11%. They've been growing three to four times as fast as sugar drinks for twenty years now."

That kind of segment growth doesn't happen without a very broad consumer base. In fact, from 1986 through 1987, Beindorff asserts that more of Diet Coke's volume growth came from males than from females.

"As the taste of diets approaches the taste of sugar drinks, more people will switch," says Beindorff. "When will Diet Coke become the number two soft drink to Coca-Cola Classic? It won't happen in 1988 or 1989. But it will happen before 1995."

To do that, Diet Coke will have to knock off Pepsi-Cola. And no one expects the guys at Pepsi to just roll over.

Still, Mike Beindorff and the Coca-Cola Company expect to be ready. If the quality of these spots are any indication, so will the folks over at Lintas: New York.

Real Life Equals Real Sales For John Hancock

HANCOCK

Client: John Hancock Financial Services
Agency: Hill, Holiday, Connors, Cosmopulos Inc.

One of the themes heard time and again in the research for this book was that Americans are in the market for emotions. Drama that grips the heart as well as the head.

Real Life, Real Answers, the powerful, image-shifting campaign created for Boston-based John Hancock by Hill, Holiday, Connors, Cosmopulos does just that. Its magic is in an approach that has seemingly been misunderstood by those in the trade and embraced by the public in almost equal measure. Of course, the proof is the sales figures. By that standard, *Real Life* has been very effective. And, fully understood or not, its success has naturally spawned imitations. While some artfully mimic the technique of the executions, few have been able to duplicate the deft fit of marketing need and appropriate creative that made *Real Life* work for viewers and for the client.

Hancock's need was familiar enough. The hundred-year-old giant is well-known as a stable, dependable insurance underwriter. But with its prime competitors—Prudential *et. al.*—moving aggressively into the financial services market, Hancock was in danger of being left behind. While it, too, offered a buffet of financial options, Hancock had to communicate that to the public. The company also wanted to convey an updated definition of the organization to the employees of its diverse divisions.

"We didn't want to change the public perception of Hancock into something the company wasn't," says Don Easdon, vice president and creative director for Hill, Holiday. "At the same time we wanted to emphasize their existing strengths.

"The insurance agent is a sympathetic figure. He comes around, sits down and listens to people, listens to their problems. That was an inherent strength Hancock had. But insurance agents aren't perceived as experts in providing financial services."

Hill, Holiday had one other strength going in: "Money is an easy

VISUAL	AUDIO

Ralph and Wendy Moxcey

Ages: 46, 44
Two children
Income (dual) . . . $49,000

VISUAL	AUDIO
Ralph and Wendy Moxcey Ages: 46, 44 Two children Income (dual) . . . $49,000	BOYS: Giggle DAD: (To boys) Boys! DAD: Man . . . that gas bill last month was a real choker. MOM: You're not kidding.

Estimated Expenses	
Mortgage, insurance, property tax	$16,500
Income Taxes	9,800
Living Costs	17,000
	$43,300

DAD: Boys! (To Mom) Did you go to the bank?
BOYS: Giggle.
MOM: Yes. This afternoon.
DAD: Good. How's work going?
MOM: Real good. (Very bright)

Needs

To supplement income
To build capital for college expenses
Long-term security

Needs

To supplement income
To build capital for college expenses
Long-term security

DAD: (To boys) Ahem. (To Mom) Do you know any good jokes?
MOM: No.
BOYS: Giggle.

Answers

John Hancock IRAs
John Hancock Mutual Funds
John Hancock Disability Income
Universal Life

DAD: Too bad (Look) These boys'd love to hear 'em.
DAD: (To boys.) Hey Boys. Get smart.
BOYS: Giggle.

Real life, real answers.
John Hancock Financial Services

Known as an insurance carrier, John Hancock sought to reposition itself in the financial services market with this series of intense, smoothly edited vignettes. Each portrays a few minutes in the life of very ordinary people. Supers give us a glimpse of the financial situation facing each of them and propose John Hancock financial products as "real answers" for their "real life" problems.

thing to advertise, because everyone is interested in money," Easdon says. "Automatically we felt we could get the public's interest. Making them believe that John Hancock would be a good financial partner for them was more difficult."

Also making the situation a little difficult was the fact that Hill, Holiday wasn't Hancock's agency of record.

The success of their new business pitch depended on coming up with real good answers to Hancock's real life problems. The agency prepared two concepts for presentation to David D'Allesandro, vice president of John Hancock.

The agency presented the "safe" campaign first: A giant hand scribing the famous John Hancock signature across a map of the U.S. The idea played into the enormous equity of the Hancock logo, painstakingly built up through years of advertising.

D'Allesandro wasn't impressed.

Then Easdon presented *Real Life.*

"Our idea was to put people first and the product second," Easdon says. "People were searching for answers to their financial problems, but they didn't know what questions to ask and they didn't want to appear stupid when they talked with an 'expert.' "

Easdon felt the agency could help allay that fear by depicting highly personalized life situations and presenting Hancock as a knowledgeable, sympathetic partner. By showing how Hancock could build an individual program for the folks in the spots, Easdon hoped to evoke empathy among viewers who'd faced similar situations.

It was a slippery concept; hard enough to pull off, but even harder to communicate to the client in rough form. Easdon did it all with a few key frames: "The spots were too complex to put on storyboards so I had to make him imagine most of it."

D'Allesandro's imagination must have been fully engaged that day: He loved it.

More important, Easdon says, he trusted the agency enough to "stay out of the way."

"We didn't have to cut through layers of bureaucracy to get our stuff approved. Our offices are in the Hancock building. Dave came down to talk with us whenever we wanted, but he sensed how fragile the concept was and let us do it our way."

That way was very, very quietly.

Easdon's concern was that the spots not put the century-old insurance company on a pedestal; that they talk with the viewers, not at them. "We tried to make the spots quiet enough that you could turn them off without thinking. "

Yow. In an age when advertisers and agencies are busting their brains over how to break through clutter, here's a guy talking about spending a whole bunch of money to make spots that are so quiet that viewers can turn them off without thinking about it.

But Easdon was planning to stack the deck with one drawing card—a very compelling one: Voyeurism. Deep down most of us are Peeping Toms. We're fascinated by the personal details of other people's lives.

Easdon proposed a series of spots, each a tightly-scripted situation: One features a couple at a bank signing a mortgage. Another shows a brother and sister discussing how they're going to take care of their aged parents. Vignettes of live action are interspersed with black screens detailing the participant's financial condition in white type.

"We hoped to intrigue viewers, to draw them into the story," Easdon says. "We weren't expecting them to absorb the whole message—all of the details—the first time around. The second time, you might watch it more carefully because you knew something was

You got to be making at least twenty five? Yes?

Thirty?

Are you making thirty? Tell me.

Thirty, right?

Well...what've you got besides the car?

Investments? An IRA? Insurance?

No?

When are you going to do something?

You're not eighteen anymore.

Michael Mark
Age: 26
Single

Occupation Sales

Income $30,000

Assets
Auto $7,200
Cash 3,000

Estimated Expenses
Income Tax $8,500
Rent 5,400
Auto Loan and Insurance 3,000
Food, Clothing 4,100
Entertainment 3,600
Miscellaneous 2,400
$27,000

Needs
To regulate spending
To limit taxes
To begin an investment program

Answers
John Hancock IRAs
John Hancock Life Insurance
John Hancock U.S. Government Guaranteed Mortgages Trust
John Hancock Auto Insurance

Michael Mark had a long talk with his older brother last night. He reached the conclusion that things weren't as great as they could be.

Later on, he had a conversation with a John Hancock representative. These are the types of products we recommended given his situation in life.

Think about where you are right now. Perhaps you'll give us the opportunity to help you make the most out of your real life situation.

Real life, real answers.

Michael Mark
Single, professional

Margaret and Tom Fitzgerald
Married, no children, dual income

Greg Clow
Divorced, remarried, one child
from each marriage

After this we'll have lunch.

We'll close 'on the house.

Then, we'll have our first big lunch as homeowners.

If we have any money left.

Margaret and Tom Fitzgerald
Age: 30, 31
Married; no children yet

Income
Combined Salaries $42,000
Bonus 2,000
$44,000

Assets
Home Equity $20,000
Furniture, Misc. 10,000
Cash, Savings 4,000

Estimated Expenses
House Closing Costs $4,000
Mortgage, Property Tax, 10,000
Insurance
Income Tax 9,200
Auto Loan and Insurance 2,400
Food, Clothing, Misc. 14,000
$39,600

Needs
To protect housing investment
To develop a long-term investment strategy

Answers
John Hancock Homeowner's Insurance
John Hancock Universal Life
John Hancock IRAs
John Hancock Growth Trust

Tom and Margaret Fitzgerald closed on their house this morning. Their first house.

A short while later they talked to us to find out ways they might protect this investment and discover other investment options.

A John Hancock representative furnished them with the recommendations you see above. Maybe you'll see in the plan we described for them an opportunity for yourself.

Real life, real answers.

GLOSSARY

Some of the terms and product names used in this supplement may be new to you. The descriptions below will help you understand the kinds of financial products and services John Hancock offers and how they might fit into your life. Contact your nearest John Hancock representative for more information or a current prospectus.

Real life, real answers.

John Hancock
Financial Services

---

different about it. The third time, you'd start to read the information in the black areas."

The spots were more than a little different. The John Hancock logo never appears until the very end of the spots.

"Our goal was to reposition Hancock. If we'd used the logo in the beginning, the viewers might have been turned off early. They'd have drawn on their existing impressions of Hancock, drawn their own conclusions about the situations we were posing. They wouldn't have given us the credibility we needed to offer Hancock as a financial services company."

Easdon wanted the spots to appear as one unbroken take. "People have labeled the technique documentary, but it's not true documentary. I objected to doing documentary early on because I felt the style could have been imitated too easily. Also, we'd have had to spend a lot of hours shooting and couldn't control the copy.

"On the other hand, we also wanted the spots to appear very spontaneous. It's hard to get that feeling when you control the copy tightly. We had a terrific copywriter, Bill Heater. On the set, he listened to the way the actors read and then rewrote the dialogue to better fit their natural speech patterns. The final spots sound as though we used real people and let them say what they wanted."

What Easdon and Heater had

The media department at Hill, Holiday suggested that the campaign could be extended into print, diversifying the audience and extending the reach of the campaign. Two eight-page inserts were prepared. Each featured three case histories, some of which were picked up from the television executions. Although not as emotionally compelling as the videos, the inserts carried a great deal more details, proposing specific Hancock financial products for each situation. The last page of each insert carried a glossary explaining features of the various products and some of the terms used by financial services companies.

	VISUAL	AUDIO VO:

Jean Wolf
Divorced
Custody of son, David

Jean Wolf
Divorced,
custody of son, David

Income/Assets

Salary and		
child support	. . . .	$40,000
Condominium	. . . .	90,000
Investments	. . . .	10,000

How are you.
Yes. Yes I'm fine. Ya. Um. Well I'm
calling because you forgot David's
birthday yesterday.

Needs
Fund college costs
Protect assets
Long term financial security

Needs
Fund college costs
Protect assets
Long term financial security

Ya, ya…I'm busy, I have responsibilities but I manage. Well enough.

Answers
John Hancock Term Life Insurance
John Hancock Variable Annuity
John Hancock Condominium
    Insurance

Look. I can't. I can't. Uh…I'm at a pay
phone. Ya. Call tonight.

John Hancock
Financial Services

Real life, real answers.
John Hancock Financial Services

Creative director Don Easdon says this video execution is his personal favorite. A divorced woman stops by the side of the road to call her former spouse. The conversation is awkward and halting. She wants to tell him that he forgot their son's birthday. The supers tell us what we already know: Divorced women with children have a hard row to hoe financially.

Aside from the gripping emotion in this spot, it is compelling because it positions Hancock as a financial partner for people who aren't upscale, dual-income, childless and super-affluent.

hit upon was a principle articulated by Mark Twain nearly a century ago in an essay, *Fenimore Cooper's Literary Offenses.* In it, he listed "eighteen rules governing literary art in the domain of romantic fiction." Rule number five is, "[These rules] require that when the personages of a tale deal in conversation, the talk shall sound like human talk, and be talk such as human beings would be likely to talk under the circumstances, and have a discoverable meaning, also a discoverable purpose, and a show of relevancy, and remain in the neighborhood of the subject at hand, and be interesting to the reader, and help out the tale, and stop when the people cannot think of anything more to say."

Anyone who's watched even a few spots for toilet paper or dish soap knows that this rule is not universally appreciated. I have never in my life tap danced into the kitchen, plucked my wife's soapy hands out of the dishwater and said, "As soft as kid leather, honey!" Maybe that's why I'm not actively engaged in matrimony.

In his essay, Twain also wrote that, "[The rules] require that when a personage talks like an illustrated, gilt-edged, tree-calf, hand-tooled, seven-dollar Friendship's Offering [Bible] in the beginning of a paragraph, he shall not talk like a Negro minstrel in the end of it." Far too many advertisers succumb to the temptation to "lighten up" serious subjects by having a super-competent executive or lawyer devolve into a babbling sub-normal I.Q. "Everyman" in the course of thirty seconds. It just doesn't wash.

Heater's scripts were the perfect antidote to such silliness. The dialogue pauses at natural break points as the copy screens interrupt the live action. The intention was not to break the rhythm of the scene in any way. "We didn't want to be obtrusive," Easdon says.

Working the copy screens in between the vignettes was

handled very artfully.

"We found that a cut to black or even a normal dissolve to black didn't work because they were too abrupt," he continues. "We decided to fade to white and then fade up to black. We reversed the order going out of the copy screens. The fades were very long. That makes it easy to watch the copy screens because they come on very slowly. They don't jar you."

The last two black screens carried the theme lines "Real life" and "Real answers." After that, the John Hancock logo finally appeared. All of this took eight or nine seconds in a fifty-second spot. That's eight or nine very expensive seconds with no voice over, no music. Just black screens with white type.

"I wanted to end the spots quietly," Easdon explains. "I wanted the viewers to think about what was just said. Even though I knew how expensive it was, I wanted to create a pregnant pause before the next spot appeared. Usually you're backed up to another spot or run into programming. The pause gives people time to reflect on the message."

Hancock loved the finished spots. They proudly previewed them for their agents in the field, fully expecting a rousing cheer of approval.

They didn't get it.

"The agents were deathly afraid of this campaign," Easdon says, but Hancock was undaunted. The spots broke in the most prime of prime times: the Super Bowl.

And the rest, as they say, is history.

"When the phone calls started coming in the agents got behind the campaign," Easdon chuckles. "There was an amazing, genuine feeling among viewers. They appreciated the approach of the advertising perhaps more than they needed financial services.

"The campaign did two things right away. It changed the perception of Hancock from an

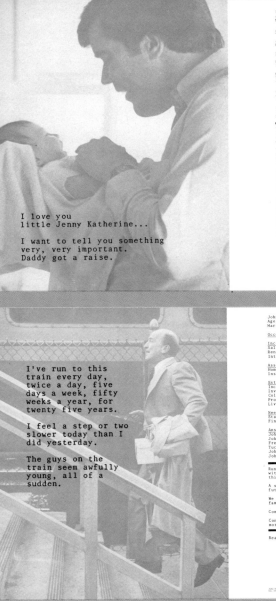

I love you
little Jenny Katherine...

I want to tell you something
very, very important.
Daddy got a raise.

John Hancock
Financial Services

I've run to this
train every day,
twice a day, five
days a week, fifty
weeks a year, for
twenty five years.

I feel a step or two
slower today than I
did yesterday.

The guys on the
train seem awfully
young, all of a
sudden.

This is no knock on
your mother.

Your mother is a very
good person.

She's just not a very
good swimmer.

I'll teach you how to
swim.

Your mother can teach
you...you know...how
to cross the street
and that.

Okay?

```
Greg Clow
Age:  35
Divorced; remarried
Two children (one from previous marriage)

Income
Greg                                          $42,000
Wife                                           28,000
Interest income                                 5,000
                                              $75,000
Assets
Home Equity                                   $50,000
Investments                                    50,000

Estimated Expenses
Alimony, Child Support                         $8,000
Income Tax                                     19,800
Mortgage, Property Tax, Insurance              15,000
Loans, Life Insurance                           3,200
Living Costs                                    14,500
                                              $60,500
Needs
Long-term security for two families
To shelter taxable income
To develop a plan to meet educational needs of
both children

Answers
John Hancock Tax-Exempt Income Trust
John Hancock Tax-Deferred Annuity
Tucker Anthony Securities
John Hancock Variable Life
John Hancock IRAs
John Hancock Special Equities Trust
```

Greg Clow is a father to two children, in two
different families. It's his job to provide for
both. He spoke to us recently about developing a
plan to help him. We recommended the investment
products above--given his income, his obligations and
the goals that both he and his present wife had set
for themselves.

Maybe you find yourself facing similar challenges and
obligations. Perhaps we can help you as well.

Contact your nearest John Hancock representative for
more information or a current prospectus.

Real life, real answers.

John Hancock
Financial Services

John Hancock Mutual Life Insurance Co., Boston, MA 02117, John Hancock Variable Life Insurance Co., John Hancock Advisers, Inc./Distributors, Inc., Tucker Anthony & R.L. Day, Inc.

insurance company to a financial services company. For a short while, it made them a leader in the market."

With only $5 million behind the initial effort, media selection and placement were crucial. Easdon credits the media team with not only meeting this challenge, but also with suggesting that the theme be extended to a series of preprinted magazine inserts and run-of-book magazine spreads.

"It's really a television idea. The impact has to come from the reality of watching somebody like you who's in a situation you can empathize with. You can't do that in print," Easdon points out. "What we could do was remind people of the television spots and play up the words. We made the personal stories much more important and put in many more financial details."

The public reacted as vigorously to the print as to the television spots.

"People ripped out the ads and sent them in, asking for special attention for a situation they had that was similar to one we'd portrayed. And, of course, in print we could afford to present more stories. We needed to show as many different kinds of stories as possible to appeal to as many people as possible."

Why did these mini-soap operas touch so many so deeply? A good concept, certainly. Great execution, without doubt. But the real power of *Real Life* goes back to something Mark Twain said: The words have to ring true. In no small measure, these scripts ring true because every one was written straight out of the life experiences of the creative team. Easdon's favorite features a divorced woman calling her ex-husband. Easdon had just been divorced at the time it was written.

"Some people here weren't very comfortable with that particular spot at first," Easdon says. "But it meant a lot to me because I'd just been through it. Until you actually go through a divorce, you have no idea how gut-wrenching it really is."

Easdon persevered and the spot was eventually done. Like the other executions, this one could have been seriously damaged anywhere along the way from copy concept to the editing room by unfelicitous fiddling about. Instead, both Hill, Holiday management and the client were wise enough to let the creative team handle the scripting and the shoot. The results are gripping.

How does Easdon explain the deep impression the campaign made on its audience?

"We'd always been told that the people out there aren't terribly well-educated. We were amazed to find that after viewers had seen the spots two or three times, they could play back not only the story line, but the details of the copy screens. Right down to the exact penny the characters were making. People are pretty smart when it comes to spending their money. They will listen to an ad if it's important to them."

John and Sandy Wilder
Age: 46, 44
Two children

Occupations
John: Personnel Director
Sandy: Homemaker

Income
Salary $45,000
Interest Income   1,000
                                          $44,000

Assets
Home Equity $52,000
Savings, Investments   10,000

Estimated Expenses
Income Tax $10,500
Mortgage, Property Tax,
  Insurance   5,300
Education Expenses   4,000
Loan Payments, Credit   2,000
Food, Clothing   13,000
Miscellaneous   2,400
                                          $37,200

Needs
To supplement income
To accumulate capital for children's education
Long-term security

Answers
John Hancock Life Insurance
John Hancock IRAs
John Hancock Bond Trust
John Hancock Cash Management Trust/Transactions Account

John and Sandy Wilder are mother and father in
what modern sociologists might call a
"traditional" family.

They came to us recently for our recommendations
on ways to both supplement their income and
accumulate capital to provide for their
children's education.

A John Hancock representative made the
recommendations you see above given their
situation, income and goals. Compare them with
your own family situation. Maybe we can help
you, too.

Real life, real answers.

You know that your mother and
I love you.

And that no matter what you do
we'll continue to love you.

Because we're family.

But if you don't stop laughing at the
dinner table we can change all of that.

Do you hear me?

John and Sandy Wilder
Married, two children, single income

Linda Fuller
Single, working mother

John Avery
Married, three grown children,
facing retirement

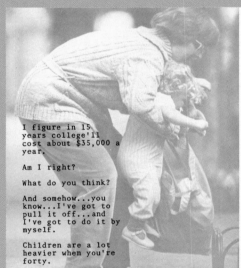

Linda Fuller
Age: 37
Divorced; one child, age 2

Occupation Librarian

Income
Salary $20,000
Child Support   6,000
                                          $26,000

Assets
Apartment Furnishings $6,000
Photograph Collection   4,000
Cash, Savings   4,150

Estimated Expenses
Income Tax $6,400
Rent   3,600
Renter's Insurance   150
Daycare (3 hours daily)   2,000
Food, Clothing   5,000
Auto Loan and Insurance   1,700
Miscellaneous   3,000
                                          $21,850

Needs
To provide for child's education
To save money
Long-term security

Answers
John Hancock Bond Trust
John Hancock Disability Income Insurance
John Hancock Universal Life
John Hancock Cash Management Trust/Transactions Account
John Hancock Auto Insurance

One morning, taking her two-year-old to daycare,
Linda Fuller began to think of college.

Look at John Hancock's answers to see the types
of products and plans we'd suggest given her
goals, her income and her obligations.

What we'd like you to see is Hancock's ability to
meet real life problems with real life answers.

Real life, real answers.

I figure in 15
years college'll
cost about $35,000 a
year.

Am I right?

What do you think?

And somehow...you
know...I've got to
pull it off...and
I've got to do it by
myself.

Children are a lot
heavier when you're
forty.

Although Hancock's field agents
weren't enthusiastic about the
campaign initially, they warmed up
when their telephones lit up with calls
from people who'd seen the ads and
wanted to talk.

The print ads turned out to be a
key indicator of the campaign's
effectiveness: Readers ripped pieces
of the ads out and sent them to
Hancock asking for help with their
own situations, many of which were
similar to those portrayed in the ads.

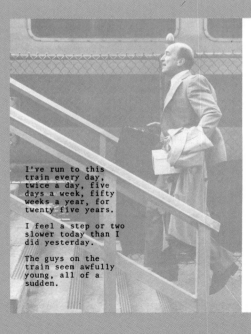

John Avery
Age: 54
Married; three grown children (one still in
college)

Occupation Sales Manager

Income
Salary $65,000
Rental Income   5,000
Interest Income   5,000
                                          $75,000

Assets
Home Equity $100,000
Summer Cottage Equity   20,000
Insurance, Investments   75,000
Home Furnishings, Valuables   25,000

Estimated Expenses
Income Tax $23,000
Investments, Tax Shelters   10,000
College Expenses   8,000
Insurance   3,000
Property Tax   1,500
Food, Clothing, Utilities   9,500
Miscellaneous   5,000
                                          $60,000

Needs
Stable transition to retirement
Financially secure future

Answers
John Hancock Tax-Exempt Income Trust
John Hancock Variable Life
Freedom Income Trust
Tucker Anthony Securities
John Hancock Cash Management Trust/Transactions Account
John Hancock Tax-Deferred Annuity

Running to the train one day, John Avery caught
up with himself and for the first time ever he
began to think seriously about retirement.

A short while later, he sat down to talk about
his future with a John Hancock representative.

We made the recommendations you see above given
his family situation, income and retirement.

Compare them with your own near or long-term
goals.

Real life, real answers.

I've run to this
train every day,
twice a day, five
days a week, fifty
weeks a year, for
twenty five years.

I feel a step or two
slower today than I
did yesterday.

The guys on the
train seem awfully
young, all of a
sudden.

Della Femina, Travisano's "Lies" Hit The Mark For American Isuzu

ISUZU

Client: American Isuzu Motors
Agency: Della Femina, Travisano & Partners

Perhaps no recent campaign has sparked the kind of vitriolic reactions inspired by the *Liar*, produced for American Isuzu Motors by Della Femina, Travisano & Partners of California (DFTP). The effort was particularly unpopular with some practitioners of the advertising craft who called it everything from despicable to demeaning. The reason is easy to surmise. The campaign's chief protagonist is a sleazy pitchman who lies about Isuzu cars. It's all in fun, of course, with the appropriate corrections to his outrageous statements superimposed on the screen as he talks. What outraged the critics was that DFTP had the temerity to make a joke out of a sad truth: The public knows that, at best, advertising is only one side of the story. Alas, the Emperor has no clothes. Fortunately, the critics aren't the ones who get to vote whether a campaign stays or goes. The client does. And since the public loved seamy Joe Isuzu—despite reports to the contrary, the campaign is selling cars—the client voted to renew Joe (played by versatile character actor David Leisure) for the 1988 television season.

Ironically, *Liar* was almost a fluke. It was never intended to run as a national campaign.

DFTP has held the Isuzu account since 1981, the first year the company exported vehicles to the United States. Although Isuzu has been building cars in Japan since 1914, longer than rivals Toyota and Nissan, it was late entering the North American market. Isuzu's primary products are trucks, not autos. The first Isuzus to appear in the U.S. didn't even wear the company's distinctive red emblem: They were imported as Chevrolet Luv pickup trucks.

From the beginning, DFTP's biggest challenge has been to build name recognition for the company. With a total budget of about $45 million (plus another $10 million from the regional dealer accounts also held by DFTP), Isuzu has a tiny share of voice in the hyper-competitive auto market. The agency worked valiantly and with some success to overcome the limitations of budget and unfamiliarity with a succession

of efforts. Some humorous (one featured an American trying to pronounce Isuzu and a Japanese salesman trying to enunciate Chevrolet), others were more traditional, focusing on the car maker's long heritage in Japan.

It wasn't until 1986 that lightning struck.

The juice came from a routine assignment given to art director Jeannie Marie Obeji and copywriter Matt Bogen. Their mission was to create a spot for Isuzu dealers in Southern California. The traditional formula is to take some stock footage of the car on a test track or out on the highway and superimpose "Great values now at your local dealer" over a few frames. Pretty routine, unexciting stuff for an agency the size of DFTP. What came out of the assignment was anything but routine. Creative director Rick Carpenter suggested the two try something a bit off the wall—a parody of a sleazy snake-oil salesman, the kind who would sell his own mother so long as he

got a commission.

Bogen and Obeji's storyboard probably wouldn't have passed management review in two-thirds of the agencies in America. To its credit, DFTP showed it to the client.

"The dealers in Southern California understood that, given the limited budget they had relative to Toyota and Nissan, they needed a spot that was splashy," says Charles Koch, who manages the Isuzu business for DFTP. "They also understood the subtlety of the humor. Whatever reservations anyone had, we all knew we needed something to cut through the clutter, and this spot seemed to do it in a humorous way that people would remember."

The account team got approval for the young upstarts (Obeji is 26, Bogen is 25 and Carpenter a ripe old 28) to cast and shoot. Their first impulse was to use the appropriately slippery John Lovitz, whose habitual lying on *Saturday Night Live* made him one of the strongest members of the

Calling the *Liar* campaign, created for Isuzu by the Los Angeles office of Della Femina, Travisano & Partners, controversial is like calling Robin Leach boring—a vast understatement. Evolved from a single spot for Southern California Isuzu dealers, the initial spots featured character actor David Leisure lying on behalf of the client. Appropriate corrections appeared superimposed over the bottom of the screen. The spots drew ample criticism from the advertising community and ample customers into the showrooms. The 1988 spots, including the effort above which purports to demonstrate that the Isuzu Impulse is faster than a speeding bullet, drew heavy fire as well.

The *Liar* campaign was expanded from television to print (opposite) in late 1987 with a series of single pages and spreads working the now-familiar formula. Actor David Leisure prevaricates and the accompanying type corrects. The pages were run in *Money*, *Popular Science* and *Popular Mechanics*, among other publications.

regular troupe. Lovitz wanted too many bucks to bend the truth for Isuzu, however, and after a cattle call, the agency ended up with character actor David Leisure. That stroke alone may have destined the campaign for greatness. Leisure was totally believable as a pathological liar.

The dealer promo aired for two months in early 1986 and received favorable reviews from *Adweek*, among others. People thought it was fresh and funny. So much so that, when Isuzu got ready to put on a $12 million summer television blitz, the ground was prepared to take the *Liar* national.

The blitz was intended to promote factory incentives and rebates, something the company had never offered on its automobile line.

"The agency creatives sat down to figure out an approach, and they considered several alternatives," Koch says. "Finally, John Armistead (creative director) and Jim Weller (senior vice president) decided we should try to extend the dealer spot."

Of course, everyone at American Isuzu Motors had seen the *Liar*, and they thought it was funny and effective.

"The dealer spot acted as a kind of demo for the initial national pool," Koch explains. "By the time the major presentation was made to the corporate marketing staff, they all understood the concept."

There was just one small hitch. The spots had to be shot almost immediately and Leisure, whose on-screen oozing had made the dealer spot so effective, had just broken his leg ice skating. The agency felt strongly that Leisure was important to the spots, so they decided to shoot around the disability.

"We looked at our five storyboards and saw that we could have him stand behind the car in one spot and hide his cast behind a rock in another," Koch recalls. One of the funnier storyboards of the group even took advantage of the injury. The spot had Leisure dressed as a race

driver on crutches. He tells viewers he crashed at LeMans. A super corrects the misstatement with "He slipped in the bathtub."

Because Leisure was relatively immobile, the spots had to be shot with very little camera movement. Koch thinks the inconvenience may have made them stronger. Without a lot of camera movement to distract the eye, the supers are much more visible and are easier to read.

The spots broke in June 1986. The public's reaction to the *Liar* was phenomenal: Isuzu's sales—helped along by first-time factory incentives—jumped during the first three months of the campaign. By November, Video Storyboard Tests ranked the *Liar* number ten on its list of the ten best-known television commercials. That list included such stalwarts as Coca-Cola, McDonald's, Pepsi, Bartles & Jaymes, Miller Lite, Bud Light and Jell-O. Quite heady company for a campaign with only three months of history.

The best was yet to come, however. By December, Isuzu's sales had surged to an all-time high of almost 14,000 units (including cars, trucks and the four-wheel drive Trooper II), about half again better than the volume of any month prior to the *Liar*. Video Storyboard Tests' rankings for the final quarter of 1986 showed the *Liar* number six.

Isuzu's own research shows that total advertising awareness among people intending to buy a car in one of the categories Isuzu competes in was up from about 40% before the campaign aired to nearly 65% nine months later. Isuzu's "likeability" rating increased as well, scoring positive gains in attributes such as quality and "manufactures cars for people like me."

Among people intending to buy a small car, awareness of Isuzu jumped from 75%—below Toyota, Nissan and Mazda—to almost 100%, even with category leader Toyota. Awareness of the Isuzu Impulse, which had been

"One of the reasons the Isuzu Impulse is faster this year."

He's telling the truth.

We did put a big, new engine under the hood of our Impulse. It's not *exactly* like the one in the photo. But it is big. Big enough to increase horsepower by 22%.*

Big enough to increase torque by 18%.* Even big enough to force our engineers to redesign the hood. And the hood wasn't the only thing that had to be redesigned.

To handle the increase in power, a more sophisticated suspension was called for. Naturally, we called Lotus. The world renowned experts in performance car handling designed a system that makes the Impulse as agile as it is powerful. Sort of like one of their Formula 1 race cars. Only better. Because an Impulse also comes standard with air conditioning, 6-speaker stereo and power everything you could possibly imagine.

All for about $13,000.** Which means that even though the Impulse definitely does not come with a jet aircraft engine.

We know for a fact they'll go awfully fast.

*Increase versus previous year's model. **Based upon manufacturer's suggested retail prices P.O.E. excluding tax, license and transportation fee as of 8/1/87. Dealer prices may vary. Prices subject to change.

Proud sponsor of the 1988 Summer Olympics on NBC.

Good luck, Mom.

You have my word on it.

One of the difficulties of keeping a humorous campaign on track is keeping it fresh with new ideas and new executions. In 1987, viewers were introduced to Joe Isuzu's family, including his mother (top). When Joe asked that his mother be struck by lightning if he weren't telling the truth, the super said "Good luck, Mom." Naturally, she evaporated in a puff of smoke before the end of the spot. Joe even struck out for exotic climes, claiming he'd saved enough on his new P'up pickup to buy "this island and all of the fish." To prove his point, he produced a fish from the inside pocket of his suit jacket. Joe then signed off in flawless Pidgin Polynesian: "Bene mele, iki bobo."

languishing down around 25%, doubled to better than 50%. Awareness of the Trooper II, which had been at 15% before the *Liar* began running, leaped to 50%, just behind Ford's Bronco II.

In general, the media reacted favorably to the *Liar*. Stories began popping up everywhere about the campaign and David Leisure. *People* magazine did a feature. So did the *Washington Post*, the syndicated *Evening Magazine* and *PM Magazine* television shows, *Good Morning America* and even a German television supplement called *Gong*. Never one to tread lightly, the paragon of the automobile press, *Car and Driver* magazine, said "Isuzu gets our nod this year for having the guts to go for this funny and original campaign. Every other car ad snores in comparison."

The number of individual exposures netted by this press coverage was phenomenal—150 million or more according to the count of Freeman/McCue, a Newport Beach, California, public relations firm that tracked publicity for the *Liar*.

To be sure, not everything printed about the campaign was congratulatory. A deep-founded suspicion of modern journalists is that nothing is ever as good as it is made out to be. When the positive press accorded a person or organization reaches a certain zenith, news folks begin sniffing around for a hint of scandal, something to "put it in its proper perspective." Said another way, when we've built something up high enough, there must be a way to bring it down. And Isuzu was getting just too darn popular.

Accordingly, in August 1987, a reporter for the *Los Angeles Times* broke a story which suggested that, cute as it was, the *Liar* campaign just wasn't selling cars.

What he neglected to mention is that Isuzu isn't really a car company. Its primary products are trucks. And most of its sales volume is in trucks. To be sure Isuzu's sales had slipped a bit

He's Lying.

House Not Included.

DFTP's strategy assumes that its audience is watching the spots, not just listening with their heads tucked inside the refrigerator.

Notwithstanding the media's doubts about the campaign's effectiveness, Isuzu dealers know the spots worked because large numbers of customers showed up jokingly asking about the free house Joe promised them on television. The fact that Isuzu's sales outpaced auto industry averages in 1987 and 1988 probably didn't hurt their spirits too much either.

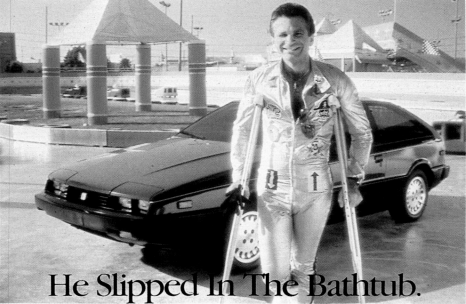

Joe's wife and kids got into the act in 1987, too. The kids don't lie because "they're adopted," although the boy looks suspiciously like Joe. But then, he also looks like Eddie Munster. The 1986 spot in which Joe claimed to have injured his leg at LeMans was shot at a go-cart track. In this case, Joe was almost telling the truth: David Leisure really did have a broken leg when the first pool of commercials were filmed. Leisure claims he broke it ice skating with his daughter. Sure.

after the banner months immediately following the *Liar* introduction. But Isuzu's sales have to be viewed in the context of an auto market that was in a serious slump.

The total auto market had dipped by 5%. Japanese auto sales were down 1%, while Isuzu's sales were actually running 11% ahead of previous year-to-date figures. Overall, car sales were off 9%, with domestic models down 14% and Japanese imports up 1%. Sales of Isuzu cars were up 17%, ahead of all but one of its Japanese competitors. The I-Mark sedan was up 63% over the previous year, while the Impulse was down 46%. The truck market was up 4% overall although Japanese trucks were down 4%. Isuzu's trucks were doing well—up 9% (ahead of domestic and import trucks). The Trooper II was doing even better: Up 57% over 1986.

The *Los Angeles Times* article acknowledged a "slight rise" in sales of Isuzu's light trucks, but concluded that the *Liar* wasn't selling vehicles very well without providing background on the weakness of the U.S. auto market.

Unfortunately, the piece was picked up and syndicated nationally. *The Wall Street Journal* even picked up statistics from the article without relating other pertinent industry sales figures.

Isuzu was lambasted in the advertising community as well. The ad press gave the campaign high marks for originality. But some agency executives felt the effort was downright blasphemous. The basic complaint was that, by portraying a television pitchman as a liar—even in jest—Isuzu was reinforcing the public's already skeptical attitude about the veracity of advertising.

The answer to that, of course, is that not talking about a problem doesn't make it go away. No less an authority than the U.S. Supreme Court has commented on this issue. Remember the old Wonder Bread television ads of

He's Lying.

The Trooper II four wheel drive contributed strongly to Isuzu's sales in 1986 and 1987. The first spot for the Trooper showed it perched on top of an oft-photographed butte in Utah, the very same rock used in a number of Chevrolet truck commercials in the 1970s. Joe assured us that he drove the Trooper up there himself. In the 1988 spot, Joe stands next to the Trooper II on the top of Mount Everest. He sells it to a group of mountain climbers. When one asks if it's safe to drive down, Joe tells them not to worry. As the Trooper plunges toward the bottom of the mountain, he calls after them "You have my word on it!"

Probably the best of the 1988 spots pictures Joe in front of Buckingham Palace where, he informs us, he has just sold an I-Mark to the Queen ("He telleth a lie"). Joe manages to work in a number of the sedan's features, telling us it has "an air conditioner so Her Highness won't sweat and an AM-FM stereo to drown out the cries of the peasants. Prices start at seven pounds, four ounces but I traded one to what's her name for this hat," he says, pointing to a bejeweled crown.

yesteryear? The product slogan at the time was "Wonder builds strong bodies twelve ways." The visual was a time-lapse sequence showing a boy and a girl growing right before your very eyes.

Wonder was called on the carpet by a citizen's action group which argued that the advertising was deliberately deceptive, calculated to convince youngsters that, if they ate Wonder Bread, they'd grow two feet in thirty seconds. How insidious, right? Well, the Court found that argument specious. In ruling against the complaint, the justices noted that, by the age of 6, all kids know that not everything they see on television is true.

The question now is, should we credit the viewing public with having less intelligence than a 6 year old? Of course not. Consumers know when they're not being told the whole truth, which—whether the subject is products, politics or the local weather—is most of the time.

DFTP meanwhile readied a new slate of executions for the 1988 model year. With name recognition no longer a problem, the advertising focused more specifically on attributes of the various models. Again, the spots were cleverly scripted and the transition to product benefits was almost transparent to viewers. David Leisure was back in the saddle (sans leg cast). The scripts managed to work in the features of various models (the speed of the Impulse, the creature comforts of the I-Mark, the toughness of the Trooper II) while maintaining the high level of witty dialogue of the earlier spots.

Isuzu is happy. Despite the flak they've taken from their peers the people at DFTP seem happy. And if we can believe what he says, David Leisure is happy. Whatever it's done for Isuzu, the *Liar* campaign has made Leisure a hot property in Hollywood. The spots have assured his place in history as the man we love to disbelieve.

"Isuzu Trooper II.
The 4x4 that conquered Everest."

What a snowjob.

The truth is, if you want to reach the top of Mt. Everest, you'd be better off driving a yak. On the other hand, you don't have to beat a Trooper II with a stick to get it moving.

Simply shift into 4-wheel drive and its fuel-injected 2.6 liter engine will eagerly take you just about anywhere.

Shift back into 2-wheel drive, and it'll eagerly take you through long stretches of highway or cramped supermarket parking lots. Or fold up the rear seat and you've got over 71 cubic feet of storage space.

And unlike a yak, a Trooper II can be ordered with automatic transmission, captain's chairs, and 2-door or 4-door body styles. The result is something that handles like a station wagon. Hauls like a Sherpa. And looks like nothing else on or off the road.

All for thousands less than other comparable vehicles.

Looks like our rivals have slipped.

ISUZU

Proud Sponsor of the 1988 Summer Olympics on NBC.

Young & Rubicam Makes Money For Jamaica Again And Again

Client: Jamaica Tourist Board
Agency: Young & Rubicam/New York

Occasionally in this field one has the chance to serve the gods of commerce and humanity at the same time. In 1981, Young & Rubicam (Y&R) got such an opportunity when it won the Jamaica tourism account. And while they were getting one of the true plums of the Caribbean (lush tropical island, great place to shoot on location in February), they were also inheriting a problematic business situation. The country badly needed tourist dollars to earn foreign exchange, increase employment and provide for the basic needs of its people. "Tourism has become our life line," confirms John Lynch, director of the Jamaica Tourist Board (JTB) in New York. The tourists, however, were staying away in droves.

The late 1970s were hard times for Jamaica. World markets for bauxite, sugar and coffee—the country's chief exports—took a nosedive. These financial woes were compounded when internecine political squabbling frightened away the tourists, 80% of them Americans, who were next on the list of contributors to Jamaica's foreign exchange earnings. To be sure, there were gun fights in the ghetto in Kingston. But the world media also wrung every last ounce of drama out of the situation. The newsreels made downtown Kingston look like Beirut on a particularly bad day. Obscured by the smoky televised images of burning tires was the fact that the victims of this sporadic violence were Jamaicans; no foreigners need apply. Symptomatic of our appalling ignorance about our neighbors to the south, American network news clips failed to mention how atypical the unrest was. Jamaica's parliamentary system predates our own, yet in the preceding century and a half, the country's entire experience with civil turbulence had been two riots and one localized rebellion. To this day, Jamaica has had nothing to match what happened in Miami in 1980 or in Watts in 1965, not to mention the Chicago Haymarket Riot or our Civil War.

The emerging recognition of the Rastafarian religious sect and the

JAMAICA

Come back to tranquillity.

Here you are, at home in Jamaica in your very own villa, all pastels and privacy.

With Evangeline to pamper you: she's going shopping soon, to surprise you with a lobster for dinner. Madly extravagant? Not at all.

There are hundreds of villas for rent, all over Jamaica.

Bring your family, or share one with your best friends, and the cost becomes irresistibly attractive.

And what nicer way to experience the bountiful wonders of Jamaica

than to have your own special place to return to each evening, where you can sit back with a rum punch, talk about tomorrow, and say to yourself, "There's no place like home."

MAKE IT JAMAICA. AGAIN.

The Jamaican people were the central focus of Young & Rubicam's first round of executions for the Jamaica Tourist Board.

The friendly faces and lyrical accents were put center stage to remind Americans of the island's most popular virtues prior to its "troubles" of the late 1970s.

The commercials were "horribly expensive" to shoot, according to Y&R vice president Ed J. Daley, because the crew had to take everything—from cameras to helicopters—with them from the U.S.

rise of reggae music roughly paralleled the increasing crescendo of violence and became entwined with it in the minds of Americans. Whatever the underlying reality, the perception among travelers was that Jamaica was not a fun place to vacation.

That was the perception Y&R was hired to overcome. The reality they had to work with—never as dismal as the media painted it—was improving. The elections held in the fall of 1980 brought the opposition party to power, and with it, a new prime minister, Edward Seaga. The violence abated. Without gunfire to punctuate the sound tracks of their news footage, the networks lost interest in a land returned to normalcy and Jamaica quickly faded from American television screens.

To obtain the dimensions of the problem the situation had left, Y&R did some research.

"There were a lot of negative perceptions. And, perception

being reality, no one wanted to go to Jamaica," says Ed J. Daley, vice president of Y&R. "Not only that, but travel agents weren't recommending it to their customers.

"Jamaica had once had a core of loyal visitors in the U.S. Our suggestion to the JTB was that we play on the memory of what the island had been in the past, its old virtues."

That led to the theme line of the first wave of the campaign: "Make it Jamaica—again."

"We never confronted the safety aspect head-on," Daley says. "It was done more subtly. We intentionally avoided the issue. Instead, we wanted to paint impressions of Jamaica. The accent and language of the people is very lyrical and it has a fascinating history. It's also very beautiful."

Despite this focus on the visual, Daley says, the first step was to complete a piece of music. The agency bought the rights to an old

Make it Jamaica.
Again.

JAMAICA

A man. A woman.

As it was meant to be.

Come Back To Romance.

JAMAICA

Suspended above a turquoise sea.

Bathed by gentle breezes.

Every tension melted away.

Come Back To Yourself.

The campaign hit a land mine in 1985, when domestic unrest erupted over government hikes in the cost of essential goods. To revive the campaign, Y&R picked up on a series of sub themes, including one which had been running in bridal magazines (opposite) since 1982. The themes—come back to romance, come back to excitement, come back to yourself—targeted three specific and distinctly different types of travelers.

Peter Paul & Mary tune, *Stewball*, and added a new set of lyrics asking travelers to "come back to Jamaica, what's old is what's new, we invite you to join us...."

Several executional avenues were explored, but the one that won the hearts of the JTB, and ultimately won the business for Y&R, paired images of the people of Jamaica with the music. Over and over, they looked straight into the camera and asked the viewer to "come back." They were really quite compelling.

"The criticism of that approach has been that it looked a little pleading, a little imploring," Daley says. "The other executions we tried were actually much closer to the spots we're running today. The music was more upbeat. But at that time, we couldn't use reggae for our sound track. To Americans it conjured up all those negative images we were trying to fight."

The usual way to sell a destination is to first sell the travel agents. But travel agents were wary of the island. Even the apostles among them who knew of the improving climate weren't going to spend a lot of effort talking recalcitrant travelers into buying Jamaica when they could sell them the Virgin Islands or the Bahamas much more easily. Y&R elected to concentrate its forces in another direction: Directly on the consumer.

The agency also proposed another unorthodox move—to put the limited resources at its disposal (less than $5 million) into television instead of print.

Fortunately, the consumers they needed to reach weren't spread evenly and thinly across the breadth of the continent. Half of the visitors to Jamaica each year come from the Northeastern U.S. A large percentage of the rest come out of a dozen charter gateways.

By concentrating its media dollars in those television markets, the JTB could create a high profile for the island while its chief competitors were

JAMAICA

COME BACK TO ROMANCE.

To a place where romance is carefully nurtured. And where love, it seems, is everywhere.

In the early morning mist. In star-dappled nights scented with passion flowers.

We've long considered ourselves experts on love. Perhaps it may've something to do with our known place.

Together with your travel agent, we'll help you find the most romantic places. On this most romantic island.

We'll make it sweet for you. So you'll make it Jamaica. Again.

MAKE IT JAMAICA. AGAIN.

spending their efforts in trade promotion and consumer print. A complementary print effort was designed by Y&R for use in select consumer publications, such as the bridal magazines.

The first spots aired in June of 1981, and their effect was felt immediately: Even though the entire winter season (traditionally the heaviest travel months in the Caribbean) had been lost, the number of visitors went up by 14% over 1980. The trend continued through 1982, with visitors up 19%, and the following year, with another 28% increase. From 1981 to 1984, the number of visitors jumped by 45%. They brought with them sorely needed American dollars, and combined with the government's other fiscal programs, the country's cash crisis eased.

The amount of exchange earned was impressive. In 1983, tourism brought in $399 million. In 1984, that rose to $406 million. Y&R felt pretty good about its work. Then a disaster struck.

In January 1985, the administration raised the price of gasoline and certain other essentials. The citizenry was not pleased. For a short time, it was 1979 all over again—people in the streets burning tires, riots. All of which attracted the attention of the news media. And sleepy Jamaica, which had been scarcely mentioned on the network news during the four years of peace, was back in living color. Rioting.

"Overnight, the momentum we had built up was halted," Daley recalls grimly. "It was right at the beginning of the 1985 winter season. The damage was worst where the media has its greatest penetration—the Northeast— which of course is also Jamaica's largest market. We went out a

week later and did a study. All the old negative perceptions came right back. It killed the credibility of the campaign. You can't be out there saying 'come back to tranquility' when *The New York Times* says they're burning tires in the streets."

Y&R literally went back to the drawing board. It took them the rest of 1985 to find the answer they were looking for.

"We could no longer show the people because the riots had made the people unacceptable to the American public," Daley says. "We decided to go back to something called the product. Of course, every destination shows the product. Beautiful mountains and blue seas get to be generically Caribbean after awhile. We needed something that would differentiate Jamaica."

The agency's four years of experience on the account proved

"The execution that's won all the awards and which is the favorite on the new business reels here at the agency is *Come Back To Yourself*," says Daley.

The execution was calculated to appeal to travelers looking for solitude, to get away from the pressures and get in touch with themselves.

Despite the highly intellectualized strategy, the spot didn't have any copy until it was being cut. The copywriter, seeing the footage and listening to the sound track, a reggae song called *Woman No Cry*, was inspired to create copy for what had been a silent spot.

a tremendous boon. The team had observed that there were three very different consumers who could be persuaded to visit Jamaica. The first were affluent, older visitors, probably repeat customers. The second were younger, carefree couples, the kind who make up their minds on Tuesday to fly to the sun and arrive on Thursday. The third were independent travelers, people traveling alone or perhaps with one other person; those looking to get away from everything, including the standard beach-and-bar tourist hustle.

"Research told us that not everyone goes on vacation for the same reason," Daley explains. "It has to do with whether they're older, younger, single, married, with girlfriend or without.

"We designed three separate sub themes and created spots for each of these three primary groups."

As it had before, the agency had the music long before it had its visuals. By 1985, reggae had found its way into every kind of popular music with the possible exceptions of gospel and classical. It was acceptable, and being a uniquely Jamaican art form, the perfect way to set the tone for the new effort.

For the older crowd, the theme line was "Come back to romance." For the live-it-up types, "Come back to excitement." And for the misogynists, the line was "Come back to yourself." A slow, tempered tune was crafted for the *Romance* execution, while *Yourself* was accompanied by a rendition of reggae king Bob Marley's classic *Woman No Cry. Excitement* ran with a spicy version of *Buffalo Soldier*, another reggae classic.

In contrast with the first round

Make it Jamaica.
Again.

Make it Jamaica.
Again.

of spots, which generally featured long shots with smooth camera movements, the new executions were almost visual collages. *Excitement*, the most extreme, had seventy-three cuts in sixty seconds.

"Strategically, we varied the appeal and executionally we varied the tone of the music," Daley says. "Variety has always been one of our creative objectives. These spots show the variety. While there were three main executions, we made sixty-second versions, twenty-five-second versions, even some fifteen-second versions. They're cut so many different ways, you'd never know you're seeing the same piece twice."

Given the expense of carting production crews and equipment down for each shoot, that helps stretch the JTB's valuable dollars.

With a higher budget, up to $10 million this year, the campaign has spread and is now playing in about twenty markets—the major gateways and regional centers behind the gateways.

While the disaster year, 1985, was flat in terms of tourism revenues, the new campaign got things moving again. In 1986, revenues leaped to $512.6 million and the JTB estimates that when the figures are in, 1987 will weigh in at better than $600 million.

"Our big increase in 1987 came because we hit the soft spot, the summer season," Daley chortles. "Who wants to go to the Caribbean in July? Well, we've developed a terrific business from the Southwest and Texas all the way across the Gulf Coast and over to Miami. We have charters out of Los Angeles now. We got more than a million people down there in 1987, and most of the growth came from promoting off-season travel using the television spots. Now we'd like to see the

JTB increase the amount of money it spends in working media to push that up even further."

The JTB seems to share Daley's optimism. With six jets already in the national Air Jamaica fleet, Lynch says the airline is negotiating for more airplanes to help carry the increasing traffic.

"Tourism has replaced bauxite as the principle earner of foreign exchange," Lynch says. "Our occupancy rate is around 70%, a far cry from what it was in 1981."

Perhaps it's all in a day's work. But Ed Daley sounds like a man who's happy to help out by doing his job just a little bit better.

The name and destination of this rural bus, featured in *Come Back to Yourself*, reflects the island's fascinating history. The name is English while the destination, Savannah La Mar—on the southwest coast near Negril—is most definitely Spanish.

Jamaica became English by accident. During the Puritan Revolution, Oliver Cromwell sent Admiral William Peim and General Robert Venables to loot Portobello, Panama. One of the chief Spanish ports in the New World, Portobello was the site of warehouses containing gold, diamonds and emeralds the Spanish had lifted from South America. After finding Portobello's fortifications too strong for their tastes, Peim and Venables turned back for England. Knowing they would not be greeted warmly by their master, the two looked around the Caribbean for a consolation prize—something they could conquer without a lot of bloodshed and take back to Cromwell as a sop. Bereft of gold and jewels, Jamaica, settled by the Spanish a century earlier, was virtually undefended. When the English troops landed in Kingston on the south coast, the Spanish governor left for Cuba simultaneously via Runaway Bay on the north coast.

After 1985, the campaign focus shifted from the people to the landscape and activities. The television executions for the *Come Back To Romance* (top) theme example targeted older, more affluent visitors.

"This group includes a lot of high-level business managers, company presidents and board members who can help bring convention business and even new enterprises to the island," Daley observes.

Despite a strong back-up in print, the campaign has always been primarily a television effort. Where print explains and builds knowledge (which, depending on the possessor may or may not lead to understanding), television may not give much intellectual meat but it can rapidly and effectively change viewers' emotions and perceptions. It has obviously made Americans feel good about Jamaica, as the number of visitors exceeded one million for the first time in 1987, and revenues were up from $399 million in 1981 to an estimated $600 million in 1987.

JAMAICA

Hurtle through a wall of warm air.

Swoop and soar above the turquoise sea.

And laugh aloud with the sheer joy of it.

Come Back To Excitement.

JAMAICA

<u>Take tea by the sea.</u>

If living well is the best revenge, it's sweet indeed in Jamaica.
Many of our hotels cherish the rituals of life: tea by the sea in all
appropriate splendor, and dinner at eight amidst candlelight and old silver.
But Jamaica's accommodations are as varied as its landscape
and its people, and if you feel overdressed in more than shorts and sandals,
Jamaica has hotels that couldn't agree more.
So whether your taste is for watching peacocks on the lawn, or chasing
a volleyball into the surf, you will find your kind of place in Jamaica.
Which, after all, is the true meaning of accommodation.

<u>Make it Jamaica</u>. <u>Again.</u>

Jamaica Tourist Board

Ken-L Ration Spins A Shaggy Dog Story

Client: Ken-L Ration/Quaker Oats
Agency: J. Walter Thompson/Chicago

Oh the trauma of the modern world. Feeding Rover used to be easy. You went in the kitchen, pulled out a bag of crunchies, poured them in a bowl—maybe threw in some table scraps—and whistled. That was it. Are we to believe that we have a humane obligation to *shop* for potables for the pooch?

The short answer is no. Any brand name dog food that makes it onto the shelves of an American supermarket will keep a dog healthy and happy. But there *is* a difference between compulsion and desire. We are an indulgent society. Pets are full-fledged members of the family; they now get the same consideration as other family members when it comes to their food.

And thereby hangs a tale, if you'll pardon the pun—a classic brand roll-out that built $44 million in sales for Ken-L Ration Tender Chops within *six months* of its introduction. The story shows how much can be accomplished when client and agency work together on an image-driven product from concept all the way through to couponing.

When you get down to it, dog food is dog food. For years, Lorne Greene and various other spokespersons have tried to make us feel obligated to seek out nutritious fare for our dogs. They succeeded beyond their wildest hopes. In fact, consumers now assume—correctly—that all national brand dog foods are nutritious. Saying a dog food is good for dogs is saying that it's the same as all the other stuff on the shelves. Which is why we're treated to so many spots featuring dogs nosing each other away from a bowl of dog food that "tastes better." Dogs can't very well discuss matters of palatability with their owners, so the real point of differentiation has become the *image* of the dog food. And what better way to create image than through advertising?

Over the years, J. Walter Thompson/Chicago has handled the Ken-L Ration business ably and well for client Quaker Oats. Ken-L Ration made history in the $1.8 billion dry dog food segment with Tender Chunks, a product that features dry nuggets with a soft, pliable core. When it became apparent that sales of Tender Chunks were plateauing, Ken-L Ration asked JWT to look into repositioning the product.

"We didn't have a lot of success finding a new positioning for

J. WALTER THOMPSON COMPANY

DATE: January, 1987
PRODUCER: The Haboush Company

CLIENT: The Quaker Oats Company
PRODUCT: Tender Chops
FILM NO.: OAKD3093
TITLE: "The Hook" :30 TV

ANNCR (VO): You're about to witness a crime.

The Hook.

LADY (OC): "Oh, poor little doggie."
ANNCR (VO): The Lift.

The Choplifter.

He's desperate for those...

...luscious new Tender Chops...

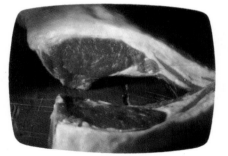

...that look like real meat chops...

...with a savory meaty middle surrounded by the crunch of bone.

Don't let your dog...

become a Choplifter. Buy 'em new meaty...

...Tender Chops. In All Tender style too!

To focus attention on the dogs, make them the stars and use their inherent charm to help sell the product, the agency auditioned 49 women and dressed the set carefully. The actress, who may be familiar to you as the woman who served the minister in the feature film *10*, was chosen partially because she is very short. All elements in the shots were scaled down to make the dogs appear larger in the frame.

much they will *steal* for it. The logic was to create a spot to show that dogs will do anything, even steal, to get Tender Chops."

This could give a whole new meaning to the pejorative "dog thief." At first, there was a concern that the negative imagery associated with shoplifters would rub off on JWT's felonious fleabags. The answer? Be whimsical and charming. Like a Disney movie. It was something DiGiuseppe was comfortable with. He'd worked with Lassie on the Recipe dog food commercials twenty years before. This is a man who understands the psychology of dogs, and of their owners.

"People like to think their pets have human personality, emotions and motivations," he says. "Our objective was to bring out that personality in our 'chop-lifters' and draw on the idea that dogs are charming."

Even with the kind of experience DiGiuseppe brought to the project, it wasn't off to the Coast for a one-day shoot and back to the lab for a quick edit. The agency wrote and pitched two other spots first.

JWT's initial concept was to have a dog sitting in a pair of pajamas which were hanging on a clothesline between two apartments. The dog's partner is pulling on the clothesline with his teeth, moving the pajamas toward a balcony across the air shaft. A juicy steak is sizzling on a barbecue on the balcony, and the dogs are after it. The spot tried to say that if the dogs wanted the meat on the barbecue, they would want Tender Chops. After doing an animatic, JWT rejected the concept as being too complicated to explain in thirty seconds.

The second try featured a policeman who arrives at a home with the family pooch in tow. He knocks on the door and informs the woman of the house that the dog has been caught choplifting.

"The spot put the people at center stage. The dogs were shown as criminals, but not in the act of thievery. The animals were

one-dimensional, so the charm factor wasn't working as strongly as we wanted," says DiGiuseppe.

Despite these drawbacks, the spot was filmed and scored well—above average—in testing. Better yet, the spot was finished and would be ready for a scheduled product roll-out in January 1987. But neither Ken-L Ration nor JWT were convinced they had the best solution.

The crew went back to the well. In their third spot, a team of dogs pulls off a "sting." A cute Benji-type dog limps up to an elderly woman coming out of a supermarket. When she puts down her groceries to comfort the dog, a second dog pulls the Tender Chops out of her grocery bag and passes it to a third dog in a getaway car. The "gang" meets up later to share the booty.

Undoubtedly, it was a cute idea. But so were the first two. The difference this time would be execution; everything in the spot was focused on the dogs. The props on the set were carefully chosen not to overshadow the pooches. The elderly woman was quite short. And while the dogs weren't auditioned at all, director

Victor Haboush says 49 actresses auditioned for the one human part in the script.

Haboush was JWT's first choice to direct because he'd done the original spot as well as an earlier spot for Smorgasburgers.

With the January roll-out already bearing down on them, the team went to Hollywood to shoot at Warner Brothers.

After two days on the set, the crew had it in the can. According to DiGiuseppe, the cuts had been carefully worked out and the final spot went together "like butter." Avenue Edit edited the footage, slowing it down slightly to smooth the transitions.

Tender Chops appeared on the shelves as scheduled, though the spot wasn't aired until March. With a limited budget, the agency decided that the best way to create awareness was to schedule a limited flight backed by full-page color magazine insertions.

The result was a phenomenon. In six months, Tender Chops had a two and a half share of the dry dog food segment. At $17.6 million per share point, that's just a tad over $44 million. Not bad for a shaggy dog story.

The last shot was a great payoff, and a tribute to the prescience of client Quaker Oats.

"We took a chance spreading the product out on the bare floor," DiGiuseppe says. "A lot of clients would have insisted that the product be in a bowl. But we wanted it to look authentic. If these dogs had just stolen a bag of food, they wouldn't pour it into bowls before eating it."

MICHELOB

Night Moves Are The Right Moves For Anheuser-Busch And Michelob

Client: Anheuser-Busch, Inc.
Agency: DDB Needham Worldwide/Chicago

While they seem to have become a part of the business landscape, not everyone agrees whether the creative slugfests known as submitting speculative campaigns are good for advertisers or agencies. However, as *The Night Belongs to Michelob*, produced by DDB Needham for Anheuser-Busch, proves, the process can sometimes produce spectacular and effective advertising. The pressure of the situation helped focus the agency's energy and perhaps encouraged the client to take risks it might have declined in other circumstances.

"It was one of those situations where you had everybody coming in with their campaigns," says Susan Gillette, executive vice president and director of creative services for DDB Needham Worldwide/Chicago. "I think one of the reasons we ended up winning the business was that we committed fairly early on to a single idea."

That idea was to stake out a psychological territory for the brewery's flagship Michelob brand as *the* beer for the night. The way the creative team went at it is about as unorthodox as they come in the straight-ahead world of beer advertising. And while the pressure put on the creatives spurred them to commit to a single idea very early, market pressures bearing down on Anheuser-Busch probably helped win acceptance for their unconventional approach.

Sales of Michelob peaked in the late 1970s and early 1980s. In 1981, sales began to drop at an alarming rate of almost 10% annually. Sales of superpremium domestic beers—Michelob, Lowenbrau and a few other small brands—were steadily drying up. Imported beers were taking an ever-increasing share of the American beer market. Naturally, most of their gains came at the expense of the higher-priced superpremiums. At the same time, light beers—Bud Light, Miller Lite *et. al.*—were chomping away at Michelob sales from below. Pricing came into play as well. Budweiser, also produced by Anheuser and America's largest-selling brand, had been upgraded and its price had crept up to within a nickel a bottle of Michelob.

"Michelob drinkers were getting older," Gillette adds. "As young people came into the market, they were choosing either light beers or imports as their beer of preference."

In the 1980s, falling sales and an aging customer base spell trouble for any brand. By the time the account came up for review in 1986, Anheuser-Busch knew it had a problem with Michelob.

The problem, as defined by DDB Needham, was that Michelob had once been a beer for special occasions. But the tide of exotic imports—Corona, South Pacific, St. Sixtus—had pretty much drained Michelob of its status.

"The quote we were using was 'Michelob was my Dad's country club beer,' " says Gillette.

Knowing what the brand had been, the agency probed further to find out where there was an opportunity for making Michelob special again. As it is with most things, sex turned out to be a key consideration.

"Our research showed that the presence of women in a social situation was key to the consumption of Michelob," Gillette explains. "While women have always consumed Michelob, they aren't as heavy beer drinkers as men. When men are out with the guys, they don't necessarily care what kind of beer they drink. But when they're out with a date or their wife, they tend to drink a higher-priced higher-status beer. We found that superpremiums weren't sports and activity beers or after-work Miller Time beers. They were consumed at night, usually when women were present."

NOW APPEARING AT A STORE NEAR YOU.

The Genesis Concert Tour Poster. Available free, wherever exceptionally smooth Michelob beer is sold. Or, send $3.00 to Michelob Genesis Poster, Box 9035, St. Louis, MO, 63102. *The Night Belongs To Michelob.*™

While staking out a territory for Michelob as a nighttime beer had a lot to recommend it, there was too much at stake not to consider alternatives.

"The agency looked at literally dozens and dozens of ideas, everything from humor and lifestyle to product-focus themes. We tested campaigns that talked about the quality of Michelob, the 100% imported hops, but none of that was compelling to beer drinkers," Gillette says. "When we saw how they reacted to the nighttime idea, we decided to put all our energy into convincing the brewery that this was the right way to go.

"There's a mystery about the night, an allure. Everything looks different at night. People look different, scenery looks different. And products look different at night. We hoped some of that magic would rub off on the brand."

The creative team wanted to do something extremely non-verbal so they got every night movie, every night commercial ever made and studied them. In the end, they took bits of footage from a number of sources and patched together something that looked remarkably like the first execution.

That first execution, which broke in June of 1986, was a montage of footage suggesting a rendezvous between a man and woman. There were no words; the sound track consisted of singer Phil Collins doing his popular *Coming In The Air Tonight*.

"In fact, the proposed spot we showed the brewery used that song as the sound track," Gillette says. "I don't believe this campaign would have worked if we had used a jingle. If we hadn't been able to get people like Phil Collins to work with us, it would have died."

Sometimes fate smiles at the most unlikely times.

"We had no idea that

(MUSIC UP) COLLINS (SINGS): I CAN FEEL IT

COMING IN THE AIR

TONIGHT...

OH LORD.

(MUSIC UP)

WELL, I'VE BEEN WAITING FOR THIS MOMENT FOR

ALL MY

LIFE...

OH LORD...

OH LORD.

ANNCR (VO): So exceptionally smooth...

(MUSIC UP)...

...

...

...

...

...

...

...

ANNCR (VO): The night belongs to Michelob. SINGER: I CAN FEEL IT COMING IN THE AIR.

According to creative director Susan Gillette, the use of first-rank talent, rather than a jingle, was crucial to the campaign's success.

"It's almost like a celebrity testimonial in the most subtle way," she explains. "If people like Phil Collins and Eric Clapton will give their name to the product, it has to be a pretty sophisticated, world-class product."

Through a fortuitous circumstance, the first musician DDB Needham proposed, Phil Collins, was already considering an offer from Anheuser-Busch to sponsor his solo tour. The first execution (above) was a montage of images, a half-completed story suggesting a night rendezvous between a man and a woman.

"There's a certain mystery about the night," Gillette says. "Everything looks different, more alluring. The commercials have been described as metaphors for the ideal beer use occasion. They are the way you wish your night was. Some of them skew more toward couples, others more toward pursuit and people meeting each other, but there's always an element of sensuality, which is something new in beer commercials."

Gillette credits art director Bruce Ritter with creating the look for the campaign. Before producing the initial test spot, the agency team reviewed every night movie and night commerical ever made.

"The musicians were extremely pleased that we didn't bastardize rock'n'roll," Gillette says. "We didn't put beer lyrics into their songs. If there was a lyric that might not be acceptable to the mass population, they occasionally did substitute the words for us. It's been a lot of fun being associated with these talented people."

So far the list of celebrities lending their sound to Michelob's videos includes Eric Clapton (above), Roger Daltrey (opposite), Wang Chung and Phil Collins and Genesis.

Anheuser was negotiating with Collins to sponsor his solo concert tour," Gillette laughs. "When we made the presentation, we said we didn't know if we could get Collins. They told us not to give up, that they might be able to do something to help. In fact, they did get him for the spot and for the concert tour."

Despite the good luck of proposing a rock star the brewery was already negotiating with, the campaign was not an automatic sale. There were other agencies and spots still in contention, and most were a lot more mainstream than DDB Needham's. Six months lapsed before the agency knew it had won the shootout.

"One of the fears was that, if we said the night belongs to Michelob, would people drink it during the day? Also, Anheuser-Busch buys its own media, including a lot of sporting events. How would a commercial filmed at night look on a one o'clock football game?" Gillette recalls.

"The people at the brewery said, 'We're not sure about this. If feels risky. It also feels like, if it works, it will be one of those campaigns that everybody talks about.' "

There is a way to resolve such issues. More research.

"All of the competing campaigns were tested. The brewery uses a lot of one-on-one interviews and a lot of focus groups to evaluate advertising. Our night spot just seemed more compelling than everything else. We got the business on the basis of that one execution. We wouldn't have won if it hadn't out-tested everything else on the plate."

The campaign represented a risk that Anheuser probably wouldn't have taken five years ago, Gillette adds. "At that time, they didn't need to run anything but mainstream advertising. By the time we got

the business, they had to do something that said different, unique, special. If I went back to the vaults of our agency and looked at the best advertising we've done, a lot of it has been created in market situations where clients knew they had to do something that wasn't safe. That's how a lot of the best advertising is born."

With the client behind the effort and Phil Collins on board, the agency hired director Joe Pytka to get the footage for the first spot.

"Phil Collins was pretty much of a sweetheart. With all of our spots, we've had as many cameras going as possible to catch those magical moments when celebrities are just being themselves. In the second spot we did with Phil, there was just a second when his eyes shifted right into the camera. It's very subliminal, but that's the kind of thing that makes the film really work."

How long were they in post-production? "You don't want to know," Gillette chuckles. "There's so much room for individual interpretation and *everybody* has an opinion. We did four or five versions of the spot. Joe Pytka even did a two-minute version and spent his own money to run it on some obscure station so he could enter it in competition.

"It's surprising how faithful the finished spot is to the original test version. It's really a study in something that was so seductive it didn't get messed with along the way."

The magic was apparent even in the editing suite. Gillette says the crew was there at all hours cutting, and other editors would drift in at two o'clock in the morning and sit, riveted, in front of the editing board. The appeal isn't limited to other creative types, either.

"On our second production trip, we were sitting in a bar in California when the first spot came on the television,"

Gillette recalls. "A hush fell over the bar and everyone was watching the commercial. The fact that people really enjoyed the spot was quite a rush."

Almost immediately, awareness of Michelob's advertising went up 50%. Just about everyone was happy.

"Anheuser-Busch is a great client. Their goals for Michelob aren't unrealistic. They know the brand isn't going to grow 20% a year like Bud Light. They'd be happy to stem the decline and have Michelob be the flagship of quality for the brewery. It's their most luxurious, most expensive product to brew. They're very proud of it. What's nice is that we've been able to restore the status of the brand.

"We can't do much about on-premise sales. If a bar doesn't carry Michelob, you can't order it. That's as much a wholesaler issue as an advertising issue. But if you look at package sales, where advertising can have a big impact, sales have stabilized. In some areas, such as Atlanta and the Southeast, where Michelob has always been strong, there's been substantial sales growth. In other areas, like California, the declines have been huge. It takes an awful lot to turn around a brand that's gotten so far down in a market."

The success of the initial execution prompted a spate of follow-ups, all using first-rank rock superstars: Eric Clapton, Roger Daltrey, Wang Chung and Phil Collins with Genesis.

The target demographics are 21 to 35, and within that range, there are two groups: Drinkers under 27 and those over 27.

"The advertising itself works as a sort of magnet," Gillette points out. "People over 45 are going to scratch their heads and wonder what it's about. People under 45 are going to think it's pretty neat. The music, much more than the

(MUSIC UP)... ... ...

... ...

... ... SINGER: I MOVE BETTER IN THE NIGHT. (MUSIC UP)...

... SINGER: I WON'T STOP UNTIL THE DAYLIGHT. MMM. MAKES ME FEEL RIGHT. ANNCR (VO): So exceptionally smooth...

SINGER: I MOVE BETTER IN THE NIGHT. ANNCR (VO): The night belongs to Michelob.

The Michelob video spots have been criticized as "mere music videos." Gillette admits the pieces are not copy-driven, but points out that a lot of communication is non-verbal.

"Your advertising says things it doesn't explicitly say," she explains. "There isn't a word in the television spots about product quality, nothing about a cut above the rest or use on a special occasion. But when we play these commercials to our target, they tell us that the spots conveyed that Michelob is a better quality beer, one for drinking when you're out with friends, a beer to drink when you want to impress someone.

"One of the things our viewers really like about the Michelob ads are that they allow consumers to draw their own conclusions. We don't hit them over the head or scream at them. The stories are vague on purpose. Our focus groups would actually argue about what they thought the scenario was. In the end, they didn't care what the 'right' answer was, but they did like the fact we didn't tie everything up neatly with a bow. There seems to be an element of fun for them to sit out there and decide for themselves what we're trying to say and what it all means. We're leaving them enough room to be part of the creative process."

CLASSICS VARY.

QUALITY DOESN'T.

Michelob, Michelob Light, Michelob Classic Dark. Whichever you choose, you're choosing a classic. Brewed from the world's most expensive *ingredients with unsurpassed care for over 90 years. The Michelob family of beers. What they have in common isn't common at all.*

TASTES VARY.

visuals, determines which end of the age scale an execution appeals to. Wang Chung skews younger than Phil Collins."

In 1987, Anheuser told DDB Needham that its Michelob Light account—which the agency had held since 1982—was to be put up for review. Sales had been heading up, but advertising awareness for the brand had never broken the bank by any measure. Again, the brewery invited a number of agencies to participate in a free-for-all.

DDB Needham proposed bringing all three Michelob brands—original, Light and Classic Dark—together as nighttime beers.

"We felt very strongly there were efficiencies to be gained by having all the brands at one agency. If you had two agencies, or three if you add in the Michelob Dark business, it would fragment the effort. The budgets for all three of these brands are very small compared to the budgets for Budweiser or Bud Light. In the end, research and common

sense prevailed."

The research was a bit of intelligence gathered by the agency that showed the nighttime campaign had done more for the sales of Michelob Light than it had for the sales of Michelob itself.

"The Michelob ads were so strong that Michelob Light drinkers were saying, 'That's my advertising,'" Gillette explains.

The result was the *Light Up The Night* execution. The visuals are a whirlwind montage of young people partying, dancing and generally having a great time—at night. Instead of celebrities singing their own material, a pulsating four-beat jingle was written and the film edited to take advantage of the musical riffs. In *Dance*, for example, shots of a woman spinning around are intercut with shots of beer swirling out of a bottle of Michelob Light. The effect is captivating. Gillette describes the spots as "fun, electric and high energy."

"So far sales of Michelob

Light have responded but the jury is still out on awareness. That surprises me because if anything, the spots are more intrusive than the Michelob spots. They're much more product oriented. You'd have to be brain dead not to see them on the air because the film is so hypnotic," she muses.

The cuts are so well timed and the images so unexpected that it isn't possible to be in the same room with them and not look at the screen. Gillette hopes the Michelob Light campaign will bolster Michelob's appeal to drinkers under 25 as well.

"The brewery would also like to see us broaden the Michelob campaign to appeal to those at the top end of our target," she notes. "This is the type of campaign that requires constant surprises. We need surprising executions in terms of story lines and in terms of the celebrities we choose. It's surprising how comfortably the campaign can move from a fairly complicated story to a totally impressionistic appeal.

QUALITY DOESN'T.

Michelob, Michelob Light. Or Michelob Classic Dark. Whichever suits your taste, you're assured of the very best. The world's most expensive ingre- *dients, naturally brewed, with unsurpassed care for over 90 years. The Michelob family of beers. What they have in common isn't common at all.*

We're look for startling commercials."

Gillette looks forward to directing the attack on these new beachheads. "It's fun to be working on ads that are doing what they're supposed to do—working in the market-place and garnering a lot of attention for the brand.

"There are people in the advertising business who see our work and scratch their heads because these pieces are not copy-driven. If you look at the Clio Award reels, almost everything is one-line humor. Some people say that we're just doing music videos, that it isn't advertising at all because it has no 'idea.' That kind of makes me laugh. It's like saying there's no 'idea' to Marlboro Country. A territory use oc-casion is just as valid a concept as a competitive stance. It's just a different cut at advertising."

Whatever the advertising world thinks about Gillette's "different cut," the crew at DDB Needham has made that difference a positive one for Anheuser-Busch.

STYLES VARY.   **QUALITY DOESN'T.**

Michelob, Michelob Light, or Michelob Classic Dark. Whichever style you choose, you choose the best. Brewed from the world's most expen- *sive ingredients with unsurpassed care for over 90 years. The Michelob family of beers. What they have in common isn't common at all.*

The print ads are much more specific than the video spots. DDB Needham created a pool of executions for use in specific kinds of magazines. *Tastes* (top) was run in consumer and food magazines, while *Styles* was shot for use in fashion magazines. The print ads are a good example of how the agency was able to gain efficiencies in media by holding the business for all three Michelob brands.

The video spots for sister brand Michelob Light were intended to compliment the Michelob *Night Moves* spots. Instead of celebrity singers, the agency chose a high-energy jingle backed by a montage of youngish-looking people partying in a variety of situations. The visuals are truly hypnotic, as in the *Concert* execution (right), where time-lapse photography of a lightning storm over Manhattan was used as a visual counterpoint to the music.

Light beer drinkers tend to be a bit younger and more active than Michelob's primary target, and the agency hopes that *Light Up The Night* (below) will extend the reach of *Night Moves* to these consumers.

Aside from the executions, the agency has concentrated on media scheduling for both efforts. "We were successful in getting some real special media buys such as the Grammy Awards, and we run a lot of *Late Night With David Letterman* and so on," Gillette says. Anheuser-Busch does its own media buying in-house, so Michelob has to compete with Budweiser and Busch for choice bits of air time from the corporate kitty.

SINGER: L-L-LIGHT | UP THE NIGHT. | WHEN THE SUN GOES DOWN, | GONNA LIGHT UP THE NIGHT.

SILVER LABEL, RED RIBBON, | A TASTE THAT'S RIGHT. | GONNA LIGHT UP | THE NIGHT...

MICHELOB LIGHT. | GONNA LIGHT UP | THE NIGHT... | GONNA LIGHT UP

THE | NIGHT... | GONNA | LIGHT UP THE NIGHT...

(MUSIC) | M-M-MY | MICHELOB | LIGHT.

SINGER: WHEN THE SUN GOES | DOWN, | GONNA LIGHT UP | THE NIGHT.

SILVER LABEL, RED RIBBON, | A TASTE THAT'S RIGHT. | GONNA LIGHT UP THE NIGHT... | MICHELOB LIGHT.

GONNA LIGHT UP | THE NIGHT. | TWIST IT, POUR IT, | LIGHT UP THE NIGHT.

CAN'T WAIT | FOR IT, | LIGHT UP THE | NIGHT. SHOW YOUR GOLDEN

BODY, MY MICHELOB | LIGHT. | GONNA LIGHT UP THE NIGHT... | GONNA LIGHT UP THE NIGHT.

Tonight, what's par for the course just isn't good enough. Make it Michelob. So exceptionally smooth, the night belongs to Michelob.

The night belongs to Michelob.

Two of the best things on ice. Hockey. And Michelob.

The night belongs to Michelob.

Clever word play is the key to the print executions. The agency trusts the audience to know that "icing" refers to a hockey infraction and to associate "eagle" with golf and with Anheuser's corporate symbol. For the special promotional ad at left, the team left out most of the words, opting instead for a jet-set rebus. The ad was run in *Rolling Stone* and *Spin.*

CAROLINA

An Active Culture's Just The Thing For North Carolina

Client: North Carolina Department of Tourism
Agency: McKinney & Silver

One of the more perceptive statements ever made about promoting tourism was unintentional. It was a poster, popular some years ago, showing a couple in the desert wearing snow skis. The headline read "Ski Arizona."

When you're selling a destination, there's no possibility of reformulating the product or changing the packaging. You can't dress the entire state of Iowa like a Hollywood set. What you have to sell is what the area already possesses. And you hope it's what the traveling public wants.

What might that be? Some years ago the state of North Carolina commissioned a research study to find out. What they discovered wouldn't surprise even a hermit: When people travel, they want to see something different from their everyday surroundings. They want to eat well and shop. They want a choice of activities.

Taken to an extreme, that would make New York City the ideal domestic travel destination. In fact, the state's long-running campaign shows pictures of Elizabeth Taylor at her most pulchritudinous standing in front of Lincoln Center, presumably on her way to yet another society benefit.

North Carolina has no Lincoln Center, no Empire State Building, no Grand Canyon, no *La Grenouille* to tout. Yet its advertising has been both effective and extraordinary; the state's print effort won the prestigious Stephen P. Kelly award for superior magazine advertising in 1987. And tourism revenues are up by a third over the past four years. That's quite an achievement for an area characterized in too many otherwise educated people's minds by visions of overalls, tattered flannel shirts and crock jugs.

The success has come from character; the character of North Carolina and particularly of the creative professionals behind the advertising.

In North Carolina, some of our greatest works of art
never hang in a museum.

Dove-In-The-Window. Star of Bethlehem. Wild Goose Chase. Wedding Ring. High in the North Carolina mountains, quilts are made to be purely practical. Yet their ageless patterns make them purely beautiful. Quilts, however, are just one expression of our highland artistry.

Some people can put their penknife to a block of sugar maple and magically reveal the form of a wild turkey or a good hunting dog.

Others make sturdy pots with glazes as guardedly secret as prized family recipes.

And still others display their art in jars of jam and jelly, or in jugs of amber apple cider found at roadside stands.

Wherever you travel, from our mountains to our shore, you'll be certain to find art that exhibits itself proudly.

So, if you're the kind of person who appreciates finer things, you really don't have to visit the museums.

Come to North Carolina, and visit us instead.

North Carolina

For our new travel package, just write NC Travel, Dept. 589

Raleigh, NC 27699. Or, in Michigan, Ohio, Illinois and Indiana, call (weekdays 8 a.m.–5 p.m.) 1-800-VISIT NC. Operator 589

For much of the past 20 years, Charles McKinney, now chairman of McKinney & Silver, has been associated with North Carolina's tourism advertising. Jan Karon, who wrote the pieces that won the Kelly Award, also worked with McKinney on the very first state tourism ads. Michael Winslow, creative director, has worked on the account for 11 years. Like a good novel, their advertising challenges and changes the stereotypes by explaining in short, telegraphic bursts of prose and image the richness of the state's landscape and culture.

"We think the unusual thing about these ads is that they have warmth and character, which are two things the people here have," Karon says. "Even when we're talking about the scenery, we cast it in such a way that it presents something of who the people are. It has to come at the readers through our own filter. And we want that filter to be one of warmth and—I don't hesitate to use the word—love. Michael and I are both natives. We love North Carolina. And we literally love our ads; we work so hard on them. This is one of our smaller accounts; it only bills about $1.5 million. But it gets the lavish attention of a $30 million account. We don't spare anything."

Sure, sure. That's what everyone says about their small accounts. But in this case, it certainly appears to be true. Not only through their intimate knowledge of the state but also through dint of hard work, they consistently find things to feature in their ads; things that other states don't have or which they haven't merchandised. And they manage to portray them in a way that's uniquely reflective of the people, the landscape and the culture of the state.

Stereotypes notwithstanding, they have a wealth of material to draw on. The western boundary of the state splits the ridges of the Great Smoky Mountains, a mile above sea level. The place names—Cullowhee,

It's not the Guggenheim or the Met, and it doesn't have a passel of Picassos, but this print campaign for North Carolina sells what the state does have—charm and character. And it does it so convincingly it took top honors in the Stephen P. Kelly Awards program for 1987. The Kelly Awards, named for the former president of the Magazine Publishers Association, is the most prestigious competition for print ads in the U.S.

An early execution, this spread lays out the cornucopia of country pleasures available in North Carolina. Backlighting rims the udders of the Holsteins and infuses the home-canned goods in the foreground with a warm orange glow. The careful attention to detail in the photograph is echoed by the economic use of language in the accompanying copy.

Subsequent executions (following pages) expand on the theme, each one zeroing in on a single, engaging vignette.

WELCOME TO MILK AN

The long rows of jars on a roadside stand shine like soft, sweet gold in the morning sunlight.

Green pastures climb slowly through the mist to join the rising mountains.

The air is so fresh, you'd think somebody had washed it. The sound of a lone bird mingles with the sound of a stream.

To the East, the ridges flatten into hills, then into farmlands stretching away toward the island beaches of the Atlantic Ocean.

The fields are rich with crops. The waters are rich with fish. The air is rich with the smell of flowers.

And the land is rich

Stecoah—remind that this was the sacred land of the Cherokee Indians. The Cherokee were one of the Seven Civilized Tribes. They had a written language, invented by Sequoia, for whom California's giant redwood trees were named. Before being packed off to exile in Oklahoma, they even had a newspaper.

From the mountains, the land slopes down to the surrounding piedmont. This fertile area embraced the hardy Scotch, Irish and English settlers who came to farm. Much of the country's tobacco industry is centered here,

in Winston-Salem and in Raleigh. Appropriately, these reminders of the Old South sit cheek-by-jowl with what the promoters like to say is the New South—the massive light industrial-educational-research complex contained within the Raleigh-Durham-Chapel Hill triangle.

The state has a great stretch of coastline, as well. From Cape Fear and Corncake Inlet in the south, past Pamlico Sound and up around the Outer Banks to the border with Virginia, the Atlantic shore abounds with historical associations and long strips of

THE LAND OF
O HONEY.

in history. It is the land
of colonists, of pioneers, of
the Cherokee Nation.

North Carolina. It is a
land of promises kept. A
land of plenty. A land that

civilization has touched,
but never destroyed.

It is a land filled with
good things. And it is a
land that reaches out and
invites you to share them.

secluded white-sand beach.
During the golden age of piracy,
just before and after the War of
the Spanish Succession (1712), the
labyrinthine waterways of
Pamlico and Albermarle sounds
were a haven for English
freebooters. Edward Teach, the
notorious Blackbeard, fought his
last battle at Blackbeard's Hole.
Teach lost his head in the fighting,
and legend has long had it that
those who are spiritually inclined
can occasionally see Blackbeard
swimming in circles, searching
vainly for his head.

"One of the first ads the agency

did when it got the account eleven
years ago was captioned
'Welcome to an Old-Fashioned
Family Reunion,' " Karon says.
"The photograph showed all of
these wonderful-looking men in
their kilts standing on an
outcropping of rock with a view
of Grandfather Mountain. While
other states have Highland
Games, no one else was talking
about them. In fact, we've
featured a number of things
which aren't unique to North
Carolina. But we seem to be the
only ones talking about them."

The team is not above seizing

COME AND SEE A PLA REPEATS ITSE

The brick sidewalks are worn by generations of patient footsteps.

The sun shines down on green gardens and tall half-timbered houses.

In the little shops, the people of Old Salem go about their daily business. Very much as their Moravian ancestors did.

You can take home a skein of bright yarn. A tin teakettle. A loaf of bread.

None of it marked "Souvenir of Old Salem." You won't find long lines. Or roped-off rooms. Or people selling balloons.

You will find a kind of peace the modern world has almost forgotten.

And a deep sense of commitment to what is

CE WHERE HISTORY
LF EVERY DAY.

worth preserving.

In fact, you'll find the same kind of commitment all over North Carolina.

In colonial homes and country inns. Unspoiled beaches and virgin forests.

Because this is a place where people work to keep their history alive. Not just to re-create it.

You see, you don't have to re-create something that never went away.

If you are what you eat,
make you a very interesting

Grits Souffle. Squash
Pie. Wild Persimmon Pudding.
Chow Chow. Corn Dodgers.
Across the gently rolling

midlands of North Carolina,
what we eat is hardly the same
old blue plate special.
To family reunions and

church dinners across
the state, we bring dishes like
our Green Tomato Pie and
Pig Pickin' Cake, which puzzle

visit to North Carolina could
erson, indeed.

sample our great homecooking. Because we also cook like this away from home.

Which means you'll find these interesting dishes in small cafes and old inns, when

you travel from our Blue Ridge mountains to our shore.

So, come. Because a visit to North Carolina is more than food for the appetite.

It's also food for the soul.

the uninitiated and thoroughly delight the oldtimers.

But you don't have to call North Carolina home just to

For our new travel package, write North Carolina Travel, Dept. 457, Raleigh, N.C. 27699. Or call 1-800-VISIT NC, Operator 457.

North Carolina

COME TO A PLACE WHERE YOU CAN STILL FIND BURIED TREASURE.

Two centuries ago, the pirate Blackbeard roamed the rugged coastline of North Carolina.

It was here he won his legendary treasures.

And it was here that, in the end, he lost his life.

The pirates and their gold have come and gone.

But the treasures are still here for the taking.

The ocean, gold in the sunset, diamond-sparkled in the cool Atlantic dawn.

Gleaming shells in jewel colors, half-buried in pearl-white sand.

Silk-surfaced lakes. Bright rivers winding like silver threads through the soft, rich tapestries of growing fields.

Sapphire mountains, set into emerald valleys.

The perfume of pines and azalea blossoms and fresh-turned earth.

In North Carolina the treasures are everywhere. From the Appalachians to the rolling farmlands, all the way to the secluded cove where Blackbeard fought his last battle.

Some, like the shells, are the kind you can carry away in your hands.

But most of them are the kind you'll probably carry away in your mind.

NORTH CAROLINA

For more information, and the free North Carolina Travel Package, write North Carolina Travel, Department 000, Raleigh, NC 27699.

opportunity and wringing it for all it's worth. The recent discovery by folks of the Northern persuasion that Southern home cooking tastes really terrific is a case in point. Five years ago, writing an ad touting grits would have been suicide. But that's one of the pieces that won the 1987 Kelly Award.

"We wouldn't have run that ad five years ago," Karon agrees. **"We'd have come off as hillbillies. But Craig Claiborne [food critic for *The New York Times*] had** made a pass through North Carolina just before I wrote that ad. He acclaimed our restaurants, including Dip's Country Kitchen. Dip's is run by a strapping black woman who must be six and a half feet tall, wears a rag on her head and works all of her kids in the kitchen. Claiborne had a plate of fried chicken gizzards and waxed rhapsodic about them. I knew that if Claiborne could **review Dip's fried chicken gizzards in *The New York Times*, we could write an ad about North Carolina cuisine."**

The execution of that ad reflects the punctilious oversight exercised by the agency. To get a window on the graciousness of the Old South, the team went to Old Salem, the restored historic district of the city of Salem.

"I styled that particular shot," Karon confesses. "For us, having a writer go on a shoot to style a photo is unusual, but this ad was very close to my heart. I wanted it to be just right. Take the pewter pitcher in the back. Instead of arranging the flowers, I simply went out to the meadow and into the neighboring gardens and gathered up armloads of flowers while the dew was still on. I just set them in the vase without any arrangement. I knew that however they fell would be perfect. My grandmother had something like the old jam cupboard in the background, and I remembered she always hung her dishtowel from it. The model was Violet, a wonderful Moravian lady who works in Old Salem. We put a cup of coffee in her hand because a woman who's just set out all that

Our cruise lines may not be known for elegant dining, but they'll take you to some beautiful islands.

Drive to the bank of the Cashie River in North Carolina, and honk the horn. And when the ferry chugs over to pick you up, you can cruise to the other side. Free.

Or, you can take a ferry to faraway places with strange-sounding names like Hatteras, Ocracoke, and Rodanthe.

Several of these rugged barrier islands are so remote, the people speak a foreign language: Olde English. And some are so unspoiled, you can still see the same pristine beauty that enchanted our first settlers from Wales, Scotland and England.

Whether you explore 25 miles of national seashore or visit our colorful fishing villages, you'll discover this: Our cruise lines may not offer elegant dining.

But they can help satisfy your appetite for adventure.

For our new travel package, write North Carolina Travel, Dept. 466, Raleigh, NC 27699 Or call 1-800-VISIT NC, Operator 466

North Carolina

---

food *needs* a cup of coffee."

The comestibles on the table? Grits souffle. Squash pie. Wild persimmon pie. Fried chicken. Fried okra.

Every authentic Southern kitchen has some tomatoes ripening on the window sill and at least one jar of pickled peppers on the sideboard ready to be poured over a steaming heap of collard greens. This one is authentic.

The attention to detail isn't accidental. It's part of the agency's way of life.

"Mr. McKinney sees everything that goes out of here, from hang tags to the video spots," Karon says. "He has a ceremonial office up on the administrative floor with the velvet couch and marble this and marble that. It's like a mausoleum. He also has an office on the creative floor; that's where he spends most of his time."

Undoubtedly, more than a few of the four or five million tourists who've been introduced to the delights of North Carolina by way of these ads are glad he does.

Although the account bills less than $2 million annually, McKinney & Silver pulls out all of the creative stops, even sending senior creative director Michael Winslow into the field to scout locations and occasionally sending copywriter Jan Karon on the shoots. The photographs for the series were done by Harry DeZitter, a South African photographer living in Paris.

Pepsi: The Strength Of Youth And The Wisdom Of Age

Client: Pepsi USA
Agency: BBDO New York

"Do not bring me mortal men, bring me giants!" — Cyrano de Bergerac

Cyrano knew there was no glory in conquering the ordinary; that the realm of mythic fame is inhabited only by Titans. There's plenty of excellent advertising done for clients which most of us will never hear of. And there are certain businesses whose protagonists rise quite naturally to the Pantheon of promotional warfare, namely any business in which the president of a company with a one point share of the market can afford a private jet and Armani suits. The auto market is one; the soft drink business is another. In the latter, case sales and dollar volume continue to rise like the silvery vapors from a just-opened bottle of that protean brew. In 1987, the U.S. soft drink market weighed in at a tad over $45 *billion*, making one share point worth $450 million.

For nearly a century, Coca-Cola was the number one soft drink. In 1930, Pepsi Cola was teetering on the brink of bankruptcy. In fact, Pepsi Cola offered to sell out to Coke, but was rebuffed. Pepsi managed to buy some twelve-ounce beer bottles. Other soft drinks, including Coke, were sold in six-ounce bottles. Pepsi priced its twelve-ounce drinks at a nickel, the same as Coke, and coined the slogan "Twice as much for a nickel." In the midst of the Great Depression, this was welcome news for beleaguered consumers. However, it left Pepsi with a distinctly second-rate image. People would pour Pepsi in the kitchen and serve it in the living room under the guise of Coca-Cola. For the next half-century, Pepsi cooperatively played the role of aggressive underdog. All of that changed when Pepsi's share briefly edged past Coke's in 1985. While not everyone—especially Coca-Cola—agrees on how to measure soft drink sales, the battle between these Leviathans has seesawed back and forth, with one camp claiming the lead for a while, then conceding it to the other. However, everyone, even Coca-Cola, agrees that Pepsi's advertising had a lot to do with its move from impoverishment to parity.

The theme of that advertising is almost prosaic: "The choice of a new generation." Its effect has been anything but commonplace. The shockwaves it set off toppled Coke from its century-old pedestal and,

Since the first days of its association with Pepsi in the early 60s, BBDO has turned out round after round of finely-crafted executions, first for the *Pepsi Generation*, and more recently for *Pepsi—The Choice of a New Generation*. BBDO has hitched Pepsi's wagon to a succession of celebrities running the gamut from Michael Jackson to Michael J. Fox.

many observers feel, was one factor that led Coke to rewrite the Sacred Formula and release "New Coke" in the spring of 1985.

To find the genesis of the campaign, we have to journey back nearly to Biblical times (Biblical by the standards of the ad business anyway). It was a time when giants ruled the Earth—or at least that part of it most familiar to the New York advertising world, which is to say midtown Manhattan and southern Westchester County. Bernbach and Ogilvy held sway. In Detroit, the word was tailfins. It was 1960, and there aren't a handful of account execs this side of the pension pool who still remember the tremors that flowed up and down Madison Avenue when upstart Pepsi left Kenyon & Eckhardt for Batton, Barton, Durstine & Osborne (BBDO).

Alan Pottasch, vice president of Pepsi Cola USA, who has been with the company since 1958, dates Pepsi's modern era of advertising to that switch. "The last campaign done by Kenyon & Eckhardt was called *The Sociables*," he recalls. "It depicted such things as people going to a wedding, and there was a bottle of Pepsi in the champagne bucket. It stretched too far trying to upgrade Pepsi's image."

That prompted Pepsi to reevaluate its advertising and ultimately resulted in the move to BBDO. And there it encountered a phenomenon by the name of Tom Dillon, chairman of BBDO. He thought about Pepsi. He thought about its problems. Then he wrote what is now known as The Necktie Memo. "It impressed me as it impressed a lot of the people here," Pottasch says. "Essentially it said you can tell a lot about a man by the necktie he wears, just as you can tell a lot about him by the car he drives, the cigarette he smokes and the soft drink he has in his hand. If a soft drink is used by people he likes and admires, he'll be proud to be seen with that soft drink, just as he'll be proud wearing a classy tie. It becomes part of his self-image and the image he wants to project.

"Up to this point, our advertising and that of our competitors focused on the product: 'The Pause That Refreshes' and so on. From 1960 on, all of our advertising has dealt with *users*. We tried to distinguish the user of Pepsi from the user of

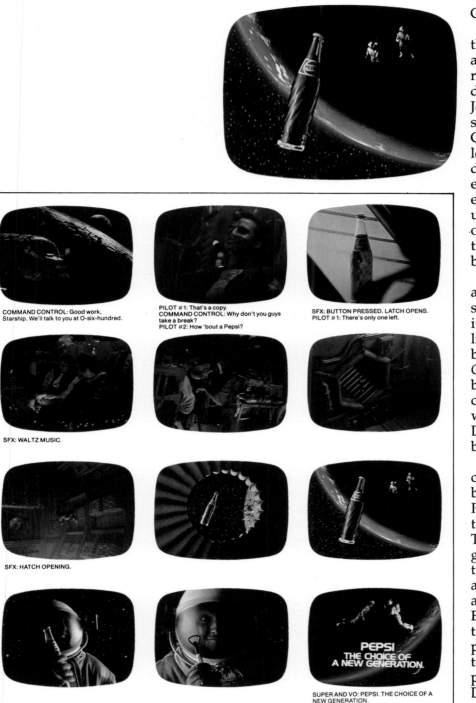

COMMAND CONTROL: Good work, Starship. We'll talk to you at O-six-hundred.

PILOT #1: That's a copy.
COMMAND CONTROL: Why don't you guys take a break?
PILOT #2: How 'bout a Pepsi?

SFX: BUTTON PRESSED. LATCH OPENS.
PILOT #1: There's only one left.

SFX: WALTZ MUSIC.

SFX: HATCH OPENING.

PEPSI
THE CHOICE OF
A NEW GENERATION.

SUPER AND VO: PEPSI. THE CHOICE OF A NEW GENERATION.

This execution, *Floats*, won a big handful of awards. A group of astronauts take a Pepsi break, only to find there's only one left. The Pepsi floats out of the spaceship and is chased through space by the crew. The attention to detail in this spot is phenomenal. In contrast to the usual view of tomorrow's spacecraft—gleaming, sterile, clean—the styling of this ship more closely resembles a beat-up World War II bomber.

Coca-Cola."

In 1963, that attempt resulted in the original *Pepsi Generation* advertising. It ran and ran and ran. Pepsi hired the best directors. Guys like Rick Levine. Joe Pytka directed for Pepsi while still in his early twenties. Michael Cimino was shooting for Pepsi long before *Heaven's Gate* shot down United Artists. Brilliant execution followed brilliant execution. And Pepsi's sales went up and up and up. The campaign outgrew more changes of clothes than a roomful of adolescent basketball players.

Beginning in 1975, Pepsi had actually been running two separate campaigns. One featured its traditional feeling-good-about-life-in-America spots. The other became infamous: *The Pepsi Taste Challenge*. That year, the Pepsi bottler in Dallas asked the company for some help. Pepsi wasn't even number two in Dallas; it was a distant third behind Coke and Dr. Pepper.

"The operation in Dallas is company-owned, and we were being outsold eight to one," Pottasch says. "The guys down there were doing everything right. They had good shelf space in the grocery stores. They had a well-trained delivery staff and absolutely no product problems at all. They had clean trucks. Everything was by the book. But they were in a terrible sales position. They asked me for a tough product-oriented campaign. I had started my career in Dallas and had a good friend there, a very creative fellow by the name of Bob Stanford, who had an agency. Bob agreed to do some research to find out if people in Dallas had a negative attitude toward Pepsi. He did blind taste tests and recorded them on audio tape. When people didn't know what they were drinking, the majority of them said they liked Pepsi better.

"He sent up the tapes and I said, 'Gee, it would be wonderful if I could see the faces of these people while they're tasting the products.' So Bob went out with a hidden camera and filmed the first *Pepsi Taste Challenge.*"

What happened next was classic sales slapstick.

"For the first *Taste Challenge* we marked the Pepsi bottle 'M' and the Coke bottle 'Q.' The person tasting the sodas would indicate they liked 'M' better, then we would reveal that it was Pepsi. Coke went into an absolute panic over this thing because they had done some taste tests of their own and they knew that what we were saying was true. Legally, there wasn't anything they could do to force our spots off the air because we could substantiate our claim. In the middle of this panic, they quickly put a spot on the air in Dallas. The script said, 'Isn't it interesting that this taste test labeled the bottles M and Q? Everybody knows that people prefer the letter M over the letter Q. Why did Pepsi choose to call itself M and call Coke Q?' That was the whole commercial. It was funny because we'd already shot *Challenge* spots using letters L and R, R and G and so on. We let them run their spot for three days, then put our new spots on the air."

The *Taste Challenge* was originally designed just for Dallas, but it worked so well the company couldn't resist moving the spots to other markets. In time, 80% of the country saw the *Pepsi Taste Challenge.*

By 1984, both Pepsi and BBDO were concerned. The *Pepsi Challenge* was on the verge of eclipsing the *Pepsi Generation* in the minds of consumers, threatening the tremendous equity built up over twenty years. Also, Coke had made significant inroads into Pepsi's stronghold—adolescents and young adults. But the *Challenge* was still selling soda, and it was hard for the company to let it go. How could they fly in the face of Rule Number One ("If it ain't broke, don't fix it")?

As things turned out they didn't have to.

The creatives at BBDO seem to have a sixth sense for finding associations that are destined for stardom. This parody of *Close Encounters* featured an alien mothership hovering over a Pepsi machine and a Coke machine. At the end of the spot, the Pepsi machine is shown being levitated up to the ship.

The solution has the surface simplicity that is the hallmark of most great advertising themes: *Pepsi—The Choice of a New Generation.* It allowed Pepsi to continue to talk about taste while reestablishing its traditional claim on the psychological territory "youth."

"It seemed that everyone was doing lifestyle advertising, so we felt it was time to jump onto a new track," says Phil Dusenberry, executive vice president of BBDO. Dusenberry, a creative director, has been associated with Pepsi's advertising almost as long as Pottasch, starting work on the account in 1963. "We wanted to separate ourselves not only from soft drinks like Coca-Cola, but from what advertisers in other categories were doing as well."

Another influential memo, this one known as The White Paper, was prepared. It mapped Pepsi's future, how to fold in the impact of the *Pepsi Challenge* and hold onto the equity of the *Pepsi Generation.*

Why the accent on youth when the market growth in soft drinks is among older consumers?

"The growth of the soft drink market among older consumers is primarily with diet soft drinks. At a certain age, folks tend to veer off and use a diet product, Diet Coke or hopefully Diet Pepsi," Dusenberry explains. "So the bulk of the market for full-calorie soft drinks is still very youth-related. Also, you can't talk to young people with an older voice. But you *can* talk to older people with a younger voice. Everybody wants to be young. We've always looked at *Pepsi Generation* advertising as being more a state of mind than a matter of age."

One of the first *New Generation* spots featured a young man in a van equipped with a big amplifier and roof-mounted speakers. He drives onto a beach. Hot July weather. Heavily-tanned sweating bodies cover every square inch of sand. The kid parks in a central location and unveils his secret weapon: He turns on

Small glimpses of a big celebrity—the first Michael Jackson spot for Pepsi—almost single-handedly unmade the way we look at television spots. The cost to Pepsi was a then-enormous $5.5 million, but the impact The Gloved One had on Pepsi's awareness levels made it all worthwhile. Despite the price, Jackson insisted that his face be on the screen for no more than two seconds. Pepsi's Alan Pottasch says that Jackson taught him that sometimes less is indeed more.

the amplifier and then opens and slowly pours a bottle of ice-cold Pepsi into a glass about two inches away from a microphone. That wonderful "whooosh-sssfffzzz" blasts out across the baking bodies. Heads pop up. Sunglass-covered eyes turn to the van. The next scene shows the kid opening the van's side doors to reveal a Pepsi stand. A crowd of thirsty young sun worshippers mobs the van and spills out of the frame camera right.

The executions were memorable and effective, but the next step turbo-charged the campaign and forever changed the ground rules of celebrity advertising.

"Up to this point, the *New Generation* was dialogue and visuals. It was definitely leading edge, but it wasn't music," says Dusenberry. "We felt we had to fill that gap because music is one way of speaking to young people. It's a universal language. But we felt that if we were going to do something musical it couldn't infringe on the other elements of the campaign. It had to be dramatic. It couldn't be just a music spot with the typical singing and dancing. It needed a celebrity."

As luck would have it, there was one high-profile celebrity who suddenly made himself available: Michael Jackson. For a mere $5.5 million, Pepsi could get a piece of a singer who was about to go thermonuclear with *Thriller*, a mega-album and mega-tour. Of course, Pepsi had no way of knowing what was coming. All they knew was that this reclusive, oddball pop singer was asking them to fork over about 100 times the largest fee the company had ever paid anyone to make a commercial. He also demanded the right to approve the final spot. And he insisted that, for their $5.5 million, Pepsi not show his face on camera for more than two seconds.

In his 1986 book, *The Other Guy Blinked*, Pepsi president Roger Enrico describes his state of mind leading up to the decision to use Jackson. Enrico was the youngest president in the history of the company. He'd been on the job less than a year, succeeding the immensely popular John Sculley (currently president of Apple Computer, another BBDO client). And now he was being asked to bet $5.5 million on the future popularity of a rock star who hadn't even released an album in two years.

Enrico said yes.

Pottasch and Dusenberry both give Enrico a great deal of credit for the ultimate success of *New Generation*.

"It was an awful lot of money at the time," Dusenberry concedes. "Since then, many celebrities have been offered more. There's a rumor that Bruce Springsteen was offered $20 million by one of the car companies. I don't know if it's true, but the fact that people in the business would give credence to the rumor indicates what the market value of a true superstar is today. In retrospect, getting Michael Jackson for $5.5 million looks like a bargain."

The Jackson spot was shot by Bob Giraldi, who also directed the MTV video for *Thriller*, in itself a budget-busting enterprise. There was an unfortunate incident during the filming; a fireworks device landed in Jackson's hair and set it on fire. Naturally, this led to great consternation and gnashing of teeth in Pepsi's Purchase, New York, headquarters. But Jackson never considered suing anyone for the mishap. The filming was finished and the spot cut. That was when the real problems started.

"In an early meeting with Michael he said he didn't want his face on camera for more than two seconds," Pottasch says. "I thought he was talking figuratively. He meant it literally. So when the final cut showed up with five or six seconds of close-ups, he wasn't happy. He told us we could show as many close-ups of his gloves, his feet, his clothes

or whatever else we wanted."

The spot was recut numerous times with a deadline dangling over everyone involved—Pepsi had committed itself to debuting the spot on the 1985 Grammy Awards telecast, where Jackson was heavily favored to win multiple awards. Every afternoon, tapes were sent across the country from New York to Los Angeles and hand-delivered to Jackson. Every night, Jackson called Alan Pottasch to convey his comments.

"Michael would call about nine p.m. Pacific time, about midnight on the East Coast," Pottasch chuckles. "One night I wasn't in, so he called Roger Enrico at home. Roger had been asleep. He reassured Michael that I would talk to him about that day's cut the first thing the next morning. Roger went back to sleep. About a

half hour later, Michael had another thought, so he called Roger back. He started the conversation by saying, 'Mr. Enrico, I don't know if you remember me. I'm Michael Jackson, the fellow you were just talking with.' Roger got a big kick out of that. But Michael was being genuine. He's very self-effacing. He really didn't expect Roger to remember who he was!"

Pepsi and BBDO worked diligently on the spot and a version acceptable to Jackson was created in time for the Grammy broadcast.

"Despite our misunderstanding about the close-ups, I learned something from Michael," Pottasch admits. "He was absolutely right about limiting close-ups of his face. It worked very well because a certain

Stylistically, *The Kid* is almost a frontal attack on Coca-Cola's franchise on small-town America. A young boy approaches a Coke machine and a Pepsi machine. In the background, the soundtrack is that of an announcer calling a baseball game. The announcer describes the pitcher making his choice, winding up, making the delivery. The boy meanwhile is choosing a Pepsi and putting coins in the machine. The combined effect of the cheering baseball crowd and the freckle-faced boy is irresistible.

Having monopolized the stratospheric zone in the celebrity sweepstakes, Pepsi is no longer satisfied with having one superstar per spot. In late 1987, BBDO unveiled this fantasy execution with David Bowie *and* Tina Turner. Bowie plays a nerdy professor. Entering bits and pieces of personalities and looks into his computer, Bowie accidentally spills a Pepsi into the keyboard and winds up with the perfect woman: Turner. They perform an electric *pas de deux* which ends in a shower of sparks.

mystery builds through the spot. In this case, less was more."

The phenomenal success of Jackson's album gilded the executional lily. Without the extraordinary public relations generated by the fireworks incident and Jackson's sweep of the Grammys, a lot of folks might have second-guessed Enrico's decision to swallow hard and reach for his wallet. Instead, everyone started looking for celebrities to sign.

Over the next eighteen months, Pepsi followed the Jackson spot with executions featuring Lionel Ritchie and one starring *Miami Vice* heartthrob Don Johnson and Eagles rock legend Glenn Frey. The choices haven't been random: "We seek young actors, vital people of any age who are young at heart, who think young and act young," Pottasch says.

Staking out the psychological dimension of youth as its turf gives Pepsi the latitude to move in many different directions without going outside of the arena viewers have come to expect. Spots such as the *Top Gun* execution, which features jet fighter pilots enjoying Pepsi inflight and which was timed to coincide with the release of the movie *Top Gun*. Or *Floaters*, a future-fantasy depicting a space crew chasing a wayward bottle of Pepsi in outer space. Both won numerous honors. But perhaps the most highly-honored recent additions to *New Generation* have been the two spots—one for Pepsi and one for Diet Pepsi—starring comedian Michael J. Fox. The spots work so well because they're brilliantly scripted, Michael J. Fox is one of the funniest men working in Hollywood today, and because Fox appeals to a very broad audience. His All-American good looks (or All-North American, he's actually Canadian) and "aw shucks" personality appeal to young and old alike.

In the fall of 1987, Pepsi released a spot with two more

mega-stars: David Bowie and Tina Turner. A second Michael Jackson spot was in the can and BBDO would say only that it might be released by the end of the year. Whatever pain might have been felt when Enrico signed that first check for $5.5 million, Jackson's second deal is rumored to have cost the company more than $10 million. Could he possibly be worth $10 million to Pepsi?

Probably. Jackson isn't an American superstar. He's a global superstar. According to the Japanese trade journal *Food News Review*, Coca-Cola has 93% of the Japanese soft drink market while Pepsi has just 6%.

When Jackson visited Japan in September 1987, Pepsi sponsored his tour. The 370,000 tickets to his various performances there sold out in a matter of hours. In July and August, Pepsi ran a promotion offering free tickets and 35,000 Michael Jackson jackets, key rings and T-shirts. For those two months, Pepsi sales

doubled over the same period in the preceding year. Ecstatic Pepsico Japan Co. executives predicted a 20% growth in sales volume for 1987. If realized, that growth would still leave Pepsi with just 7.5% of the Japanese market; a gain of one and a half share points. And share points in Japan aren't worth anywhere near the $450 million they're worth in the U.S. Still, the promotion "put Pepsi on the map in Japan," company executives say. And the promotion dramatically demonstrated the power that celebrities like Jackson can exercise when intelligently utilized by advertisers.

For Pepsi, it's a game they have learned to play well and with finesse. That finesse has not gone unnoticed at another soft drink company whose headquarters are in Atlanta. Since the advent of the Jackson era, a number of celebrities have been signed to push Coke, though the Coke officials express an almost

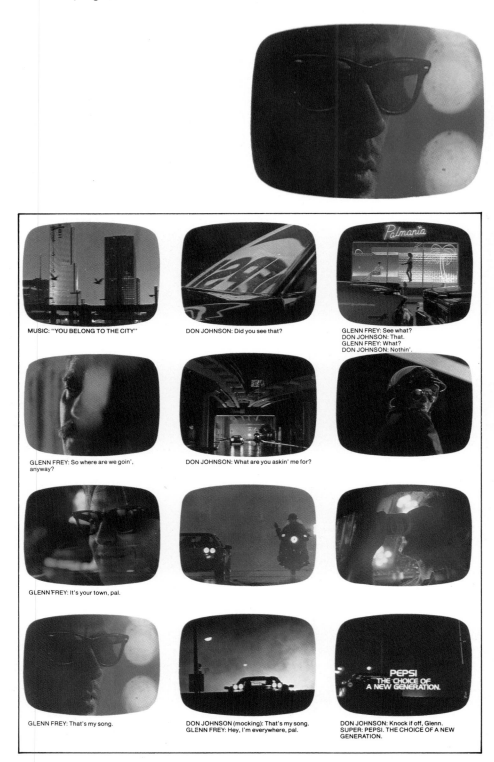

MUSIC: "YOU BELONG TO THE CITY"

DON JOHNSON: Did you see that?

GLENN FREY: See what?
DON JOHNSON: That.
GLENN FREY: What?
DON JOHNSON: Nothin'.

GLENN FREY: So where are we goin', anyway?

DON JOHNSON: What are you askin' me for?

GLENN FREY: It's your town, pal.

GLENN FREY: That's my song.

DON JOHNSON (mocking): That's my song.
GLENN FREY: Hey, I'm everywhere, pal.

DON JOHNSON: Knock if off, Glenn.
SUPER: PEPSI. THE CHOICE OF A NEW GENERATION.

This 1986 effort was another dual-rocker superstar spot. It featured *Miami Vice* heartthrob Don Johnson and Eagles singer Glenn Frey. If celebrities are your vehicle, what could be better than the man with the number one television show and a man with a string of number one radio hits stretching back to the late 1970s? The spot was a hard one to shoot, Pottasch says, because the crew had to work around Johnson's hectic *Miami Vice* schedule.

A medal at Cannes resulted from BBDO's collaboration with Canadian comedian Michael J. Fox (opposite). Pottasch couldn't say enough good things about Fox, who shot take after take running through a rainstorm in the cold post-midnight atmosphere of Los Angeles.

religious aversion to paying Pepsi prices for talent. And they've had some successes, signing the immensely talented Whitney Houston to sing for Diet Coke when she was virtually unknown, for example.

Punch. Counterpunch. Flinch, duck, retaliate. The marketing juggernauts that are Coca-Cola and Pepsi could likely flatten any other first-rank consumer products company in the world if one of them chose to turn its firepower to some other field. But the opponents are so evenly matched that they seem to be able to do no more than dent the other's armor.

And who's getting hurt by this incessant warfare? Nobody. While share points are grudgingly traded back and forth, the total market for soft drinks is increasing. Both consistently realize gains in unit and dollar volume. As consumers born after World War II make up an increasing portion of the population, the per capita consumption of soft drinks continues to climb. Latest word has it that the colas are going after the breakfast market, mounting a challenge to coffee and tea as the early-morning beverages of choice. Makes sense to me. I don't drink coffee. For years I started each day by turning on a typewriter, tearing into a pack of peanuts and popping open a Pepsi .

Meanwhile, Roger Enrico relishes his role as field marshal in the cola wars. He thinks that more publicity about the Coke-Pepsi feud equals more liters of soft drinks sold. He's probably right. Alan Pottasch looks forward to the day he can retire to Grand Cayman to teach scuba diving (he's tried several times). At BBDO, Phil Dusenberry is passing the torch to a new generation of Pepsi creatives such as Ted Sann, who wrote and produced the Turner/Bowie spot. Their work promises us years of contentious, highly effective and supremely entertaining advertising to come.

SFX: FOOTSTEPS CROSSING LIBRARY FLOOR.

SFX: M.J. FOX DROPS BOOK ON TABLE.
M.J. FOX: Hmmm.

SFX: BOOK DROPS LOUDLY ON COPIER MACHINE.

M.J. FOX: Somebody have any . . .

STUDENT: Ssssh!
M.J. FOX: . . . change?

SFX: SNAPS FINGERS. CLAPS HANDS. COPIER MACHINE MAKES PHOTOCOPY OF PEPSI CAN.

SFX: PICKS UP PHOTOCOPY.

SFX: CAN OPENING SOUND.

SFX: FIZZING NOISE.

SFX: SQUEAK OF MOISTURE ON CAN. SOUND OF PHOTOCOPY BEING ROLLED INTO A CAN.
M.J. FOX: Whistles.

SFX: DRINKING SOUNDS.
M.J. FOX: Ahhh.

STUDENT: Ssssh!
SFX: CAN CRUSHING. CAN BANGING IN METAL GARBAGE CAN. M.J. FOX: Ssssh!
VO AND SUPER: PEPSI. THE CHOICE OF A NEW GENERATION.

BBDO Helps Make Spectra An "Instant" Success

POLAROID

Client: Polaroid Corporation
Agency: BBDO New York

Does this sound familiar? You're selling the same thing everyone else is selling, the market is saturated with product, price points are critical and the industry is in danger of discounting itself into bankruptcy. What you wouldn't give for a crack at selling something totally unique, something as different as Xerox copiers when they first appeared.

That may be a wish you don't want to have fulfilled. Ask the Polaroid Corporation. Instant photography has been the proprietary property of Polaroid since Dr. Edwin Land first released it in the mid-1950s. For a spell, Kodak also made instant products until a federal court forced it to quit. From a distance, Polaroid seems like a dream assignment. The product definitely has a unique selling proposition. The price points are high but not outrageous. So why were sales in a tailspin from 1981 to 1986?

The truth is that while unique products are common enough, products that truly have no competition are very, very rare. Even the Xerox copiers, when they were first released, had to compete with carbon paper. For Polaroid, the ogre is inexpensive 35mm point-and-shoot cameras. Polaroid found itself, as marketers of unique products sometimes do, odd man out in a high-stakes game with fierce and well-funded competitors. Although Polaroid has the only entry in the instant photography category, it has to battle Nikon, Canon, Olympus and Minolta—not to mention Kodak—for a piece of the overall consumer photo market.

That was the wall facing BBDO New York when it picked up Polaroid in 1986. After a little research, the agency team found that was only the tip of the iceberg. Polaroid was perceived as delivering inferior quality pictures compared to 35mm cameras; having inconvenient, bulky cameras requiring expensive film; making cheap cameras; and having low social approval—it just wasn't "serious."

There was some even worse news. The likelihood that someone would own or consider buying a Polaroid camera was directly correlated to age. Polaroid's greatest penetration was among people 45 or older and plunged rapidly with decreasing age. Not only was the company in trouble, it didn't have a base of future customers. The mission was not just to sell some products. It was to save a company.

WHICH 35MM CAMERA TOOK THIS PHOTOGRAPH?

Introducing the Polaroid Spectra System. A revolutionary photographic system—camera, film, accessories and laser-copy prints and enlargements—that captures reality in a way we've never done before.

THE CAMERA. THE VERY PICTURE OF HIGH TECHNOLOGY.

Continuing a long tradition of Polaroid innovation, the Spectra camera has an interior filled with some truly remarkable electronic and optical breakthroughs.

In all, over 40 advances.

Including advances that help make over 30 complex focusing and exposure decisions, all within 50 thousandths of a second.

Which means you'll get beautiful photographs. Instantly and automatically.

And the camera's sleek, computer-designed exterior fits in your grasp so comfortably that taking pictures with it becomes second nature.

©1986 Polaroid Corp. "Polaroid"® Spectra™

NONE.
IT WAS TAKEN WITH THE NEW POLAROID SPECTRA SYSTEM.

Polaroid did, however, have what it considered to be a "secret weapon." The Spectra was a new camera and film system that Polaroid hoped would help change the way people felt about instant photos. What it needed was someone to sell it. That's where BBDO came in.

"Polaroid wasn't adding new customers," says Lonny Strum, management supervisor for the Polaroid business. "The perception among younger people was that Polaroid just wasn't relevant to them. Historically, 35mm cameras had been bulky and expensive. The technology was intimidating. But the advent of the 35mm point-and-shoot models changed that. These are really high-tech Brownies. They're easy to use, they make very good

photographs and the price is right, less than $100. Whatever the brand, the product is ideally configured. It's what consumers at almost every demographic level want. They get the feeling they're using professional type equipment, but they don't have to know anything or spend a fortune for it."

Spectra solved some, but not all of the perceived problems with Polaroid products. It was just as bulky as previous cameras, but it was more highly stylized. The film costs were about the same. But the picture quality was demonstrably superior to any previous Polaroid. That helped with the price/value relationship. "Our strategy was to position Spectra as a sophisticated photography system using state-of-the-art technology. We used

35mm photos as our point of reference. We didn't say Spectra made better photos than any 35mm camera. It can't. But compared to a 35mm point-and-shoot model, it makes comparable photos. And you get to see them in a minute," Strum explains.

That's a good story. Especially since it's true. But who was going to listen? Polaroid was an older-folks product. Talk about the Golden Market all you want; the folks who buy film are people with kids who aren't old enough to borrow the car keys.

BBDO felt that the opportunity for Spectra was with people who already owned 35mm cameras—generic upscale households: 25 to 54 years of age with household incomes of $30,000 plus. Specifically, the agency was looking for people who adopt

AN AUTOFOCUS SYSTEM THAT DOES EVERYTHING EXCEPT CHOOSE YOUR SUBJECT.

As you peer through the incredibly accurate Spectra viewfinder, slightly depress the shutter release and the sonar ranging system displays an exact readout (from 2 to 20 feet) of your subject's distance from the camera.

Press the shutter release and the autofocus system snaps the 125mm lens into precise focus. It's our exclusive Quintic lens.

Its surface is molded to within a tolerance of 20 millionths of an inch, so you get sharp images with virtually no optical distortion.

Since this new lens also allows your subject to fill more of the picture area, it's ideal for landscapes as well as portrait and group shots.

So you can not only take those group shots but be in them as well, we've built in a self-timer. It actually has an audio signal telling you how much time you have before the picture is taken.

The Spectra control panel allows you to override the flash or the autofocus, engage the self-timer and even vary the exposure.

| The sonar transducer emits sound waves to precisely measure distance. | The Quintic lens produces sharp, brilliant images. | This flash can recycle faster than you can read this sentence. |

A FLASH THAT'S ALWAYS READY IN A FLASH.

Life doesn't stand still waiting for a flash to be ready. And neither should you.

That's why Spectra's flash can usually recycle in less than one second.

Outdoors or indoors, the unique Spectra fill-flash automatically blends just the right amount of daylight and flash, which helps eliminate the shadows that have marred your pictures in the past.

SPECTRA MEASURES LIGHT YOU CAN'T EVEN SEE.

All of this automation would be useless without a highly accurate autoexposure system. That's why our dual silicon photo diodes measure two kinds of light—visible and infra-red. Which results in more evenly exposed pictures and truer skin tones.

YOUR EARS CAN EVEN HELP YOU TAKE BETTER PICTURES.

So no detail escapes your attention while you're concentrating on the big picture, Spectra has a special audio-signal system. This system chimes in when you're too close to your subject or the lighting is too low and you need flash.

It even chimes when you're out of film, so chances are you'll never miss a shot.

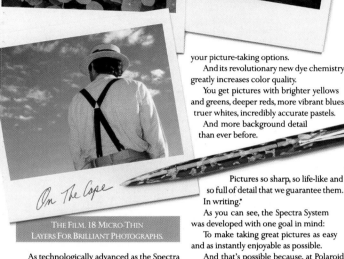

Produced from actual, unretouched Spectra photographs.

On The Cape

THE FILM. 18 MICRO-THIN LAYERS FOR BRILLIANT PHOTOGRAPHS.

As technologically advanced as the Spectra camera is, it's still only as good as the film you put in it.

Enter the amazing new Spectra instant film. Its larger rectangular format greatly increases your picture-taking options.

And its revolutionary new dye chemistry greatly increases color quality.

You get pictures with brighter yellows and greens, deeper reds, more vibrant blues, truer whites, incredibly accurate pastels.

And more background detail than ever before.

Pictures so sharp, so life-like and so full of detail that we guarantee them. In writing.*

As you can see, the Spectra System was developed with one goal in mind:

To make taking great pictures as easy and as instantly enjoyable as possible.

And that's possible because, at Polaroid, we take your pictures seriously.

PolaroidSpectraSystem
WE TAKE YOUR PICTURES SERIOUSLY.

*See dealer for film replacement details or call 800-225-1384 from 8am to 5pm Eastern Standard Time.

---

technology early on, the ones willing to spend a little extra to have a new gadget before it becomes widely available and the cost drops due to production efficiencies.

Polaroid ponied up $35 million for a war chest. That would be enough to give it a 27% share of voice in the category and position it number two behind Kodak. Despite the healthy budget, BBDO was still concerned that the general public wasn't ready to listen to the Polaroid story. They needed to be softened up first, so the agency prepared a massive teaser campaign.

BBDO contracted a computer animation production house, Dreamquest, to produce a teaser video spot called *Worlds*. While a cultured-sounding announcer intones, "The worlds of science and art will become one," the viewer is treated to a burst of surrealistic images: The Mona Lisa wrapped around a globe, floating pyramids and the like. No product news, no hint as to what is going to follow. Just a stream-of-consciousness visual treat and the message that something was about to be announced.

Worlds ran heavily in the spring of 1986, preceding D-Day by six weeks. When they felt they had everyone's attention, the agency followed with the introductory spot, *Journey*. To tell the technology story, BBDO threw in a fair amount of techno-talk. The spot is entirely point-of-view camera. The viewer enters the lens of the Spectra, and after bouncing off of various high-tech components, winds up at the

This six-page insert was also run as a three-page unit in a wide variety of upscale consumer magazines. Although two-thirds of the media budget was spent in television, BBDO boosted Polaroid's expenditures in magazines from $3.5 million in 1985 to more than $5.7 million in 1986. Newspaper insertions went up from $500,000 in 1985 to more than $1.7 million in 1986.

Polaroid followed the Spectra with the release of the Onyx (overleaf), a more expensive version of the same camera. Its smoked-plastic casing allows consumers to look right into the camera's inner workings.

Subsequent ads for Spectra emphasized the system accessories, comparing Spectra to a 35mm camera.

PHOTOGRAPHIC WORKS OF ART BY A WORK OF PHOTOGRAPHIC ART.

Introducing the world's first transparent camera. The Polaroid Spectra System Onyx.

As you can see, engineering can be considered an art form in more than one sense of the word.

But it is a beauty that is more than skin-deep. The camera's sophisticated sonar ranging system, full-information viewfinder, dual silicon light metering system and automatic fill-flash virtually assure you a beautiful shot every time.

Yet all of these advanced electronics would be wasted if it weren't for the Spectra Instant Film. 18 micro-thin layers of advanced chemistry which produce the finest instant pictures you've ever seen.

Pictures with brighter, truer and more accurate colors and more background detail than ever before. Pictures so sharp and lifelike we guarantee them. In writing.*

The Polaroid Spectra System Onyx. It's as beautiful as the pictures it takes.

POLAROID SPECTRA SYSTEM ONYX
— WE TAKE YOUR PICTURES SERIOUSLY. —

Introducing a total photographic system designed for those who appreciate the difference between a photograph and a snapshot.

The Polaroid Spectra System.

Its camera, film, accessories and laser reprints, together offer a new dimension in serious photography.

Like a 35mm, the new Spectra camera has a very precise autofocus system. It's linked to our exclusive Quintic lens. Its unique surface is molded to a tolerance of 20 millionths of an inch for sharp images with virtually no optical distortion.

The Spectra camera also has a full-information viewfinder. It gives you a digital readout of your subject's distance from the camera and tells you when conditions are right for taking a picture.

The camera's sophisticated light-metering system (dual silicon photodiodes) measures light you can't even see. But you definitely see the results.

INTERCHANGEABLE FILTER SET.

Truer skin tones and more evenly exposed pictures.

The quick recharge flash, at times as quick as 1/10th of a second, automatically blends just the right amount of daylight and flash.

This is designed to help eliminate the shadows that may have marred your pictures in the past.

The Spectra camera also has a built-in film advance. Just like many 35mm's.

Which leads us right to something the Spectra System has that no 35mm camera has.

The new Spectra Instant Film. 18 micro-thin layers of advanced chemistry which produce the finest, most brilliant instant pictures you've ever seen.

Larger, rectangular pictures with brighter, truer, more accurate colors and more background detail than ever before.

Pictures so sharp and so incredibly life-like that we guarantee them. In writing.*

INTRODUCING A POLAROID CAMERA THAT THINKS IT'S A 35MM.

Polaroid Spectra System

*See dealer for film replacement details or call 800-225-1384 from 8am to 5pm Eastern Standard Time.

PRODUCED FROM ACTUAL UNRETOUCHED SPECTRA PHOTOGRAPH.
LASER REPRINTS AVAILABLE UP TO 8"x10."

just taking great pictures. How much more? Up to 8"x10" more. Using the latest in laser and computer technology we have developed a new copy system that produces high-quality border-

RUGGED NYLON CAMERA BAG.

less reprints of your Spectra photographs.

In all, you'll find the Polaroid Spectra System is quite extraordinary.

And so are the photographs you'll take with it.

Like a 35mm system, you'll find a whole series of optional Spectra System accessories to help you get the most out of your picture-taking. Everything from interchangeable filters and a wireless remote control to a collapsible tripod and a custom designed camera bag to hold it all.

But there's more to the Spectra System than

THE WIRELESS REMOTE WORKS UP TO 40 FT. AWAY.

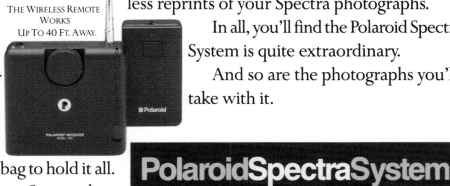

PolaroidSpectraSystem

WE TAKE YOUR PICTURES SERIOUSLY.

Journey and *Red Dress* were the introductory television executions. *Journey* was designed to convey the impression that the Spectra technology was all-new, a breakthrough. Viewers are led on a trip from the lens, through the interior of the camera to the picture plane, where an announcer explains what all the new gadgets do: Produce better instant pictures. *Red Dress* focused on the vivid color and high quality of Spectra photographs, using a woman in a red dress, a rose, a marble table and fine china as examples.

picture plane and encounters the announcer. It's a lot to take in, even in the full 60-second format.

"The technical details weren't really the focus of *Journey*," Strum explains. "Its purpose was to establish that there was significant new technology in the Spectra, that it was not a one-step camera. We weren't looking for playback on the individual elements— sonar focus and so on. We were going for a Gestalt, a net impression that the technology was a breakthrough."

Journey ran for several months into the summer on selected network programs.

"We cherrypicked programs for this campaign because we wanted to skew to upper income," Strum notes. "We used *Cheers*, *L.A. Law* and some late-night as well."

The video spots were accompanied by a heavy print schedule—more than $7 million worth. The ads took a variety of configurations: gatefolds, spreads, and three- and six-page preprinted inserts.

While it supported the television spots, the print was also cleaning up another big, ugly spot on Polaroid's horizon. The company's earlier products—the SX-70, the Sun Camera, Pronto—were self-contained. There were no accessories. And they were heavily discounted through mass-merchandise outlets such as K-mart. As a result, very few photo retailers carried the lines. Along with the Spectra, Polaroid offered a raft of accessories. A series of print ads was prepared to talk up the details of each element of the system. By making plate changes, a series of inserts directed to the trade was created and placed in photo industry publications. The trade schedule was designed to convince retailers that this camera was worth carrying, that it would offer them profit margins comparable to the point-and-shoot 35mm lines and that Spectra had accessories as well.

To support the introduction, the agency launched a mall

demonstration program to give consumers hands-on experience with the Spectra and an opinion leaders program, placing Spectras in the hands of "influentials."

Journey and its accompanying print ads were followed by two more executions, *Stolen Moments* and *Red Dress*. The new spots extended the Spectra message, focusing on the high quality of Spectra photos.

Usually, print follows the creative lead of the television effort. But in this case, the print ads were developed first and the video spots modeled on them.

As they were breaking, Polaroid introduced another new product, the Onyx. A higher-priced ($280) version of the Spectra, the Onyx was the same camera except the top of the body was made of clear, as opposed to opaque, plastic. This revealed the inner workings and was a bit more elegant than the plain-Jane black case of the Spectra.

Although not featured in the television spots, the Onyx was heavily promoted through spread ads in upscale consumer magazines including *Town & Country*, *Smithsonian* and *European Travel & Leisure*.

Obviously, you can do a lot of good advertising with $35 million. But in the end, it has to make money for the client. Awareness of Polaroid's advertising, which had been lingering in the sub-basement for years, jumped 69% within nine months. Positive perception of Polaroid was up 13%. More significantly, factory shipments outpaced first-year projections by 19%, with Spectra accounting for about 600,000 of the 4.3 million Polaroid cameras sold that year. Polaroid's sales, 60% of which come from the consumer photo business, leaped 25% to $1.63 billion while earnings more than doubled, rising 180% to $103.5 million. Operating profits shot up over

The teaser spot, *Worlds*, treated viewers to a surrealistic spin through the icons of art and science. The Mona Lisa was shown wrapped around a spinning globe. Although the commercial was shelved after just a few weeks of air time, pieces of it have been recycled for use in corporate billboards further amortizing the expensive, computer-animated footage.

Introducing a revolutionary photographic system that captures reality in a way we've never done before.

The new Polaroid Spectra System.

THE CAMERA. THE VERY PICTURE OF HIGH TECHNOLOGY.

Continuing a long tradition of Polaroid innovation, the Spectra camera's interior is filled with optical and electronic breakthroughs.

INTRODUCING THE FIRST CAMERA OF THE FUTURE FROM POLAROID.

Polaroid Spectra System

In all, over 40 advances.

Including advances that help make over 30 complex focusing and exposure decisions within 50-thousandths of a second. So you get beautiful pictures.

Instantly and automatically.

Press the shutter release, and the Spectra autofocus system snaps the exclusive 125mm Quintic lens into precise focus. Its longer focal length makes it ideal for landscapes as well as portrait and group shots.

And the camera's special audio-signaling self-timer lets you not only take those group shots, but be in them as well.

And since life doesn't stand still waiting for a flash to be ready, the Spectra flash can usually recycle in less than one second.

The camera's auto-exposure system, dual silicon photo-diodes, measures light you can't even see.

But you definitely see the results. More evenly exposed pictures and truer skin tones.

Your ears can also help you take better pictures. Because the Spectra audio-signal system chimes in when you're too close to your subject, if the lighting is too low or if you're out of film.

THE FILM. 18 MICRO-THIN LAYERS FOR BRILLIANT PHOTOGRAPHS.

The Spectra film's new larger rectangular format greatly increases your picture-taking options.

And its revolutionary new dye chemistry greatly increases color quality.

You get pictures with brighter yellows and greens, deeper reds, more vibrant blues, truer

Produced from actual unretouched Spectra photographs.

35MM IMAGES. NO WAITING.

The beautiful photographs you're looking at are certainly the kinds of images you'd expect to take with a 35mm camera.

Amazingly enough, they weren't.

Because each and every one of them was being viewed just moments after it was taken.

All of these stunning images were taken with the Polaroid Spectra System. An instant photographic system designed for those who appreciate the difference between a snapshot and a photograph.

The Spectra camera's precise autofocus system, full-information viewfinder, sophisticated light metering system and quick recharge fill-flash virtually assure a great shot every time.

Yet all of these advanced electronics would be wasted if it weren't for the Spectra Instant Film. 18 micro-thin layers of advanced chemistry which produce the finest instant pictures you've ever seen.

Pictures with brighter, truer and more accurate colors and more background detail than ever before. Pictures so sharp and so lifelike we guarantee them.

In writing.*

And no 35mm camera does that.

PolaroidSpectraSystem

WE TAKE YOUR PICTURES SERIOUSLY.

*See dealer for film replacement details or call 1-800-343-5000 from 8am to 8pm Eastern Standard Time.

© 1987 Polaroid Corp. "Polaroid"® Spectra™

fifteens for the same money as a smaller number of thirties. That extends our message and should give us very strong impact."

The fifteens seem to stand up to wear and tear a bit better as well. If you watched American TV between September and December of 1987, you should have seen the spots about twenty times. They come and go so quickly that you don't seem to tire of the message on repeated exposure. Part of the credit for that undoubtedly goes to the creative team. While the spots are cute, they aren't sappy.

"We tried for emotions that are a bit edgier than a child's birthday party," Strum says. "A child's birthday party is important, but we wanted to make Polaroid more contemporary, so the emotions we chose to portray are a little less ordinary."

Not only are they less ordinary, the situations are all targeted to a very young audience. The reason, you see, is that this is still not the end of the story. The milestone introductory campaign for Spectra and the tight, ground-breaking pool of fifteens that followed it are prologue to what Polaroid hopes will be a second coming of instant photography.

Spectra and Onyx will remain the core of the product line, but in 1988, Polaroid plans to introduce a camera priced for young consumers, the 18-year-old crowd. Back in the salad days of the late 1960s, Polaroid had a popular product called the Swinger. It used square-format pack film, sold for about $20 and came in the same basic color range as vinyl go-go boots (white, black, hot pink). It got so you couldn't get into the back seat of a Mustang or Nova without finding a Swinger on the floor. It's faintly possible that Mustangs and Mavericks came with Swingers as standard equipment there for a while.

That's what Polaroid is shooting for—a low-priced camera that could be the Swinger of the 1990s. With BBDO aiming the big guns, they might make it.

Polaroid hopes to amortize its huge investment in Spectra advertising against a wider product line. During 1988, the company plans to make Spectra film compatible with some of its earlier camera models. While the technology of the cameras themselves is not as sophisticated as the Spectra and Onyx, the new film should substantially improve customers' photos and their satisfaction with Polaroid products.

Chiat/Day Puts Porsche On The Fast Track

Client: Porsche North America
Agency: Chiat/Day

Consider the plight of the poor folks at Chiat/Day who have to create the advertising for Porsche. "What?" you exclaim. "I'd agree to write copy for Tucks pads for ten years for a shot at the Porsche business." Maybe you would. And maybe you'd enjoy it. You might even get a chance to buy a Porsche at dealer cost. But before you send in your reels, portfolios and resumes, think about this: Porsche just may be the most intellectually challenging automotive account in America.

Here's why. People buy Porsches because they're exclusive and flashy. But the folks who buy them don't want to be *thought of* as insubstantial or "Hollywood." The kind of people who have the money to afford one are solid citizens, most of them bankers and real estate agents and businessmen. They want class and exclusivity. One of the primary jobs of the advertising is to support the image of status and class that the present owners have spent anywhere from $25,000 to $80,000 to acquire. Ironically, the more you advertise the car, the less exclusive it seems to both present owners and prospective buyers.

Is it possible to advertise and sell cars without appearing to be advertising? No factory rebates. No smiling yups out for a Sunday romp. No deals from Art Grindel's Wheel Ranch.

Clive Whicher thinks so. And it's a good thing, too, because Whicher is the man on the spot at Chiat/Day, the account manager responsible for the Porsche business.

In the distinctively cultured English intonation Americans associate with breeding and quality, but without any of the duck-and-weave we've come to expect, Whicher described the situation Chiat/Day inherited in 1984, the year Porsche and Audi ended their joint U.S. marketing agreement. Audi stayed with Doyle Dane Bernbach in New York while Porsche went to the Coast.

"Porsche had lost control of the image of its cars," he explains. "An image had been formed by the media. There were newspaper stories of drug dealers arrested in their Porsches, movie stars crashing their Porsches. The image was flamboyant and transient. When you walk down the beach in Venice you see the sidewalk vendors selling posters of nude women draped over the front of a Porsche. There wasn't much to counteract that image; unless you were a Porsche enthusiast, that would be your image of the car.

"Because of the glamorous image, people tended to think of the car as being very exotic and therefore fragile, like a Ferrari. People with money were saying, 'I'm not sure I want that kind of image. And if I did, should I spend $60,000 for a car that's going to break down?'"

PORSCHE

Faster than schnell.

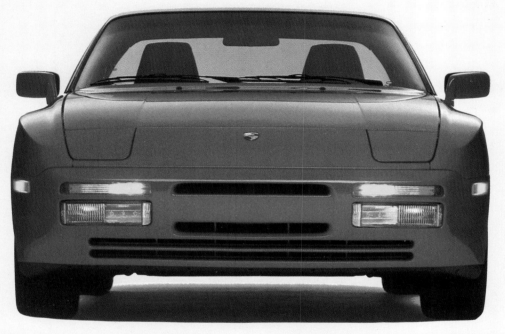

The German word for "fast" is "schnell." And the German word for "schnell" has always been "Porsche."

Most recently, the Porsche 944.

Well, this year, we've given new meaning to the word "schnell."

With the Porsche 944 Turbo.

If the performance of its normally aspirated cousin can be described as extraordinary, the performance of this machine almost defies description.

Horsepower is up 50%. Top speed is 152. Zero to 60 time is 6.1 seconds. Handling is still what Car and Driver magazine once described as "scalpel sharp."

And if you hurry, you can see the 944 Turbo at your authorized Porsche dealer, doing just what we've been talking about.

Going fast.

The Porsche experience begins with your authorized Porsche dealer.

It goes like a bat out of Zuffenhausen.

Over the years, our factory in Zuffenhausen has turned out some pretty remarkable engines.

But early in the development of the Porsche 944 Turbo, our engineers set themselves a rather ambitious goal. A 50% increase in horsepower from a 4-cylinder engine that was already one of the biggest, most powerful fours in production anywhere.

The result? A 50% increase in horsepower, of course. From 143 to 217.

Acceleration: 0 to 60 in 6.1 seconds. Top speed: 152 mph. Handling: still what Car and Driver once described as "scalpel sharp."

If you hurry, you can see the 944 Turbo at your authorized Porsche dealer, doing just what we've been talking about. Going fast.

PORSCHE®

The Porsche experience begins with your authorized Porsche dealer.
(Dealer Name)

Okay, that's simple enough to solve. Just copy Volvo's ads. Show some Porsches bouncing off a brick wall at high speed. Emphasize durability by showcasing the car's performance at endurance races. Great rational appeal. The only problem is that, as Whicher puts it, "Buying a Porsche is hardly a rational decision."

What do you do when you're stumped? Of course, you do research. Chiat/Day took Porsche's problems on the road, meeting with both owners and non-owners in focus groups across the country. They found two things. The first was that people were *very* particular about the way Porsche should be advertised.

"We showed them some concepts," Whicher recalls. "For example, we showed them a parking lot, and off to one side, parked by itself, was a Porsche. Owners said, 'Yes, that's what I always do, but I don't think I'd like to see that in an ad.' We showed them a Porsche going very fast, being glamorous. This time they said, 'Oh yes, that's why I like Porsche. But I don't think Porsche would do that; it's beneath their dignity.'"

In fact, the company found that the very act of advertising is thought to be a bad thing by its target audience. Advertising the car said two things to Porsche enthusiasts: First, that too many people will buy it, making it less exclusive. Second, that maybe the car isn't so desirable after all. Maybe people don't want it because it has to be advertised in order to sell.

Gnashing your teeth yet? The second result of the focus groups pointed to a possible solution.

"We found that performance was, of course, a critical part of their perception of Porsche. There's no good buying a Porsche if you don't want to drive fast. But you can buy lots of cars that go fast. You can buy ones that cost more, or you can buy cars that are much cheaper.

"We also found that these people viewed themselves as being very successful. Buying a Porsche was really a statement about how they

Copywriters cleverly played on two German words to create arresting full-page ads (previous pages) for the 944S. Zuffenhausen is the city where Porsches are built. The ads helped establish the 944S as a true performance sports car, emphasizing its speed.

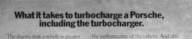

After 15 years of building the most successful sports car in history, Professor Porsche declared "We have reached the end."

But that was only the beginning.

In the Spring of 1948, the first Porsche 356 emerged, without fanfare, from a converted sawmill in Gmünd, Austria.

And changed forever the world's perceptions and expectations of a sports car.

Fifteen years of refinement and improvement followed. And during that time—on race tracks and rally circuits, highways and winding back roads—the 356's lightweight,

Professor Ferry Porsche and an early 911.

aerodynamic body, air-cooled rear engine and fully independent suspension offered a driving experience unmatched by any other sports car of its day.

So when, in 1963, Professor Ferry Porsche announced that the 356 had reached its design and engineering limits, the potential for alienating a legion of Porsche fanatics was high.

But it never materialized. Because the car that suc-

ceeded the 356, the 911, was—in the eyes of objective observer and fanatic alike—a significant improvement. While retaining the basic philosophical underpinnings that had made the first Porsche such a classic.

Once again, Professor Porsche and his staff had risen to the challenge of taking a proven idea and proving it could be better.

There was never any question, of course, that the 911's shape should evolve from the best features of the earlier design. Or that its engine should continue to be

air-cooled and mounted over the rear drive wheels for superior traction, handling and reliability.

Nor was there any question that the 911 should remain, at its heart, a product of our racing heritage—with performance as its reason for being.

Today—24 years, 7 engine displacements, innumerable engineering improvements and countless racing victories later—the 911 is better than it's ever been.

And there's no end in sight.

PORSCHE

911 Cabriolet 6-cylinder, horizontally opposed, two overhead camshafts, air-cooled rear engine, 3164cc's, 214 hp. Weight: 2756 lbs. Top speed: 149 mph.

felt about themselves. It tells the world about them. People look at them and say, 'Gee, that person is really successful.'

"In talking to Porsche, we could see that they had an attitude toward building and designing cars which was very much in keeping with the kind of attitudes that successful entrepreneurs and professionals had about their own businesses. We summed that up in our strategy by saying Porsche is fascinated by and dedicated to keeping excellence. Their attitude is, 'now that we've done that, how can we make it better?' The customers of Porsche are like that too. They want to carry on and do things to the best of their ability. That was the spirit we tried to capture in the advertising."

With a strategy in place, the agency had one more hill to climb—the lingering effects of Porsche/Audi's joint program.

"When the 944 was first introduced, it wasn't considered a real Porsche," Whicher explains. "It was a definite improvement over the 924, which came into the U.S. with an Audi engine. They had added the emission control equipment afterwards, and the engine just wasn't powerful enough. So we had an underpowered Porsche with, of all things, a non-Porsche engine. It got terrible reviews.

When the 944 was introduced, it still wasn't seen as a real Porsche. We put the 944 on television, rather than just advertising the 911. That showed Porsche was serious about the car, and that consumers should be serious about it, too. The press has helped tremendously by being very positive about the 944."

With its strategic ducks in a row, Chiat/Day recommended a series of high-visibility magazine inserts that combine an emphasis on Porsche's engineering with luscious photographs of the cars. You want to reach into the page and run your hand over the cars' creamy finish.

The quality of the photos was a major factor in the decision to preprint inserts: "We can use good paper stock and control the printing; create our own environment within a magazine by preprinting," Whicher points out. "It supports the idea that Porsche is a superior, high-status product. Consumers really do notice. They say the paper looks better, that the photos are glossier than those in the run-of-book ads in the same issue. We do the same thing in our television spots. We spend a lot of money on production, making them as perfect as we can."

For a mere $30,000 or $50,000, Porsche enthusiasts expect nothing less.

In 1948, Professor Porsche decided any car that merely got you from here to there, just didn't go far enough.

1948 Type 356/001

1949 Type 356/2 Cabriolet

1949 Type 356/2 Coupe

1952 Type 356/1500S America Roadster

1954 Type 550 Spyder

1955 Type 356/1500S Speedster

1957 Type 356A/1500GS Carrera Deluxe Coupe

1958 Type 718/1500 RSK Sebring Spyder

1960 Type 356B/1600S-90 Roadster

1960 Type 356B/1600GS Carrera GTL Abarth

1964 Type 904 Carrera GTS

1965 Type 911 Coupe

1966 Type 906 Carrera 6

1967 Type 911 Targa

1968 Type 907 Longtail

1969 Type 908/02 "Flounder" Spyder

1970 Type 914

1973 Type 911 Carrera RS

1973 Type 917/30 Spyder

1974 Type 911 Carrera RSR Turbo

1976 Type 911 Turbo

1978 Type 935 "Moby Dick"

1978 Type 928

1978 Type 936 Spyder

1980 Type 924 Carrera GT

1984 Type 962

1985 Type 959 Gruppe B

1985 Type 911 Cabriolet

1985 Type 944

1985 Type 928S 4-valve

For Christmas 1920, Ferdinand Porsche Jr. received a toy car. Not the kind you push around on the floor or wind up and let go.

The kind you drive.

Fully operational, with headlights and an engine that would push it along at a brisk 30 miles per hour.

Of course, like most 11 year-olds, young Ferry had little understanding of the practical uses for the automobile. And cared even less.

Because his car provided him with countless hours of the one thing eleven year-olds value more than anything else. Fun.

Twenty-eight years later, the first 356 Porsche was introduced. With 40 horsepower and a top speed of 84 mph. Ferry Porsche was now Dr. Porsche, but the thrill of his first days behind the wheel was etched clearly in his memory.

And with his new silver convertible, he played a strong hunch. That while everyone else was building utilitarian cars for the masses, there must be at least a few people like himself who still felt eleven years old. And who would want a car that did more than simply transport you from one place to another.

The kind of car you drive... just for the fun of it.

Thirty-seven years have passed since the car in the upper left hand corner of this page was introduced.

The hunch had become a legend. One that still thrives in the car in the lower right hand corner of this page.

The latest Porsche. Model 928S. With four valves per-cylinder, 288 horsepower and a top speed of 155 mph.

As for Dr. Porsche, he's now a professor.

On his 75th birthday, he was presented with another toy car. A scale model of the Le Mans winning 936 Porsche with a five horsepower engine and just enough room for an eager 75 year-old man to squeeze into the cockpit.

And before any pictures could be snapped or toasts proposed, the little car had disappeared.

Along with Professor Porsche. **PORSCHE**

In 1948, Professor Porsche decided any car that merely got you from here to there, just didn't go far enough.

In 37 years, nothing has changed.

There's a restlessness about Weissach.

Even in winter.

The bitter cold that keeps more reasonable Germans inside, only means Helmuth Bott and Helmut Flegl will wear fur-lined gloves to the test track this morning.

The snow has been plowed against the catch-fences.

The tarmac, freshly salted, is safe enough to test a suspension system.

If everyone is careful.

Bott, head of Research & Development, and Flegl, Director of Research, will do today what men with such titles usually prefer leaving to men without such titles.

Risk a good deal more than cold hands to do what Porsche engineers have done since the beginning.

Discover.

Discover the same kinds of things that, for 37 years, have helped build cars like the 911.

A car that is not only immediately recognizable as a Porsche, but

also universally recognized as a phenomenon.

Its basic shape and 6-cylinder, air-cooled, rear-engine design have remained essentially unchanged since the 911 was introduced in 1964.

But under that apparently familiar exterior lies 20 years of new car.

Horsepower has been increased 54%. Stroke lengthened. Wheelbase lengthened. Grills added. 5-mph bumpers and front air dams incorporated.

Grills removed. Heating improved. Sound deadening increased. Suspension modified. Gearbox improved.

Catalytic converters have replaced thermal reactors. And Quartz-Grey Metallic has replaced Anthracite.

Otherwise, the Porsche 911 remains the same study in simplicity it has always been.

Reliable. Revered. And most important, the best 911 it can possibly be. This year.

911 Carrera: 6-cylinder, horizontally opposed, two overhead camshafts, air-cooled, rear engine, 100c.c.s, 214 hp. Weight: 2756 lbs. Top speed: 146 mph.

Some of the most important discoveries we've made in racing are now vice presidents.

Wolfgang Berger wasn't always head of Quality Control at Porsche's production facility in Zuffenhausen.

Once, he was just a race fan. A 12-year-old kid who would poke his nose through a chain-link fence just to get a better glimpse of a pit crew.

He found his way to Porsche the way the best always do. By following his passion: making cars go faster.

As part of our racing department, Berger was Project Manager on the

972 Carrera. Worked on the 934, 935 and 936 race cars. Assisted Helmut Flegl with the Can Am racers. And headed up Customer Racing.

He remembers when the Research & Development Center at Weissach was just a test track. No canteen. No telephones.

He would bring his lunch and eat on the track while he and the crew put a prototype through its paces.

It was on the track that Berger learned the simple principles of racing: The importance of teamwork.

That if you aren't prepared to start, you aren't prepared to win. And the purpose behind the ongoing pursuit of "zero defects."

It was on the track that he learned to make critical decisions faster than a pit crew could change a tire.

And it was on the track that we recognized in Berger what we had recognized many times before. In Helmuth Bott, Paul Hensler, Helmut

Flegl, Hans Metzger, Heinz Dorsch, and Roland Kussmaul, to name a few.

Not the ability to set speed records, but the ability to set priorities.

A willingness to get involved.

And an unwillingness to compromise.

Qualities that have earned all of our senior people their biggest responsibility:

To build every Porsche—every Porsche, as if it were on its way to Le Mans.

To win.

956: 6-cylinder, horizontally opposed, four overhead camshafts, 4 valves per cylinder, water/air-cooled, mid-engine with two intercooled turbo chargers, 2649c.c.s, 630 hp. Weight: 1848 lbs. Top speed: 217 mph. Monocoque chassis. Ground-effect length.

As soon as we win, we change the rules.

On the wall near head-designer Tony Lapine's drafting table hangs his favorite design trophy.

The broken stem of a champagne glass mounted in lucite.

The same glass that Professor Porsche threw against the wheel of the 928 to celebrate the final approval of its design.

The broken champagne glass, after all, captures the true spirit of the accomplishment.

Calculated irreverence.

Like all Porsches, the 928 began

as a challenge: to build a car that would satisfy Professor Porsche's obsession with technological leadership. And keep R&D entertained at the same time.

Having already built the 911, neither task would be easy.

But endless arguments later, the 928 team arrived at precisely what Professor Porsche had expected.

The unexpected.

The first front-engine, liquid-

cooled V-8, transaxle, grand-touring luxury coupe ever to share his name.

A car with a top speed of 144 mph.

And an air conditioned glove box.

Of course, no sooner had the paint dried on the first production 928 in Zuffenhausen, when engineers were back to arguing over bottles of DinkelAcker at the R&D canteen in Weissach.

Someone in Engine Development with a particular fondness for

working late proposed that a 4-valve design could do for the 928 V-8 what it does for the TAG F-1 engine and the 956.

Eighteen months later the first 928 4-valve turned a test lap.

Top speed: 155 mph.

The 4-valve technology had not only added 54 horsepower, it had improved everything from the torque curve at low rpm's to fuel economy.

Meanwhile, Tony Lapine sits in his swivel chair eyeing a schematic of the 928, and wonders.

What would happen, if?

928: 8-cylinder, wide, over V, four overhead camshafts, four valves per cylinder, liquid-cooled, front engine, 4957c.c.s, 288 hp, transaxle. Weight: 3195 lbs. Top speed: 155 mph.

Fun may be the most important discipline of all.

When Roland Kussmaul is tired of meetings, tired of wearing a tie, tired of hearing his phone ring, he leaves his office in the racing compound a few hundred yards west of the test track, to do the one thing he never gets tired of doing.

Driving.

Not driving as people who wear ties know it. But driving as Kussmaul knows it.

Putting the car a little bit sideways.

Kussmaul is a professional test driver. Which means he can detect a millimeter's difference in the thickness of a sway bar or a 5% adjustment in a spring rate. In a single test lap.

Kussmaul was Project Leader for our customer-owned 956 race cars. Project Manager on our SCCA 944

racer. And when he isn't helping tune the suspension of the Paris/Dakar 4-wheel drive car, he's out crossing African deserts in one.

Needless to say, a man like Roland Kussmaul isn't easily entertained.

Which says something about the Porsche 944.

A car Kussmaul drives not

because it can do 0 to 60 mph in 7.2 seconds.

Not because its transaxle design helps make it the best handling production sports car on the market. Even when driven to Kussmaul's limit.

And no, not for its newly designed, 928-like interior.

But for what may be the best reason of all to drive any Porsche.

The fun of it.

944 4-cylinder in-line, single overhead camshaft, liquid-cooled, front engine. 2478 c.c. 143 hp., transaxle. Weight: 2778 lbs. Top speed: 130 mph.

And Professor Porsche expects still more.

The windows in Professor Porsche's office in Zuffenhausen overlook a courtyard.

A courtyard lined with Porsches parked in a patchwork of colors and model designs.

Not shiny new cars, but the ones that have already met foul weather and potholes. Survived the winding kilometers between summer picnics and winter ski trips.

To Professor Porsche, these are very important Porsches.

Because when he stands at this window, hands crossed behind his back, rocking from toe to heel, and looks down at the cars in the courtyard, he imagines.

He is reminded of how much is yet to be accomplished.

It is the reason Professor Porsche drives his company much the same way one drives his cars.

With passion. Respect. Conviction.

The result, cars that set new expectations of what a car ought to be.

Cars like this one.

Porsche's latest project, the 959. Or, more affectionately known as the "Gruppe B" car.

A car powered by the same 6-cylinder, horizontally opposed, twin overhead cam engine used in Porsche's 956 race car. Producing 400 hp.

A car with such a sophisticated

drive train you can actually dial in the power to each of the four wheels.

A car with a self-adjusting suspension system that automatically lowers it as speed increases.

Top speed: no one really knows. Yet.

And as far as Professor Porsche is concerned, it really doesn't matter.

Because no matter how close to perfection the Gruppe B car comes, there will be another day when he stands at his window.

And imagines.

959 (Gruppe B) 6-cylinder, horizontally opposed, four overhead camshafts, four valves per cylinder, water-air cooled rear engine. 2849 c.c. 400 hp. Estimated top speed: 195 mph.

Magazine inserts proved the right venue for Porsche. Chiat/Day targeted its audience carefully, choosing magazines that could provide the kind of exclusive environment that would appeal to status-conscious buyers. Also, by preprinting its inserts, the agency was able to accurately portray the lush lines and sensuous paint jobs Porsches are famous for.

The first insert, run for the 1985 model year, featured the very first Porsche—the 356-001—on its cover. The 356 model reached its nadir in the late 1950s and early 1960s with the production of the 356-C, the "bathtub" Porsche speedster.

The rest of the insert features Porsche's current heroes: The 911, 956 race car, 928, 944 and the futuristic (and phenomenally quick) 959. The pages showing the 956 were also run as stand-alone spreads in some selected publications.

The line-up says forcefully that Porsche is not just another pretty face; the car's value is built in, not just painted on.

In 1948, Professor Porsche decided any car that merely got you from here to there, just didn't go far enough.

356-001 4-cylinder horizontally opposed, air-cooled, mid engine. 1131 c.c. 40 hp. Weight: 1287 lbs. Top speed: 84 mph.

© 1985 Porsche Cars North America, Inc. 200 Ferdinand Porsche, Reno, Nevada 89511. For the location of your nearest dealer, call 1-800-252-4444.

Thirty-eight years ago, Professor Ferdinand Porsche and his son, Ferry, built the first cars to bear the family name.

As a direct result, Porsche enthusiasts of today are subject to a recurring dream. Which goes something like this:

After running out of gas on a remote country road, you hike over to a distant farmhouse, knock on the door and ask an old man with a weathered face if he has some gas you can buy.

"Sure," he says. Out in the barn, as he sets to work with gas can and siphon, something in the shadows catches your eye.

There—enshrouded in dust, sitting lopsided on a time-flattened tire—is a 1958 Porsche 356 Speedster. Left behind 25 years earlier, you discover, by a son on his way to boot camp and a subsequent commitment to marriage, family and a station wagon.

Nonchalantly, you walk around it, examine it, and realize that, under the dust, nothing is missing. It's all there. Waiting.

"Never got around to selling it," the old man says.

"Oh?" you reply, stifling the urge to hug a perfect stranger. "I might be interested."

"You would, eh? $500 be too much?"

And then you wake up.

Porsches change. What makes them Porsches doesn't.

What is it about a decades-old Porsche that makes it so very desirable—even with the $15,000-plus price tag such a car is more likely to command these days? Horsepower? Handling? Top speed?

None of the above.

Its true value lies in the total commitment of two uncompromising men to build cars that would be more than simply a means of getting from one place to another. Cars that would be a joy to drive. Cars like no one else had ever built. Or ever would.

This commitment has been passed on successfully—some might say miraculously—to the uncompromising people who build Porsches today.

The workers on the Zuffenhausen assembly line who, in their off-hours, have been known to grab their friends, point at a passing Porsche and say with genuine pride, "That's one of mine."

The quality control technicians—one for every ten production workers—whose goal is to take the ideal of "zero defects" and make it a daily reality.

And, of course, the engineers at our R&D facility at Weissach.

For them, the pursuit of excellence will never fit comfortably between the hours of 8 and 5. Or within the theoretical vacuum of an air-conditioned office.

For them, theories have value only on the inside of a Porsche, at speed, on the Weissach test track—preferably with one of them behind the wheel.

The results of their labors, and the extent of their success, is reflected in the procession of cars you see below.

From the first recorded Porsche win on July 11, 1948 to Innsbruck to the most recent victory at Le Mans, these cars have dominated the racing circuits of a world that loves fast cars.

As they have dominated the highways, turnpikes, interstates, autobahns, city streets and winding back roads of a world that loves to drive them.

We've spent the last 23 years working on the same idea.

If there's one thing which, more than any other, characterizes Porsche's approach to building sports cars, it's our preoccupation with making every 911 demonstrably better than it was the year before.

While adhering to a styling concept so unarguably "right" that it has remained essentially unchanged since it was first introduced in 1963.

Even the 282-horsepower, 157 mph, top-of-the-line Turbo shown here, with its radical "whale-tail" spoiler and considerably flared rear wheel wells, is unmistakably a 911.

Today, the 911 is perhaps the most coveted high-performance sports car in the world. A 23-year beneficiary of everything we've learned in world class endurance and sprint racing.

Built, as every Porsche, with a precision and attention to detail that's quickly vanishing in this age of rampant robotics.

The legendary air-cooled, horizontally opposed, six-cylinder, fuel-injected engine is still hand assembled by a small team of workers, any one of whom is qualified to build the entire engine from scratch.

It's still bench tested for 45 minutes at maximum rpm. By an increasingly rare breed of technician whose gloved hand, strategically placed on a running engine, is as good a judge of quality as most of his sophisticated monitoring equipment.

At the end of the assembly line, every 911, as is every Porsche, is test driven for at least 30 kilometers on both city streets and no-speed-limit autobahns.

Everything is checked. Chassis, body, engine, transmission, suspension, brakes, paint, interior finish, everything.

Any fault they uncover, no matter how minor, is located and fixed, and the car driven again before it is released.

At Porsche, we take a great deal of pride in the fact that every new car we sell is slightly used.

911 Turbo 6-cylinder, horizontally opposed, two overhead camshafts, air-cooled rear engine with turbocharger and intercooler. 3299cc, 282 hp. Weight: 2976 lbs. Top speed: 157 mph.

We wanted to see how far we could go without changing direction.

At Porsche, nearly 30% of our employees are involved in research and development.

And having developed the 911 to a state of near perfection, many of them were more than ready for the challenge of designing a totally new car.

Professor Ferry Porsche was more than happy to oblige.

He gave them something to gladden the heart of any engineer. A clean sheet of paper. And only two requirements for the finished product.

It had to be the most technologically advanced car we had ever built.

And it had to be a Porsche.

The result, in 1978, was the 928.

A car which, to some traditionalists, broke every rule in the Porsche handbook of automotive design. But which—with it's front-mounted, liquid-cooled V-8 engine and rear-mounted transmission and differential—was as ingenious and unexpected a solution as the 356 had been 30 years before.

Or as Professor Porsche likes to put it, "It was never my philosophy to ask where the engine should be placed, but which solution would bring the greatest gains."

After being named "Car of the Year" the minute it was introduced, the 928S has improved steadily every year since.

Today, it is one of the most sophisticated, luxurious sports cars you can buy.

But infinitely more important, it is every millimeter a "Porsche," the universally accepted synonym for performance.

The 288 horsepower, fuel-injected V-8—with a four-valve head design adapted from our 956 endurance racer—will propel the 928S from 0 to 60 in an awesome 6.1 seconds. And to a top speed of 155 mph.

The near 50-50 weight distribution of the transaxle drive train, combined with our patented Weissach Rear Axle, contributes to the uncanny sensation that one is cornering on rails.

And it can all be brought to a quick, sure, arrow-straight stop, regardless of road conditions, by our new electronically monitored Anti-Lock Braking System.

Assuming, of course, that you ever want to stop.

928S 8-cylinder, 90 degree V, four overhead camshafts, four valves per cylinder, liquid-cooled front engine. 4957cc, 288 hp. Automatic. Weight: 3335 lbs. Top speed: 155 mph (with manual transmission).

By the time anyone begins to catch up, we will have moved ahead again.

The success of the 928S proved that there was, indeed, more than one "right" way to build a Porsche.

It also set the stage for the next important step in the evolution of the sports car as defined by Porsche. The 944.

A car designed to benefit not only from the very latest technology, but from everything four decades of building and racing sports cars had taught us.

A car in which more people than ever before would be able to experience the sheer exhilaration of driving a Porsche.

From the beginning, the 944 was an unqualified success.

Car and Driver Magazine voted it "One of the Ten Best Cars in America" for four years running. And last year, declared it "The Best Handling Production Sports Car in America."

But, more important, people bought it. People who loved sports cars. And people who had never owned one before.

Of course, Porsche hasn't led its competitors year after year by resting on such laurels. And this year is no different. Thanks to the car you see here.

The Porsche 944 Turbo.

If the performance of the 944 can be described as exhilarating, the performance of this machine almost defies description.

Not just because we were able to increase horsepower by a staggering 50%

in a four-cylinder engine that was already one of the biggest, most powerful fours in production.

But because we didn't leave it at that. Professor Porsche's philosophy simply doesn't allow for bolting on a turbocharger and renaming the car.

Every element of the 944 Turbo—engine, transaxle, suspension, brakes, tires, aerodynamics—was re-thought and re-engineered to meet the most demanding criteria for performance and handling.

The result, for you, is a brand-new car. And for our competition, a brand-new goal.

944 Turbo: 4-cylinder, in-line, single overhead camshaft, liquid cooled, front engine with turbocharger and intercooler, 247cc; 217 hp; transaxle. Weight 2900 lbs. Top Speed: 152 mph.

Many of our future discoveries will be made in this laboratory.

These days, they say, it's possible to duplicate anything in a laboratory.

Anything, perhaps, except the way your latest technology is likely to perform in a car driven by an actual human being.

For that you need the car. And the human being.

A rolling laboratory, if you will.

Precisely the role of the technological wonder revealed, quite literally, below.

The Porsche 959.

A 190+ mph laboratory in which we are re-shaping and redefining what a sports car ought to be.

Consider the following:

A 450 horsepower, 6-cylinder, horizontally opposed, twin-turbocharged 962C endurance racer.

An all-wheel drive system that's so

sophisticated, it continually and electronically monitors throttle application, speed and road conditions, and adjusts both front and rear torque accordingly.

A suspension system that automatically stiffens the shocks and lowers the car as speed increases, to maximize aerodynamic efficiency and minimize lift.

Body panels made of Kevlar, a space-age material with twice the strength of steel. And half the weight of aluminum.

The Porsche of the future?

Perhaps. Perhaps not.

It doesn't really matter.

Because as perfect as the 959 might become, for us it will still only be the next step.

Which is not too surprising a thought when you consider a conversation that once took place between Professor Porsche and a certain visitor.

The visitor said, "Tell me, Professor, which is your favorite Porsche?"

The Professor replied, "We haven't built it yet."

PORSCHE

959: 6-cylinder, horizontally opposed, four overhead camshafts, four valves per cylinder, water/air-cooled rear engine with twin turbochargers and intercoolers; 2850cc; 450 hp; Estimated Top Speed: 190+ mph. A test vehicle, not currently available.

Thirty-eight years ago, Professor Ferdinand Porsche and his son, Ferry, built the first cars to bear the family name.

As a direct result, Porsche enthusiasts of today are subject to a recurring dream. Which goes something like this:

After running out of gas on a remote country road, you hike over to a distant farmhouse, knock on the door and ask an old man with a weathered face if he has some gas you can buy.

"Sure," he says. Out in the barn, as he sets to work with gas can and siphon, something in the shadows catches your eye.

There—enshrouded in dust, sitting

lopsided on a time-flattened tire—is a 1958 Porsche 356 Speedster. Left behind 25 years earlier, you discover, by a son on his way to boot camp and a subsequent commitment to marriage, family and a station wagon.

Nonchalantly, you walk around it, examine it, and realize that, under the dust, nothing is missing. It's all there. Waiting.

"Never got around to selling it," the old man says.

"Oh?" you reply, stifling the urge to hug a perfect stranger. "I might be interested."

"You would, eh? $500 be too much?"

And then you wake up.

Experience all the new Porsches first hand. Call (800) 252-4444 for the location of your nearest authorized Porsche dealer.

The inserts for the 1986 model year again played up the Porsche heritage by leading off with a sports car enthusiasts' dream, finding a perfect 356 sitting in a barn, unused.

Inside, illustrations of successive Porsche racing machines emphasize the company's historic commitment to excellence in engineering. In fact, Porsche works under contract to solve engineering problems for many of the world's largest auto makers—a fact neither Porsche nor the other companies disseminate too widely.

Not many of the companies Porsche works for have models that are more than twenty years old, as is the Porsche 911. The idea of a Porsche is to get better at doing the same things, rather than to follow the changing fashions in external sheet metal.

The photography for the second insert is even more lush than for the preceeding year's effort; notice how the 911 and 928 were carefully "painted" with light to reveal their smooth body lines.

At Porsche, we don't usually make comparisons with other cars. But in this case, we're willing to make an exception.

Experience all the new Porsches first hand. Call (800) 252-4444 for the location of your nearest authorized Porsche dealer.

The 1987 insert made the point that Porsches can only be compared to other Porsches, not to other makes of auto.

The piece opposite directly attacked the lingering perception of Porsches as delicate, exotic autos by showcasing their performance in endurance races. Over the years, Porsche has been very successful at LeMans, Daytona, Sebring and other long-distance events.

Zero to sixty, 5.5 seconds. Top speed, 157 miles per hour.

For nearly four decades it has been Professor Porsche's philosophy that a car should do more than simply move people from one point to another.

Much more.

And anyone who's ever had the good fortune to drive a car like the one on the left knows exactly what he had in mind.

Since its introduction in 1974, the race-bred, rear-engine 911 Turbo has stood alone as the fastest, most powerful production Porsche ever built.

The ultimate expression of Professor Porsche's philosophy.

But now turn your attention to the car on the right. The new 928S 4.

With its front-mounted, liquid-cooled V-8 engine and rear-mounted transmission, it's as different from the 911 Turbo as it could possibly be. A fact which did not

Zero to sixty, 5.7 seconds. Top speed, 165 miles per hour.

escape the attention of surprised Porsche enthusiasts when the first 928 was introduced in 1977.

But, like the 911 Turbo, the 928S 4 started as a breakthrough in sports car design. A design that promised even more than a new level of performance.

It promised a totally new driving experience. Different from the challenge of the 911 Turbo, yet every bit as rewarding.

Since then, it has evolved, year by year, to higher and higher levels of performance. Incorporating, at every step, the most advanced technology our engineers could devise.

And so today, it is the 928S 4 which stands alone as the fastest, most powerful production Porsche ever built.

The ultimate expression of Professor Porsche's philosophy.

"It was never my philosophy to ask where the engine should be placed."

"But which solution would bring the greatest gains?"

Curious words from a man who made rear-engine sports cars synonymous with high performance.

But, by 1971, the gains achieved by Professor Porsche and his engineers had already brought the 911 to such a state of perfection, they felt the need for a new challenge.

And Professor Porsche made it the challenge of a lifetime—create a totally new car with the most advanced technology, and the potential for more performance than even Porsche enthusiasts had come to expect.

The result, in 1977, was the Porsche 928. A car which, today, as the 928S 4—the fourth generation of this remarkable design—has emerged as the new benchmark of sports car performance.

This year, the front-mounted, 5-liter V-8, with 4-valve cylinder heads derived from our 956 endurance racer, produces 316 horsepower, up from 288.

It's the most powerful production engine we've ever built. And, with its network of computer-coordinated functions —ignition, fuel injection, knock sensors and new two-stage resonant induction chambers—the most sophisticated.

For us, of course, performance is not solely a function of horsepower.

The Porsche-pioneered transaxle drivetrain plays an essential part in utilizing the full potential of our astounding engine. By transmitting as much of that power to the road as possible, with a degree of control unprecedented among production cars.

As shown below, the front-mounted engine and rear-mounted transmission/differential make weight distribution virtually equal over both axles.

This, combined with the self-correcting action of our Weissach Rear Axle, helps make the 928S 4 remarkably stable.

So at higher speeds, it exhibits the kind of confident handling and cornering ability that even professional drivers find impressive.

Add to all this its advanced anti-lock braking system, and the result is a high-performance car which, in just 9.0 seconds, can take you from zero to sixty.

And back to zero.

We don't intend to make them any faster.

From the day the very first Porsche rolled out into the world, we have believed in the absolute incompatibility of building fast cars and building cars fast.

Below, you see our latest example of that belief. And the best example to date. The 928S 4.

It has long been obvious to us, if not to others, that high performance is the result not only of a superior design. But also of the production process that turns that design into reality.

That's why, for 39 years, Porsches have been manufactured with unhurried, hand-built precision. A passionate resistance to the "efficiencies" of automation. And little regard for production quotas.

The assembly process is so meticulous, in fact, that a 928S 4 takes nearly three weeks to complete.

Every minute of which involves the skilled labor of dedicated craftsmen—second generation Porsche employees, in many cases.

Engine builders who see nothing strange about a company that requires them to maintain blueprint specifications to within 1/1000th of a millimeter.

Metalworkers whose sensitive and practiced hands can detect the slightest flaws that might compromise the car's aerodynamic shape.

Assembly line workers who, rather than performing simple rote functions, take pride in mastering virtually every step in the assembly process. And make a significant contribution to the performance of the cars they build.

This kind of commitment extends even to those craftsmen who have little to do with how fast a 928S 4 can get from zero to sixty.

Like the painters and leather workers whose skill and uncompromising artistry add their own level of exhilaration to driving a Porsche.

All of which brings us back to the simple truth we started out with.

It's one thing to design a high performance car. But when it comes to building it, the key is motivation, not automation.

Quality, not quantity.

Slow, not fast.

PORSCHE

On Feb. 1, 1987, the sun rose in the east, day followed night and Porsche won Daytona.

After winning the 24 Hours of Daytona for the last 10 years in a row, it didn't come as a total surprise this year when we made it 11 in a row.

It was, however, a bit of an eye-opener when we also came in second, third, fourth, fifth and sixth.

The winning team of Al Unser Jr., Derek Bell, Chip Robinson and Al Holbert took the flag in a Porsche 962 endurance racer (seen here with its turbo afterburn giving the dawn a little competition).

That car's performance was virtually flawless, averaging 111.6 mph for 2,681 miles and a record-setting 753 laps. The sort of performance that would tempt most engineers to sit back and take a few bows.

But at Porsche we've never been comfortable resting on our laurels. Even when our laurels include an 11-year winning streak.

That's why our engineers are, as usual, back at their drawing boards, using what they learn from racing to make our cars perform even better. On the track and on the road.

So, while we wouldn't want to predict what will happen next year, there are some things we're pretty certain of.

The swallows will return to Capistrano.

Thanksgiving will fall on a Thursday.

And each new Porsche will be better than the last.

PORSCHE

Timberland And Lintas Prove That It's A Tough, Tough World

TIMBERLAND

Client: The Timberland Company
Agency: Lintas: New York

Think tough. Really tough. John Wayne on Tarawa. The Iron Man competition. G. Gordon Liddy toasting the palm of his hand with a Bic lighter. Some fool busting concrete blocks with his head at a karate match. Fortunately, none of those images came to the minds of Don Gill, Rafael Altman, Eric Jensen, Stanley Shulman or Bruce Kravetz, the Lintas: New York team responsible for Timberland's arresting advertising. Instead, they found a dozen different and clever ways to tell us how tough Timberland's boots are. Unfortunately, Timberland is tough in more ways than one. After a string of successful seasons, boosting sales for the boot and shoemaker, Lintas resigned the account late in 1987. The parting was largely amicable, but let's face it, agencies don't walk away from business without a reason.

When creative director Don Gill came to Lintas from Young & Rubicam in 1985, he was surprised to learn he'd be working on Timberland. The last he'd heard, the account had been resting happily with Ally & Gargano.

"I said 'Timberland? Why did Carl [Ally] lose Timberland? They told me that while Ally had done a good job of building the business in the East, that the brand wasn't doing as well as they wanted in other parts of the country," Gill recalls. "So that was our assignment, to broaden the brand out, move it beyond the Eastern Seaboard where they had traditionally been strong."

The Ally & Gargano ads, which Gill liked very much, were black and white spreads and were run in magazines such as *Esquire*. The tag line was "The clothes you have to wear versus the clothes you want to wear." One of the more memorable illustrations was of a youngish man sitting on the stoop of a log cabin. He's got the crew neck sweater, faded Levi's and, of course, Timberland shoes. All in all, a very Ivy League appeal. While that supported the company's main base of buyers wonderfully, it didn't play all that well in Peoria or in

TIMBERLAND BOOTS.
DON'T LEAVE NOME WITHOUT THEM.

Whether you're shoveling snow in Detroit or driving a dogsled to Nome, Alaska, you'll find that wearing a pair of Timberland Boots is practically the next best thing to staying home with your feet by the fire.

At Timberland, we are committed to building simply the finest boots in the world.

ANCHORAGE TO NOME 1049 MILES

Boots tough enough to keep you warm and dry when it's 40 degrees below zero. Boots built to endure the Last Great Race On Earth—the Alaskan Iditarod.

To meet these conditions, we developed the only insulated Pac Boots ever made that are guaranteed waterproof. A Pac Boot with high abrasion rubber bottoms thermally bonded to the waterproof leather uppers. All other Pac Boots are stitched and not waterproof.

GORE-TEX® Registered Trademark of W. L. Gore & Associates, Inc.

For those who prefer a variety of waterproof insulated footwear with B-400 Thinsulate,® two other boots are available. One is made from rare "Krymp" oxhide, the other with a breathable, waterproof inner Gore-Tex® fabric bootie.

The rest of us who will probably not take part in the Iditarod, will take comfort in knowing that Timberland Boots have

Thinsulate ® Thinsulate is a registered trademark of 3M.

been tested under the most adverse conditions known to man. Even your own backyard is no place to get cold feet.

Timberland®
MORE QUALITY THAN YOU MAY EVER NEED.

*Registered Trademarks of The Timberland Company
© 1987 The Timberland Company, P.O. Box 5050, Hampton, N.H. 03842-5050.

Petaluma, for that matter. Folks in the Midwest and West generally aren't going to pay $80 to $120 for a pair of shoes so that they can look like they went to Princeton.

So despite his personal feelings about the merit of the Ally & Gargano pieces, Gill guided Timberland straight into the valley of tough. But it's a very sophisticated kind of tough.

"I felt that if I could convince a customer that Timberland was going to give him more quality than he would ever need, I could close the sale on him," Gill says. "The first piece we wrote was called *Laces*. It says 'Years from now, you may have to replace the laces.' That ad has the same tone as the Ally ads, but anybody could put themselves into that pair of shoes. We felt it would appeal to a Harvard graduate, to a farmer in Iowa or to a cowboy in California."

Instead of black and white, the shoes were done in luscious color. Superb studio lighting reveals every nook and cranny of the

shoes' surface. You can almost reach into the photo and feel the texture of the smooth, richly-tanned leather.

While previous ads had been exposed almost exclusively to the Eastern audience, Lintas used the product line to determine the right venue for the spreads.

"We let the particular boot or shoe we were featuring determine our audience. The lightweight boots were advertised in hunting magazines—*Field & Stream*—very vertical books. If the item had the potential of being a dress shoe or a fashion shoe, we put it in *Esquire* or *GQ*," Gill says.

Gill also found another venue, which had been totally overlooked in previous campaigns for Timberland: spot television.

"I knew they couldn't afford TV on their budget," Gill explains. "However, their boot sales were starting to slide a little bit for the first time in years. That was largely due to the fact they hadn't been advertising the boots. I

Although the campaign was primarily a print effort, creative director Don Gill found a cost-effective way to bring Timberland into spot television, with an execution about the Alaska Iditarod, a grueling dog sled race. This print piece was a spin-off of the TV spot, but demonstrates the same level of tongue-in-cheek headline writing that makes the series so effective.

TIMBERLAND. FOR YET WALK

Although some of us may claim otherwise, the ability to walk on water has been mastered by very few. The rest of us would be well advised to wear Timberland Sport Boots.

Though your feet may sink in the mud, we at Timberland guarantee that they will remain warm and dry. We start with a Gore-Tex® fabric bootie, sealed with

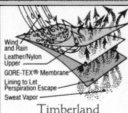

Wind and Rain
Leather/Nylon Upper
GORE-TEX® Membrane
Lining to Let Perspiration Escape
Sweat Vapor

Timberland
Waterproof Gore-Tex®
System

Gore-Seam™ tape. This combination, with a leather and nylon shell and Thinsulate,® adds up to a "two tier" waterproof barrier between your foot and the cold, wet world. We were the first to develop this system.

The entire boot is then permanently bonded to a remarkably

GORE·TEX® Registered Trademark of W. L. Gore & Associates, Inc.

Thinsulate® Thinsulate is a registered trademark of 3M.

THOSE WHO CAN'T ON WATER.

comfortable dual density sole that is vastly lighter than any regular boot.

If you have any further doubts, we challenge you to test our boots on the terrain of your choosing. Bear in mind, however, that we flexed our boots 4,000,000 times under water without detecting a single leak.

This makes us confident you will discover that Timberland Sport Boots are not built on faith alone.

Timberland

MORE QUALITY THAN YOU MAY EVER NEED.

FOR LONG WEAR AND RUGGED

Boot made in USA.
Loaned by Mr. T. Almy,
purchased Sept. 1984.

thought about the problem for a bit and came up with the idea of taking spot TV in the Northeast and Northwest.

"The plan was to run during the Saturday football games, local college games, right before the big winter selling season. Also, the commercial could be used by Timberland's sales force when they called on retailers. You can localize radio and outdoor. I figured why not try localizing spot television. We did the piece, and they broke it a lot wider than planned, putting it on NCAA football on ABC and on ESPN."

"The piece" Gill refers to so cavalierly is a wonderful bit of television. If you like the outdoors, you can't help but love it. Gill wanted something *really* tough to showcase the quality of the Timberland boots. It doesn't get much tougher than the Iditarod, the longest, coldest, baddest dog sled race on Earth. The basic plot of this annual event

is that a field of brain-dead *machismos* (and *machismas*, women also compete) leave Anchorage with a team of dogs, a sled and a bunch of food. Whoever makes it to Nome first wins. Sounds simple enough. Except that between Anchorage and Nome lies about 500 miles of frozen tundra. During the day, it might warm up to -20°; at night it gets downright chilly, maybe -40° or worse. Those numbers are *before* calculating the wind chill factor.

Terrific stuff for a sixty-second spot, no? Not if you've got to go up and get it yourself. Gill was one of the lucky participants.

"It's one of those things that you're glad you did but you never, *ever*, want to do again," he says. "It was shot in the spring of 1987. We went up in April and I was worried there wouldn't be enough snow."

Not enough snow in Alaska? Come on. The agency hired Dick Mackey, a veteran of the Iditarod

and an expert dog sledder as technical adviser. The director was Andre Barkovitz, who filmed *Pritzi's Honor*.

The group headed out of Anchorage and went up to Hatcher's Pass where Mackey assured them they'd find all the snow they needed.

"We were up there about three weeks, and I think we solved Russia's foreign debt problems with all the Stolichnaya we drank to keep warm," Gill laughs. "The scenes in the finished spot don't look dangerous, but a lot of it was filmed with Andre hanging off the side of a special sled going full speed."

The spot did its job; boot sales responded nicely as the spot broke in late fall. Overall, Timberland's sales rose about a third during Lintas' tenure on the account. In selected markets, such as Los Angeles, the figures were much higher—almost a doubling of sales volume.

GOOD LOOKS, JUST ADD WATER.

Water. It's the stuff that makes ordinary boots crack, wither, stiffen up and die. But it only makes a pair of Timberlands, with time, beautiful. And even more comfortable.

You see, water in any form simply doesn't stand a chance of penetrating a Timberland boot. We use only flawless, silicone impregnated leather on the uppers. And unlike ordinary boots, the four rows of stitching on a pair of Timberlands aren't just for decoration. They're there to create an ironclad waterproof seam. All this is permanently bonded to a rugged Timberland sole.

But simply keeping your feet warm and dry is not enough. Timberlands require no break-in. A padded collar, insole and a glove leather lining will surround your feet in comfort from the moment you put them on.

At Timberland, we don't make guarantees on the condition that you supply a shoebox full of paste, waxes, oils and elbow grease. Just add a little silicone once or twice a year. However, don't get upset if it takes some time for your Timberlands to develop the character that the simple adding of water will provide.

Timberland
MORE QUALITY THAN YOU MAY EVER NEED.

*Registered Trademarks of The Timberland Company © The Timberland Company, P.O. Box 5050, Hampton, N.H. 03842 5050

So why did Lintas and Timberland split? Unfortunately, winning or losing business doesn't always have as much to do with good advertising as we'd like. Clients sometimes fire good agencies. Agencies doing an outstanding job sometimes resign an account. They sometimes do it even when they're not chasing a piece of competitive business.

In this case, Timberland itself was in transition. The advertising manager, John Thorback, who had brought Lintas the business, was squeezed out. That left advertising decisions in the hands of a management committee, one that Gill says he couldn't quite see eye to eye with.

"They wanted to do more Ralph Lauren type advertising," he says. "My feeling was that if they became redundant to Ralph Lauren, they'd lose their originality. I'm a believer in the Vince Lombardi theory of advertising: If you have a play

that's working, keep running it until it stops working. And their advertising was working."

Particularly when it comes to making creative decisions on advertising, in fact the client isn't always right. But it remains a rule of business that the client *is* always right, even when he's wrong. Lintas just didn't see the percentage in trying to convince Timberland to continue down the creative path that had so far proven successful.

Where is the justice in this business? Well, for one thing, John Thorback ended up as the president of Bass, a rival shoemaker that's older, bigger and stronger than Timberland.

Don Gill is staying busy with other Lintas clients. And in the end, whatever Timberland's next agency does, the team at Lintas knows how many pairs of loafers they sold. And they have a passel of excellent creative to show their next footwear client.

Special markets sometimes require a special effort: This piece was created for *Rolling Stone* magazine. The odd size allowed Timberland to take one-half page on both sides of a spread, giving maximum exposure at a reasonable cost.

YEARS FROM NOW REPLACE

Shoe loaned by Mr. V. Cremer, purchased July, 1981.

Timberlands just seem to get better with age. You see, what makes them wear well is what makes them look good.

We handsew them because no machine can do the job. We make the sides and bottom from one piece of hide to cradle your foot and add a glove soft leather lining to gently coddle it as well.

As time goes by you'll notice that the solid brass eyelets are still in place, and still shining. The leather uppers will certainly have earned

YOU MAY HAVE TO THE LACES.

some memorable nicks and scars, but the nylon hand stitching will still hold. As will the rawhide laces.

And if some day years from now

you have to replace a lace, we hope you won't feel that the new one harms your Timberlands' appearance.

Timberland
MORE QUALITY THAN YOU MAY EVER NEED. ℠

*Registered Trademarks of The Timberland Company
© The Timberland Company, P.O. Box 5050, Hampton, N.H. 03842-5050

Timberland

"EXTRA COURAGE"   60 SECONDS

849 Miles From Nome.
You race at night. The track is faster.

You pray for cold. The dogs like it better.

For two weeks you push — 1,049 frozen, brutal miles.

Dick Mackey
Iditarod Winner
Nothing takes the measure of a team like the Iditarod — the last great race on earth.

If mushing across the cold heart of Alaska is the ultimate test of man and dog,

it's also the ultimate test of the bootmaker's craft.

That's why Timberland has chosen the Iditarod to test its boot collection.

Boots that keep you warm, dry and comfortable under the most inhospitable conditions known to man

are tough enough for anything.

Timberland Boots. Tough enough for the Iditarod.

More quality than you may ever need.

Timberland
MORE QUALITY THAN YOU MAY EVER NEED.

MORE QUALITY THAN YOU MAY EVER NEED.™

This sixty-second spot was the first time Timberland had tried its hand in television. The spot was designed to pique interest in Timberland's high-quality boots at the beginning of the winter selling season. As is often the case, art imitates life: To capture the impression of cold and isolation that ambush the sled racers in the Iditarod, the creative team had to spend three frigid weeks scouting and shooting in the environs of Alaska's Hatcher Pass, north of Anchorage. The resulting film worked: Exposed on NCAA football broadcasts over ABC and ESPN, it boosted sales volume for the boots, which had been declining.

   Laces, right, was the first ad in the series and the first to get away from what Gill calls the "preppy" orientation of Timberland's previous advertising.

SOME SOLES ARE MORE ETERNAL THAN OTHERS.

Upon close examination, you will discover that all loafers should not be judged on looks alone. Some have the sole of a true Timberland.

You see, Timberland loafers have unique patented, honey rubber "tap sole" inserts in the heel and sole. They act as shock absorbers and prevent wear in the places where time takes its toll on ordinary loafers. The glove leather lining will surround your feet in comfort. And the colors are tanned all the way through the hide so they won't crack or wear away.

While your Timberland loafers may not achieve immortality, you'll be eternally grateful you bought them.

Timberland
MORE QUALITY THAN YOU MAY EVER NEED.

*Registered Trademarks of The Timberland Company

© 1987 The Timberland Company. P.O. Box 5050, Hampton, N.H. 03842-5050.

WHEN IT COMES TO TIMBERLAND, SOME PEOPLE GO A LITTLE OVERBOARD.

Choosing to buy Timberlands is easy, but choosing between Timberlands can be a little difficult. That's why we can understand when some people go a little overboard.

Unlike ordinary boat shoes, our colors aren't just painted on the surface. We use only full-grain, oil-impregnated leathers that never lose their color and remain soft and supple for the life of the shoe. The eyelets are solid brass so they will never pit or rust. Our midsole construction keeps soles from flapping, and our Timberland bottoms assure a life of long wear.

A look inside explains their remarkable comfort. Our Scuppers have a soft core within the sole for the cushiest walk on land or sea. Our Super Boat shoes feature an orthotic inner sole for support.

When shoes are this well made, so comfortable and classic in design, no one really needs more than a few faithful pairs. But then again, some people can't get enough of a good thing.

Timberland
MORE QUALITY THAN YOU MAY EVER NEED.

*Registered Trademarks of The Timberland Company © The Timberland Company. P.O. Box 5050, Hampton, N.H. 03842-5050.

Transamerica Goes "Ape" With The Help Of DFTP

Client: Transamerica
Agency: Della Femina Travisano & Partners

There's nothing in the advertising world more desirable or harder to define than the legendary but elusive "big idea." Whatever the definition, we do have a relative terminology. There's the big idea, the *really* big idea and the "this is going to make the Marlboro Man look like Don Knotts" idea.

The difficulty of finding even a moderately large idea means that most campaigns are built on a carefully-constructed base of copy strategy and professional—if uninspired—execution. When lightning does strike, it's not at all certain that the client will go along for the ride. Big ideas are scary. And sometimes they're risky.

When Transamerica came to Della Femina, Travisano and Partners (DFTP) they were just looking for some good advertising. What they got was a big idea: Really big. Like over a thousand feet.

It was 1984, and Transamerica was a company in transition. After years of digesting a wide variety of unrelated businesses, a new chairman was preparing to sell off the movie studio (United Artists), airline, Budget Rent-A-Car and concentrate on the company's insurance and financial services business. Its image among insurance brokers and the public needed sharpening. The proximate cause of Transamerica's move to DFTP was opportunism: The company underwrote the insurance for the 1984 Olympics in Los Angeles. Prior Olympics had been sponsored by governmental bodies. But the L.A. Olympics were produced by a private group, and the group needed protection from the hundreds of millions of dollars of liability represented by the arrival of the world's best athletes and the thousands of spectators.

DFTP produced a campaign replete with images of athletes and talk about performance. It was exactly what the client wanted—a solid strategy and excellent execution. But DFTP wasn't satisfied. Lurking in the collective subconscious was something better. And bigger.

"We knew we had to do something with the Transamerica building," says management supervisor John Fuller. The building, with its unique profile, is one of the most widely-recognized structures in America. "We wanted to take this corporate symbol and make it an integral part of the advertising. That's when the brainstorm happened. Why not take this famous building and add the most famous building

WOULD THE
MOST INNOVATIVE
INSURANCE
COMPANY
IN AMERICA
PLEASE
STAND UP.

For over 50 years Transamerica's ... stand as leaders in their fields. A ...rica's Insurance Companies ...yramid is working for you.

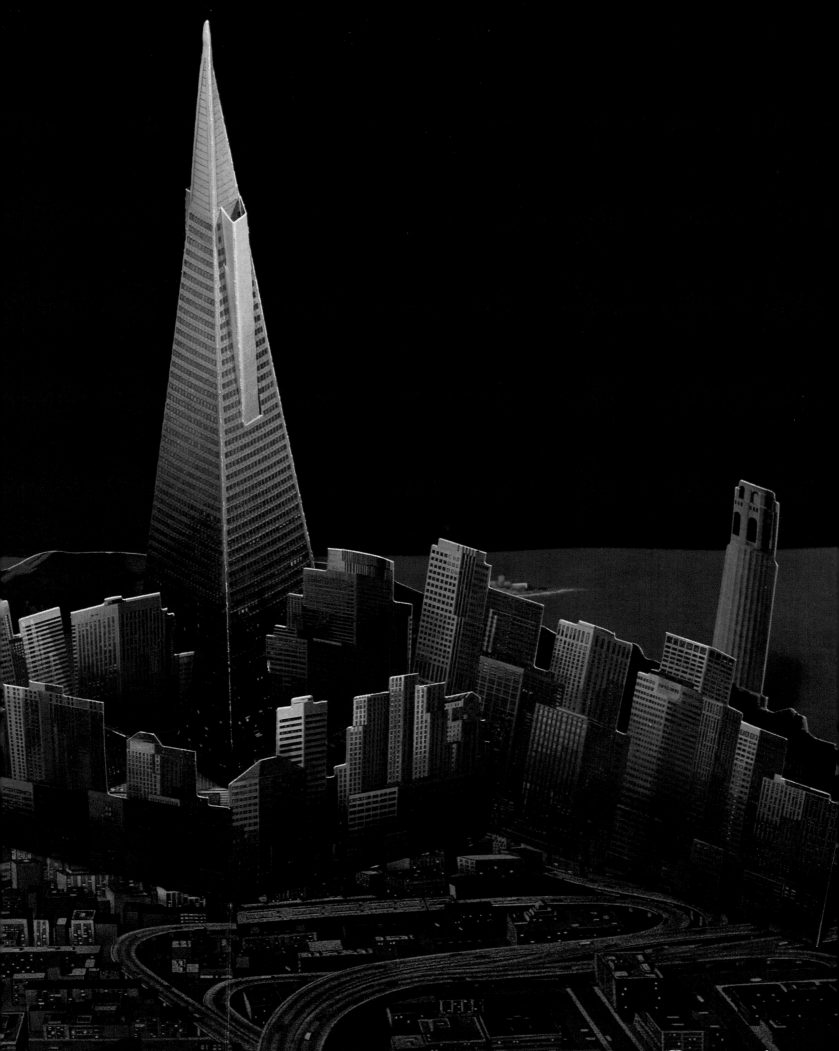

a has stood for innovation. Today, Transamerica's Insurance Companies
. And more than ever, the Power of the Pyramid is working for you.

appendage—King Kong."

The idea was to have King Kong scale the side of the Transamerica building. As he got to the top, he would knock over a flower pot, whereupon Faye Wray (actress Marilyn Beck) would come out onto the ledge and yell "Hey, you big ape. Who's going to pay for this mess?"

Talk about revisionist history. We all know that the geographic center of America's population is moving West about forty feet each year. The quintessential Manhattan playwright, Neil Simon, went Hollywood. So did Joltin' Joe Dimaggio. But King Kong and the Empire State Building are inseparable. Not even the magic of television could take that away. Or could it?

The numbers show that it did. DFTP tested the pre-exposure recall of two critical audiences. Among the general public, awareness of Transamerica increased from 23% to 35%. Recognition of Transamerica's slogan—"The power of the

pyramid is working for you"—was 39%, with 22% correctly identifying it with Transamerica. After *King Kong* began running, recognition went up to 61%, with 34% correctly identifying the company. Among corporate insurance buyers awareness jumped from 34% to 54%. The company also acquired a much higher profile among independent brokers, on whom Transamerica depends for much of its consumer insurance sales.

The numbers were so good, in fact, that DFTP walked away with an Effie for effective advertising in 1984. According to Fuller, the creative, as good as it is, wasn't solely responsible for the big movement in awareness; numbers that put them second only to Prudential, which spends many times what Transamerica spends in advertising. The media strategy has been a key to its success.

"We didn't have enough money to dominate our competitors across the board," Fuller explains, "but what we did

is pick a spot and dominate them on a small piece of turf. We call it our Sunday Strategy. That's the day when businesspeople, brokers and other busy, upscale people are likely to sit down and relax in front of the television. The two things they're most likely to watch are NFL football and first-run movies on Sunday night. We don't try to compete on the *Cosby Show* or *St. Elsewhere*, because we don't have enough money. When we were on, we ran five or six spots each Sunday instead of one each day of the week."

DFTP's media department is responsible for another big idea as well: The legendary pop-up.

"The *King Kong* spot helped Transamerica believe in big ideas. They told us to keep thinking. If we could come up with something that made sense, they'd produce it," Fuller says.

As it often does, serendipity played a role in the next big idea.

"Our media director, Vicky Gilbert, had a friend who had gone to work for Intervisual

Communications, which is one of the world's largest producers of children's pop-up books. They talked about pop-ups, which have been phenomenally successful in bookstores, and the friend mentioned that revisions to the postal regulations would probably allow magazines with pop-ups to be mailed."

That was all the encouragement DFTP needed. Transamerica had a tremendous three-dimensional symbol. Now there was a high-visibility way to deliver it.

"Our creatives got involved and created a concept. The pop-up would be the skyline of San Francisco, with the Transamerica pyramid as the star of course," Fuller says.

The only thing that stood in the way of this really big idea was a really big budget. Even with the kind of production efficiencies Intervisual can muster, pop-ups are still expensive.

"Initially, our thought was to use the pop-up simply to garner publicity. We were going to run it

The innovative pop-up ad (preceding pages) was Della Femina Travisano & Partners' second big idea for Transamerica. The die-cut magazine ad was inserted in 5.5 million copies of *Time* magazine. A phenomenal 96% of those who read the issue remembered the ad and the effect on such measures as favorable impression of the company was just as impressive.

The first big idea was the *King Kong* television commercial. In it, DFTP paired Transamerica's primary advertising equity—its headquarters building in San Francisco, called "the pyramid"—with King Kong.

The production of the spot was incredibly complex. The storyboard called for Kong to climb up the outside of the building. As he nears the top, he was to knock off a flower pot. An actress who resembled Faye Wray (the female lead in the movie, *King Kong*) was to come out and upbraid the ape.

The shoot required the director, Robert Abel, to construct a 1/24th scale model of San Francisco, complete with Alcatraz and the Golden Gate Bridge. An animatronic model of Kong was created. Its face was capable of a number of emotions, controlled by a puppeteer off screen. For the payoff shot of Kong and the actress, a mirror was used to matte the image of the puppet climbing the 1/24th scale Transamerica building into a shot of the actress standing in front of a full-scale portion of the building.

in a regional edition, something with a very limited distribution," Fuller says. "But the more we got into the project, the more we realized that if we were going to do this thing, we ought to do it in a big way."

How big? How about the entire circulation of *Time* magazine, 5.5 million copies.

"Our people went up to San Francisco with a handful of children's book and a cardboard mock-up of how this thing might look," Fuller recalls. "To their credit, Transamerica was eager to fund the project."

Production of the pop-ups ran about fifty cents each, and the total came to roughly $3.5 million. That's a pretty big pill for any client to swallow for a one-shot effort, especially one whose entire annual budget comes in at under $10 million.

So what did they get for their money? The impact of the pop-up was incredible. It generated almost 600 newspaper and magazine articles throughout the world. The pop-up made it onto both network and syndicated television shows: *Good Morning America*, *Entertainment Tonight*, *The CBS Morning News* and more. That's many thousands of dollars worth of free publicity.

"An analyst with one of the Wall Street brokerage houses wrote that Transamerica may have gotten as much as $10 million worth of publicity out of that one magazine insertion," Fuller chuckles. "*Time* did some research on their subscribers. Of the subscribers who had seen that issue, 96% remembered seeing the ad. That's the highest number the researchers had ever seen. Among those who'd seen it, 72% were aware that Transamerica is an insurance company. That compares to 22% of those who hadn't seen the ad who were aware Transamerica is an insurance company. *Time* also compared the impression the two groups had about Transamerica. Of those who'd seen the ad, 69% had a positive impression of the

company, while only 14% of the group who hadn't seen the ad had a positive impression."

The pop-up also made positive impressions in other quarters. It helped DFTP pick up another Effie in 1986.

Fuller believes that there was more to the pop-up than the gimmick factor. "We weren't the first ones to do a pop-up," he points out. "Honeywell did one in *Business Week* almost a year before we did. And Dodge trucks did one in *Sports Illustrated* a few months after ours appeared. In my opinion, the difference was that those two weren't properly staged creatively. Our ad was set up with the question, 'Will the most innovative insurance company in America please stand up?' I think that's what made it work so well."

In 1987, DFTP added a new television execution to the campaign. Creatively, it plays off the "Power of the Pyramid" slogan. The spot opens like a remake of *The Ten Commandments*. With the Great Pyramid of Cheops looming in the background, slaves roll giant blocks across the Egyptian desert. One of them stands up on a stone and makes an impassioned speech, promising the others that one day, a pyramid will be built to help people; a pyramid dedicated to good, not evil. He then dismisses the outlandish notion with a sarcastic "Naah." The scene switches to an aerial view of the Transamerica building and the voice-over assures viewers that the pyramid is ready to work for them.

The spot's debut, on NFL football, was delayed slightly by the NFL players' strike in the fall of 1987. DFTP bought a football schedule, but delayed its placements until late October, betting that the strike would last a month. They were off by one week. It was yet another gamble that payed off for Transamerica. Any bets on whether DFTP can create another breakthrough for the pyramid?

The latest addition to the stable of epics created for Transamerica is this spot, released in fall 1987. A parody of the film *The Ten Commandments*, it features slaves building a pyramid for the Pharoh. One of them decries the effort, promising the other slaves that, one day, a pyramid will be created to help people. That pyramid, of course, is the Transamerica pyramid, and the spot ends with the now-famous tag line "The power of the pyramid is working for you."

BBDO Puts Visa Right Where It Wants To Be

Client: Visa USA
Agency: BBDO, Inc. New York

VISA USA

No matter how many times it's enacted, there's always something compelling in the combat between a likable David and a big, menacing Goliath.

Certainly American Express fills the sandals of the latter admirably. From its monolithic headquarters in lower Manhattan, executives of the Big Green Machine happily look out at a world in which they seemingly have little to do except sit back and watch the nickels roll in by the hundreds of thousands.

Visa International, on the other hand, seems a bit oversized for a proper David. A subsidiary of the Bank of America, its executives supervise their dominion from an equally monolithic headquarters in San Francisco. But when the battle is for the heart and mind of the spender, the shoe fits.

A comparative latecomer to the plastic money business, Visa began as a brown-white-and-blue wafer known as BankAmericard. Two decades and a name change later, Visa has blossomed into a $650 million dollar business. But in the world of travel and entertainment cards, that only qualifies Visa as a distant, if vigorous, number two. And when the measure is media dollars, Visa is outspent not only by American Express, but by the third major player, MasterCard, as well.

In these stories, there's always an equalizer; a sling and a rock. In this case Visa had an aggressive account team at agency BBDO. And, historically, the name Visa has given it an edge over MasterCard, an increased ability to solicit members and an enhanced perception of prestige which translate into an ability to drive more retail transactions per card. But, in early 1985, that advantage began to slip.

"At the time, Visa was doing very warm, emotional advertising," says BBDO account supervisor Gary DePaolo. The spots were slice-of-life and associated the card with happy events such as the birth of a child, marriage and celebrations. Unfortunately, the campaign virtually disappeared under the superior throw weight of MasterCard's media budget and the effectiveness of its *Worldly Welcome* campaign. MasterCard began to challenge Visa's traditional advantage. Both Visa and BBDO knew it was time to make a move.

Though their immediate concern was the encroachment by MasterCard, after some thinking, BBDO and Visa realized they could

At Bret's Skysailing, you can't soar without a little daring, and you can't soar at all with American Express.

While most of his friends were just learning to drive, Bret Willat was already flying solo in sailplanes.

Now, almost 20 years later, his passion for soaring is greater than ever. And after one ride at his Skysailing School just south of San Francisco, you'll learn why.

Riding on invisible waves of rising air, Bret will bank your two-seater silently over the northern California countryside. And if that journey sparks a desire in you, Bret can teach you to soar alone. To catch a thermal above nearby Mission Peak and spiral upward in wide, lazy circles. Then to drift earthward, landing softly as a bird.

So if you go there, bring your sense of adventure and your Visa card.

Because at Bret's, you can't soar above Mission Peak without a little daring, *and you can't soar at all with American Express.*

VISA

WORLDWIDE SPONSOR
1988 OLYMPIC GAMES

It's everywhere you want to be.

© Visa U.S.A. Inc. 1987

completely reshuffle the credit card deck.

"The real standard in this category is not MasterCard or Visa, it's American Express," DePaolo explains. "American Express has all of the attributes a credit card should have. We recognized there was less equity to be had by fighting MasterCard than by competing with American Express. That competition was something consumers were willing to accept, but which Visa and MasterCard

had just never aspired to."

A simple enough plan, but where was the chink in the American Express armor? In a little over three decades, American Express had grown into a behemoth behind a media juggernaut skillfully directed by Ogilvy & Mather. But sometimes when you're very good, people think you're a bit better than you actually are. They give you credit for services you don't and perhaps can't provide. Through its research, BBDO knew that

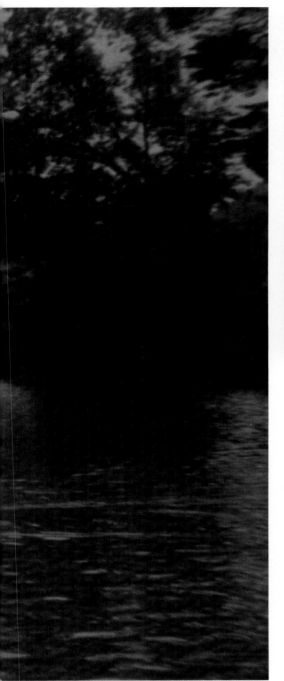

"Everywhere you want to be" is the tag line that summarizes Visa's brilliant flank attack on arch rivals American Express and MasterCard. The campaign was conceived as a television effort to give Visa the broadest possible reach across its huge base of cardholders. The spots feature the kinds of places consumers would expect their American Express cards to be accepted but where, in fact, they aren't. *France*, at left, features a Medieval chateau-turned-hotel in the majestic Loire Valley. The slightly soft focus, painterly effect of the photography romanticizes this presumably Visa-financed vacation superbly. *Boston,* above, exhorts viewers to visit a famous Beantown eatery, to bring their appetites and their Visa cards. Both succinctly make the point that many prestigious establishments don't accept American Express.

Tracking research confirms that the spots have increased consumer awareness of the appropriateness of using Visa in prestigious surroundings. It has also done something else: Presented an alternative to the Big Green Goliath. "American Express had blown away Carte Blanche and Diner's Club, and people felt a bit at the mercy of this monolith," says account supervisor DePaolo. "These spots helped them feel they had options."

consumers held some unrealistic expectations of American Express and its services.

BBDO saw this excess of confidence as an opportunity. There were enough misconceptions about American Express that merely pointing them out would enhance consumers' perception of Visa.

Obviously, when you're outnumbered you don't launch a general broadside attack. Instead, Visa would concentrate on one key attribute of people's

The Winter Games of the 1988 Olympics, to be held in Calgary, Alberta, Canada, presented Visa with an unparalleled opportunity. The Olympics have long been almost synonymous with American Express, but this time around, it's Visa who has the right to use the magic rings.

Visa launched an early promotion in the summer of 1987 urging consumers to "pull for the team." Visa promised to make a donation to the U.S. Olympic Team for each use of the Visa card.

Despite the high price tag of the Olympic deal, reported to be in the range of $10 million to $12 million, Visa stands to benefit tremendously from the heavy media coverage generated whenever the Olympics are held in North America.

experience with credit cards: Acceptance. And this was an area where Visa had a clear, if not complete, advantage.

The Visa card is accepted in substantially more locations than American Express. The reason is simple: American Express takes about a nickel of every dollar consumers charge on their cards. Visa takes about half that. Merchants make more money when consumers use Visa so more merchants accept it. At the time, Visa and MasterCard were about neck and neck in the number of locations accepting them, "But of course, we chose not to talk about MasterCard," DePaolo chuckles.

Beyond physical acceptance is the realm of psychological acceptance. "Our customers felt Visa was more appropriate for use in everyday retail trade, to buy socks or tires or whatever," DePaolo points out. "They felt Visa was less appropriate in more prestigious surroundings. In **restaurants and upscale retail stores, those with dual cards would use American Express simply because of the statement it** made about them. Ironically, the cardholders were reluctant to use their Visa cards even though merchants would accept it, and in fact many preferred Visa."

The strategy? Use Visa's advantage in physical acceptance to enhance the card's prestige.

To dispel the most dominant myth that American Express is accepted everywhere, BBDO created a series of television spots featuring places where consumers would expect American Express to be accepted, but of course isn't. The first round of executions included a luxurious chateau in France, a famous seafood restaurant in Boston and a sports shop in Florida. The tag line: "Visa: It's everywhere you want to be."

"We picked places people associate with American Express and added the provocative wrinkle that these were places where American Express was not accepted," DePaolo says.

The result was immediate and "wonderful."

"People reacted positively in almost every way we could measure," DePaolo recounts. The agency's subsequent research shows that Visa's physical and psychological acceptance has improved and that its international capabilities are more appreciated.

The campaign has had another, unexpected, effect. The retailers love it. "It flatters them and upgrades their image," DePaolo points out. "Our merchants write in asking to be considered for the campaign. Some of them have even offered to drop American Express so they can be considered."

In addition to stroking the merchant base, the campaign has proved very popular with Visa's member banks. Unlike American Express, Visa is a network of more than 18,000 institutions licensed to use the Visa name and issue Visa cards. DePaolo says BBDO has received numerous requests for twenty-three-second executions the banks can tag and run in their local markets.

In 1987, the campaign moved to a whole new level with Visa's purchase of the exclusive rights to the Winter Games of the 1988 Olympics to be held in Calgary, Alberta, Canada. The quadrennial gladiatorial contest has long been synonymous with American Express. Not only did Visa get the right to use the Olympic rings, it picked up two very choice plums in the negotiations: That Visa would be the only credit card and Visa travelers checks would be the only travelers checks accepted at Olympic sites. In past years, those privileges have belonged to American Express.

"The strategic correctness of the Olympics is that it was everywhere we wanted to be psychologically, that it has traditionally been an American Express venue, and that we could pass the use of the Olympic marks along to our member banks," DePaolo avers.

Of course, no one has publicly confirmed the price for all that correctness, but sources estimate that Visa paid in the range of $10 million to $12 million for the rights. That's no small change, but DePaolo thinks the value Visa received was well worth the asking price.

"Clearly we can get more out of an association with the Olympics than American Express can," he explains. "American Express has always enjoyed the advantage of being able to act unilaterally. Visa's always had to have ideas its franchisees could get behind. Despite their advantage, American Express had difficulty converting its Olympic association to real use. We're able to do that through the franchise network. Any bank that advertises in the context of Visa can promote the fact that it's a sponsor of the Olympics.

"In the past, when Visa has had a promotional program, they would offer it to the members and say 'use it if you like it.' The Olympics gives each of those members a role to play in a world-wide promotional program. They can participate directly in the fund-raising. It's very powerful and it's put Visa in a leadership position with its franchisees."

In the summer of 1987, BBDO began airing an umbrella ad exhorting consumers to use their Visa cards. It promised that, each time they used the card, Visa would make a donation to the U.S. Olympic team. Captioned "pull for the team," it featured a montage of footage of athletes preparing for the games.

"We wanted an early and obvious association with the Olympics, but we didn't want to just be a guy who bought the rings and put them on a box," DePaolo says. "We wanted to show what was really happening during the summer, the athletes in strenuous training. The message to the viewer is that, if you like what this person's doing, working hard to improve their

When You Go From Cutting Figure Eights To Cutting Dea

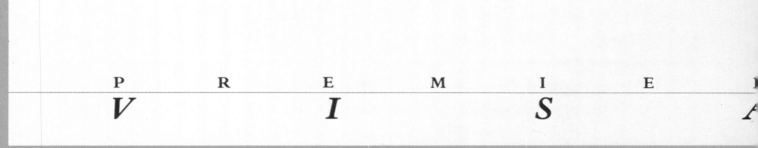

P R E M I E
V I S A

Competing with American Express meant more than pointing out its shortcomings. Visa needed a premium-class product to face off against the American Express Gold card and a vigorous travelers check program as well. Olympians Ken Shelley and JoJo Starbuck were a natural for this spread promoting the new Premier Visa, a service similar to the American Express Gold card.

As with other parts of the campaign, BBDO tries to identify Visa with people and with lifestyles that will increase the card's prestige.

When they were cutting figures in U.S. Pairs Competition, they drew raves for their style. Now that JoJo Starbuck and Ken Shelley have paired up in business, nothing much has changed. Their new production company, 'The Skate Source', has gained accolades from L.A. to D.C. by providing everything from ice-skating showgirls to entire ice-skating shows.

Outperforming American Express Gold.

Now that they've gone from single axels to big wheels, they've gone to the Premier Visa® Card. Because whether they're designing a show in Butte, or taking in a show back home on Broadway, they know the Premier Visa Card is accepted in four times as many places worldwide as American Express Gold. And it comes with a minimum starting credit line that's over twice as high.

Also, with access to emergency cash at over five times as many banks and cash machines, they're never on thin ice.

How To Get Premier Treatment.

If this sounds good to you, and you're ready to enjoy these advantages, apply for a Premier Visa Card today. Whether you're doing business or just doing the town, it's the right move.

It's Everywhere You Want To Be.

© Visa U.S.A. Inc. 1987

How to get cash in five times as many places as American Express.

Whether you need rupees for a rug in Kashmir, or dollars for an emergency in Seattle, there are over 200,000 places worldwide where your Visa® card means cash.

The Visa symbol means you have instant access to dollars or drachmas, cruzeiros or pesos at over 190,000 banks in the U.S. and abroad.

That's more than five times as many places around the world as *American Express.*

There are also over 15,000 cash machines where you just enter your personal I.D. number and Visa card, and you leave with cash.

Next time you travel, look for the Visa symbol. It means easy access to cash in any language.

VISA **It's everywhere you want to be.**

WORLDWIDE SPONSOR 1988 OLYMPIC GAMES

© Visa U.S.A. Inc. 1987

While the television spots have focused almost exclusively on the standard Visa, these print ads extend the "everywhere you want to be" theme to new products. BBDO's DePaolo stresses that while some parts of the Visa campaign exist only in print, Visa's budget won't cover a full-fledged multi-media schedule. Print is used to reach people who don't watch much television and to articulate some of the campaign's sub-themes.

It's everywhere you want to be.

Diversity—of lifestyles, uses and even financial products—is a cornerstone of the campaign. The "Doorways" ad (opposite) was the opening salvo in a broadside directed against the American Express travel products business. Given the ambivalence of many bankers toward American Express' entry into retail banking, Visa stands a good chance of making a dent in the travelers check segment in particular, as travelers checks are sold almost exclusively through banks, many of them Visa franchisees themselves.

performance at the Games, do the easy thing and help them by using your Visa card. We tried to put together a package that would be somewhat inspirational."

It had better be. American Express and MasterCard can't be counted on to sit still for this kind of promotional abuse for very long. Both have shown signs of mustering a counterpunch to take the edge off of the effectiveness of Visa's advertising.

In the fall of 1987, MasterCard countered Visa's "pull for the team" spots with an offer to donate money to charity each time cardholders use MasterCard. For the time being, it has dropped its celebrity endorsers altogether, as has American Express. Perhaps feeling a little hot breath on its neck, American Express stepped up introduction of auxiliary services for cardholders and released a slew of new executions designed to justify the expense of the green card and bolster the sagging cache of the gold card.

The retail credit segment gets more crowded every year. Along with revamped advertising from its traditional competitors, the Sears/Dean Witter Discover card and the American Express Optima card promise to help make life interesting for BBDO and Visa during 1988. But in a fundamental way, this campaign has helped turn the tables on the giants. Despite its lower media budgets, Visa has effectively used "everywhere you want to be" to position itself as a serious threat to American Express.

In the meantime, BBDO has taken great pains to pre-position Visa's Olympic tie-in so the client won't get lost in the welter of Olympic advertising that's almost certain to glut the airwaves in early 1988. When the world media shows up in Calgary, it is the Visa logo their cameras will be picking up at the bottom of the Giant Slolom, at the bottom of the jumping hill and around the sides of the speed skating arena. Those are places any advertiser would like to be.

Visa. The key that opens millions of doors worldwide.

You'll find the Visa name on millions of the world's most marvelous doorways.

Doorways that open to the silver jewelry of Taxco, Mexico. To the richly woven tweeds of Scotland or to the best blackened redfish you ever had in New Orleans.

And when the Visa name is on your travelers cheque, you can travel with confidence. Because it's nice to know you'll see this name on more than five million doorways around the world.

VISA

It's everywhere you want to be.®

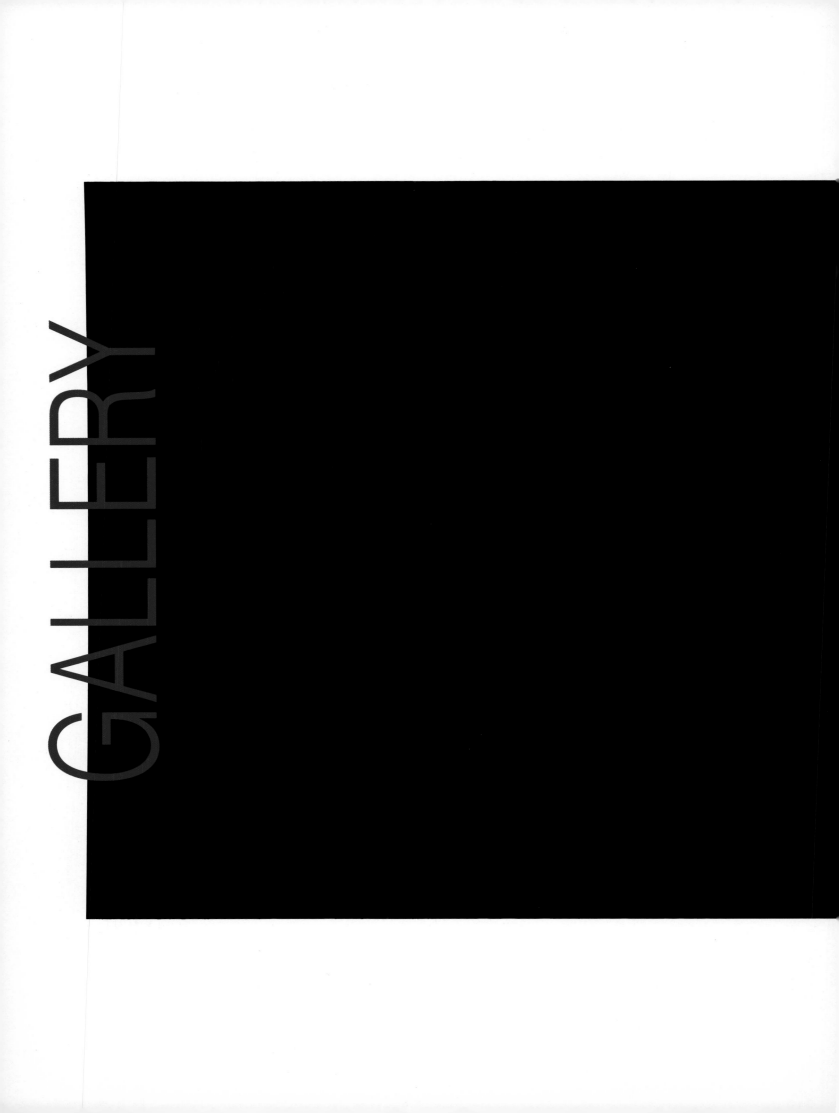

GALLERY

214 Campaigns!

Client: National Federation of
Coffee Growers of Colombia
Agency: DDB Needham Worldwide

In a series of print ads, DDB cleverly points out that nothing is more valuable than 100% Colombian coffee. The executions have retained Juan Valdez, the association's long-time mythical spokesperson as an icon, but have taken an entirely new tack, emphasizing taste and sophistication. The executions are engaging visual puns. The quality of the photography is superb and the consistent format of the pieces makes each quickly recognizable as part of the campaign. A television execution based on one of the ads shows a jetliner against a clear blue sky. As the captain talks to the passengers over the intercom, a stewardess informs him that they've taken off without the Colombian coffee. The jet makes a U-turn in mid-air, presumably heading back to the airport.

The only coffee to go with your Danish.

The richest coffee in the world.™

Remember the last time someone had a party without Colombian Coffee?

Luckily, the Colombian Coffee hadn't been poured.

100% Colombian Coffee

The richest coffee in the world.

Amaretto di Legere

56 proof © 1987, Imported by The Paddington Corporation, Fort Lee, NJ Photo: Ken Nahoum.

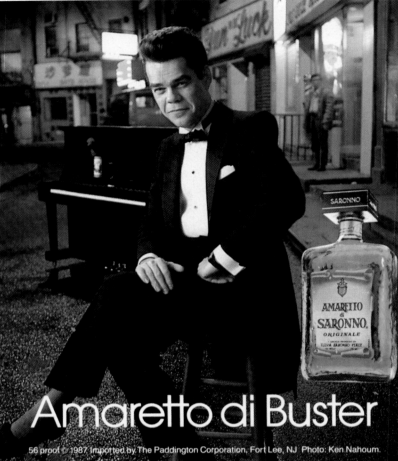

Amaretto di Buster

56 proof © 1987, Imported by The Paddington Corporation, Fort Lee, NJ Photo: Ken Nahoum.

Client: The Paddington Corporation
Agency: Geer, Dubois Inc.

There's breakthrough advertising and then there's breakaway advertising. Geer, Dubois' campaign for Amaretto di Saronno definitely falls into the second category. Previous ads for the almond-flavored liqueur have emphasized the Renaissance tradition and Italian origin of the beverage. Paddington, which imports the brand into the U.S., asked the agency for a campaign that would appeal to upwardly mobile 21- to 35-year-olds.

Amaretto di Saronno sounds ponderous and a bit overwhelming, especially to a group raised on light beers and wine coolers. First, the creative team played around with the name of the product, calling it Amaretto De-troit and a few other things, then switched to using celebrities instead. The celebrities chosen are themselves young and upwardly mobile; some are just barely well-known enough to qualify as celebrities.

The celebrities and the unusual approach garnered a fair amount of publicity, including short squibs in *USA Today* and the *New York Post*.

Amaretto di Carol

To send a gift of Amaretto di Saronno anywhere in the U.S. call 1-800-243-3787.
56 proof © 1987, Imported by The Paddington Corporation. Fort Lee, NJ. Photo: Ken Nahoum.

Amaretto di Kid Creole

56 proof © 1987, Imported by The Paddington Corporation, Fort Lee, NJ Photo: Ken Nahoum.

Amaretto di Alt

To send a gift of Amaretto di Saronno anywhere in the U.S. call 1-800-243-3787.
56 proof © 1988, Imported by The Paddington Corporation, Fort Lee, NJ. Photo: Ken Nahoum.

Create a new world where lightweight plastics can outfly metals.

Aerospace designers are limited by their materials, not their dreams.

At BASF, we looked at the design limitations of metals and saw the need for a radically new generation of materials. The result: strong, lightweight, carbon fiber reinforced plastics. These Advanced Composite Materials will enable future designs to carry more, faster, farther.

In one industry after another, from aerospace to automotive, our broad-based technologies help us create new worlds by seeing in new ways.

The Spirit of Innovation

Client: BASF Corporation
Agency: Geer, Dubois Inc.

Create a new world where nature "thinks" like a farmer.

A quarter of North America's potential cotton crop is ruined each year by weeds, insects, disease.

At BASF, we looked at the problem in new ways and saw the cotton plant's environment as an ally. The result was a BASF breakthrough: Pix® Plant Regulator. Pix causes nature to rethink the plant's growth. Incorporating natural defenses, the plant and farmer work together toward a healthier, more bountiful harvest.

In one industry after another, from agribusiness to textiles, our broad-based technologies help us create new worlds by seeing in new ways.

The Spirit of Innovation

BASF

Client: BASF Corporation
Agency: Geer, Dubois Inc.

Following a corporate reorganization in 1986, BASF Corporation asked its agency, Geer, Dubois, for a new campaign that would both communicate the company's diversity and create a unified image.

The agency's solution was a series of striking, surrealistic print ads, each showcasing a different aspect of BASF. The illustrations were executed by artists (such as Wilson McLean, previous spread) who do very little commercial work. The budget for the effort—launched in fall of 1987—was set at $8 million over two years, and will include television.

Client: Blue Chip Electronics
Agency: WFC

When this piece broke, IBM owned the business PC market. As the original IBM model was at the end of its product cycle, WFC creative director Charlie Thomas felt Blue Chip, an IBM work-alike computer manufactured in Korea, could grab some market share by emphasizing the fact that it offered more features than the IBM at less than half the price.

We've got bad news for everyone who just bought an IBM PC.

◎ BLUE CHIP

Client: Twenty-Twenty Restaurant
Agency: Heinrich + Sills

This is a *very* New York ad for a trendy New York restaurant. New Yorkers have grown accustomed to seeing a sinister form of graffiti, a shadow painted on a wall. Come across one in a dark street at midnight and it will scare the hell out of you. Who knows what food lurks in the heart of Manhattan? This shadow knows.

Pop Secret.
It's the only way to pop.™

Pop·Secret® microwave popcorn.
It's fresh. It's light. It's fluffy.
It's perfect popcorn popped
under perfect conditions.
So you get great popcorn
without a lot of unpopped
kernels. Get Pop·Secret.
And get popping.

NEW, IMPROVED CORN. POPS LIGHTER AND FLUFFIER THAN EVER.

Mills, Inc.

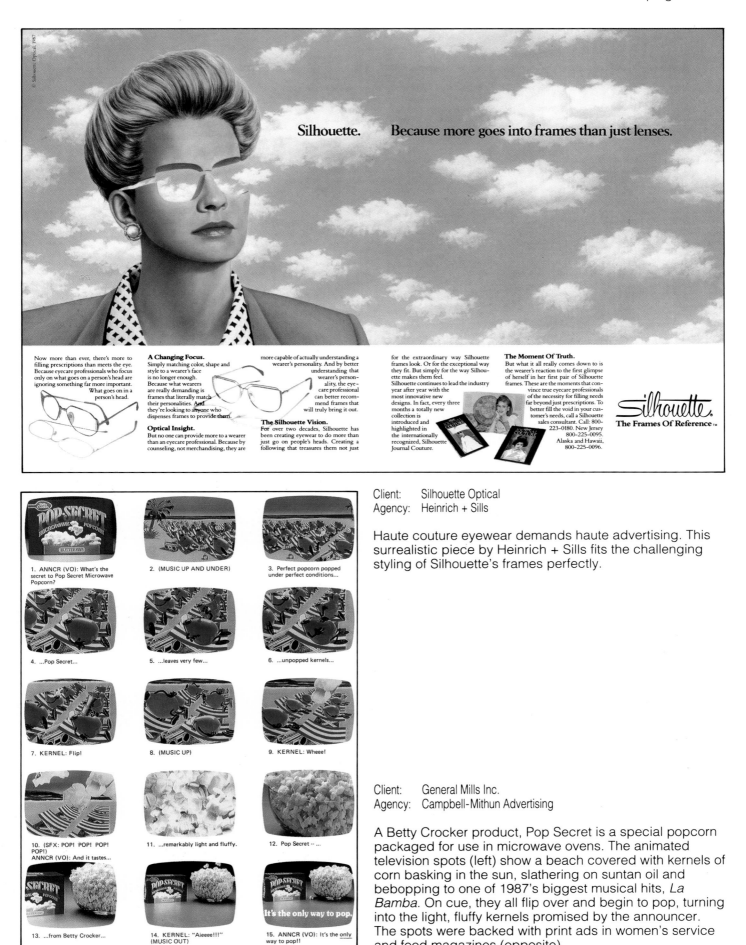

© Silhouette Optical 1987

Silhouette. Because more goes into frames than just lenses.

A Changing Focus.
Now more than ever, there's more to filling prescriptions than meets the eye. Because eyecare professionals who focus only on what goes on a person's head are ignoring something far more important. What goes on in a person's head.

Simply matching color, shape and style to a wearer's face is no longer enough. Because what wearers are really demanding is frames that literally match their personalities. And they're looking to anyone who dispenses frames to provide them.

Optical Insight.
But no one can provide more to a wearer than an eyecare professional. Because by counseling, not merchandising, they are

more capable of actually understanding a wearer's personality. And by better understanding that wearer's personality, the eyecare professional can better recommend frames that will truly bring it out.

The Silhouette Vision.
For over two decades, Silhouette has been creating eyewear to do more than just go on people's heads. Creating a following that treasures them not just

for the extraordinary way Silhouette frames look. Or for the exceptional way they fit. But simply for the way Silhouette makes them feel. Silhouette continues to lead the industry year after year with the most innovative new designs. In fact, every three months a totally new collection is introduced and highlighted in the internationally recognized, Silhouette Journal Couture.

The Moment Of Truth.
But what it all really comes down to is the wearer's reaction to the first glimpse of herself in her first pair of Silhouette frames. These are the moments that convince true eyecare professionals of the necessity for filling needs far beyond just prescriptions. To better fill the void in your customer's needs, call a Silhouette sales consultant. Call: 800-223-0180. New Jersey 800-225-0095. Alaska and Hawaii, 800-225-0096.

Silhouette
The Frames Of Reference™

Storyboard panels (left):

1. ANNCR (VO): What's the secret to Pop Secret Microwave Popcorn?
2. (MUSIC UP AND UNDER)
3. Perfect popcorn popped under perfect conditions...
4. ...Pop Secret...
5. ...leaves very few...
6. ...unpopped kernels...
7. KERNEL: Flip!
8. (MUSIC UP)
9. KERNEL: Wheee!
10. (SFX: POP! POP! POP! POP!) ANNCR (VO): And it tastes...
11. ...remarkably light and fluffy.
12. Pop Secret --...
13. ...from Betty Crocker...
14. KERNEL: "Aieeee!!!" (MUSIC OUT)
15. ANNCR (VO): It's the only way to pop!!

Client: Silhouette Optical
Agency: Heinrich + Sills

Haute couture eyewear demands haute advertising. This surrealistic piece by Heinrich + Sills fits the challenging styling of Silhouette's frames perfectly.

Client: General Mills Inc.
Agency: Campbell-Mithun Advertising

A Betty Crocker product, Pop Secret is a special popcorn packaged for use in microwave ovens. The animated television spots (left) show a beach covered with kernels of corn basking in the sun, slathering on suntan oil and bebopping to one of 1987's biggest musical hits, *La Bamba*. On cue, they all flip over and begin to pop, turning into the light, fluffy kernels promised by the announcer. The spots were backed with print ads in women's service and food magazines (opposite).

Every company has its own personality.

Maybe it's conservative.
Or flamboyant.
Or maybe it's conservative and flamboyant.
The point is your office furniture should be able to say: "This is the kind of company we are."
Something Knoll Office systems and seating happen to do very well.
They can suit almost any personality. Open plan office, private office or data processing center. From the receptionist to the CEO.
And to give all those offices their own personalities, you can choose from wood veneers like mahogany and maple. Fabrics and plastic laminates. And colors from beige to shades that can please the most flamboyant chairman of the board.
At Knoll, we offer everything from systems to seating and from desks to textiles. As well as the service that makes managing your office a lot easier.
Call 1-800-633-0034 to talk with a representative or authorized dealer nearest you.
(We promise he won't have green hair.)

Knoll

Client: Knoll International
Agency: Goldsmith/Jeffrey

We're used to seeing furniture ads that emulate the liquor bottle and glass genre—happy employees, creamy-smooth photos of dividers, modesty panels and executive chairs. Goldsmith/Jeffrey took a radically different approach in their series of print executions for Knoll. Instead of focusing on product, it focuses on users. The illustrations rely on shock value to catch your attention, and the relatively short copy is brief and to the point.

Other pieces in the series included a collage of workers caught in a visual whirlwind. The unexpected graphics are a delightful change of pace for viewers wading through the somewhat stodgy business books which are the primary venue for Knoll and its competitors.

Client: Wisconsin State Fair
Agency: William Eisner & Associates

One in a series of toungue-in-cheek ads for the Wisconsin State Fair, this poster cleverly parodies the popular Bartles & Jaymes Wine Cooler ads produced by Hal Riney & Partners of San Francisco. This is a perfect example of how advertising creates its own mythology and icons. Once they become part of the popular culture they are, of course, fair and productive targets for other advertisers.

LADIES.
MY NAME IS BRIAN.
AND I'M ASKING YOU
TO STOP WEARING
ALL THIS WILD
NATURAL WONDER
MAKEUP IT'S LIKE—
COLOR OUT OF CONTROL. THE
SIMPLE FACT IS—I CAN'T TAKE IT.
CALL ME WEAK, I'LL ADMIT IT.
BUT WHEN I SEE A GIRL IN THAT
'TIGER EYE' LIPSTICK WITH THAT
'HOT SHOT RED' EYESHADOW, I
JUST—WELL I KINDA MAKE A FOOL
OF MYSELF. I KNOW THE MAKEUP
IS GOOD FOR YOUR SKIN,

"PURE WAS NEVER SO PRETTY"
AND ALL THAT. BUT A GUY
CAN ONLY TAKE SO MANY
GORGEOUS COLORED LIPS AND EYES AND CHEEKS AND NAILS BEFORE HE...WELL,   BEFORE SOMETHING HAPPENS. THINK ABOUT IT.   100% PURE COLOR COSMETICS.

PURE WAS NEVER SO PRETTY *Natural Wonder*

Client: Revlon
Agency: Bozell, Jacobs, Kenyon & Eckhardt/New York

It's hard to be a guy in the 1980s. Take Brian (above) for example. The poor guy can't even walk down the street without being mesmerized by a woman wearing one of the wild new colors from Revlon. That's serious. The ads, however, are wonderfully flippant and do a great job of displaying Revlon's colorful cosmetics. The consolation in this, for Brian and the rest of us, is that contrary to what they may say, women still work hard to make themselves attractive to men.

Client: Sea Ray Boats, Inc.
Agency: Heinrich + Sills

A clever headline and dramatic lighting make this ad for Sea Ray (opposite, above) a welcome and effective departure from the mass of boat advertising. The copy concentrates on how good the Sea Ray will make its owner look—an important consideration for anyone willing to fork out the bucks for a high-powered muscle boat.

Client: Remington Arms Company, Inc.
Agency: Rumrill-Hoyt

To introduce Remington's new line of hunting clothes and accessories, Rumrill-Hoyt prepared a series of three spread ads. The three clothing systems were developed for the three major types of hunters: big game, waterfowl and upland game. There has been a resurgence in interest in serious hunting as a sport, perhaps reflective of America's "return to traditional values" and perhaps of hunting's appeal as a manly sport.

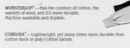

Client: Mita Copiers
Agency: HCM

The point is, folks, that, unlike its
rivals (Minolta, Ricoh, Panasonic),
Mita makes just one product—office
copiers. To make that point,
copywriter Patti Goldberg and art
director Richard Ostroff proposed a
series of thirty-second spots
featuring stereos, microwaves and all
the assorted high-tech bric-a-brac
made by the other guys being
obliterated in unusual ways.
Accordingly, one spot (above) has
football player Manuel Perry crushing
a cassette player, a camera being
run over by a steam roller, a
microwave being eaten by a shark
and a portable stereo exploding on
screen. It's all choreographed to a
version of a 1967 hit *Nobody But Me*.
The words, however, are pure
product: "We don't make vacuum
cleaners like they do; we don't make
cameras like they do; just copiers,
just copiers...." It's all very
entertaining and, for neo-Luddites in
the audience, hopefully prophetic.

HISS AND HERS.
WOODLAND PARK ZOO

I do business a little differently
than the heads of the other big seed
companies.
    Last year, for example, I drove
50,000 miles, met 50,000 farmers and
wore out my favorite pair of shoes...
just to make sure our hybrids are
the best you can plant.
    The other guys wear out business
suits in high-level meetings. I wear
out shoes looking at corn and talking
with farmers.

David Garst

I know what it's like to be in your shoes.

GARST
SEED COMPANY

Box 300
Coon Rapids, Iowa 50058

Client: Woodland Park Zoo, Seattle
Agency: Livingston & Company

If everybody hates snakes, why did this painted billboard turn up on almost every list of excellent advertising compiled this year? Aside from the obvious visual tension created by the facing snakes and their brilliant color, it makes reptiles almost—well, almost friendly. It's enough to make even the crankiest herpetologist happy.

Client: Garst Seed Company
Agency: Valentine-Radford

Empathy is the appeal of this striking trade ad for Garst Seed. Use of actual typewriter type gives the ad a homey, personalized flavor that would be hard to convey with standard typefaces. The copy stresses David Garst's personal understanding of his customers' problems.

Client: El Greco, Inc.
Agency: Janklow Bender

Candies, a comparatively recent entry in the women's footwear market, has made its mark with unusual advertising. The combination of a black-and-white photo of the model and color in the shoe effectively puts the focus right on the product in an arresting fashion. The use of black and white with color is not unique, but it is more appropriate and more deftly handled here than in executions for some other products.

Client: Gates-Mills
Agency: Janklow Bender

It's so easy to make product ads that are boring. It's refreshing to find an agency who's found a way to freshen up a concept. From the outside, Gates gloves look just like those produced by dozens of other companies. But inside, there is a terrific product story. The spread (below) was made up from two separate pages which ran in skiing magazines. They were reprinted with a cover (right) and used as a dealer promotion as well.

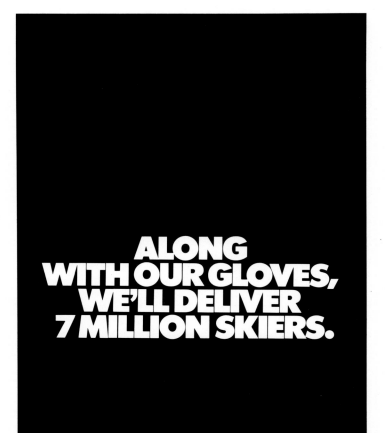

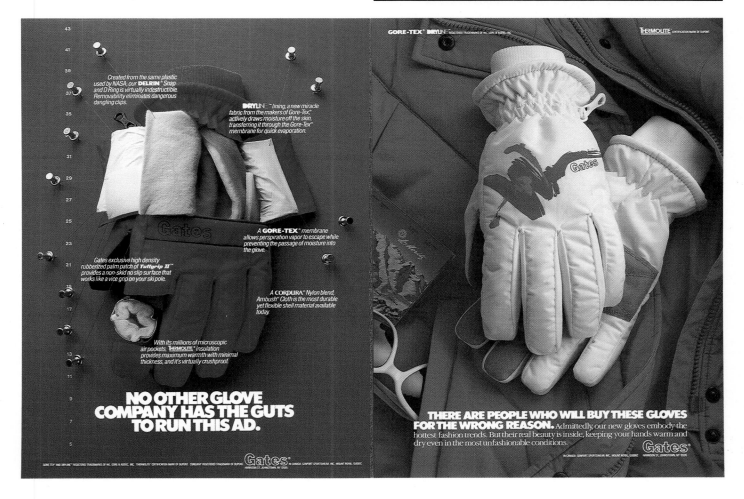

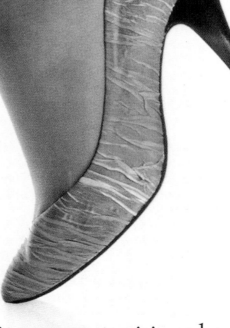

Think of it as a dramatic ending to an exciting short story.

Candie's

In the 9th century, a group of Vikings discovered an island. An island they wanted to keep to themselves. So they gave it the most unappealing name a Viking could think of. A name that has fooled mankind for over a thousand years. Iceland.

Client: Glenmore Distilleries
Agency: Grybauskus & Partners

The mail pieces (above) and print ad (right) are part of an innovative introductory campaign for Elduris Icelandic vodka which broke in September 1987. The upscale drinkers targeted by Glenmore are not easily influenced by large-scale media campaigns, so Grybauskus created a combination direct mail/media effort. Teaser postcards (upper left) were mailed to more than 100,000 households in the East Coast test markets. They were followed a few weeks later by the booklet (top), which uses photos and text about Iceland to pique consumers' interest in the country and in Elduris vodka. Finally, print ads (right) appeared in a variety of regional publications.

MEANY, M

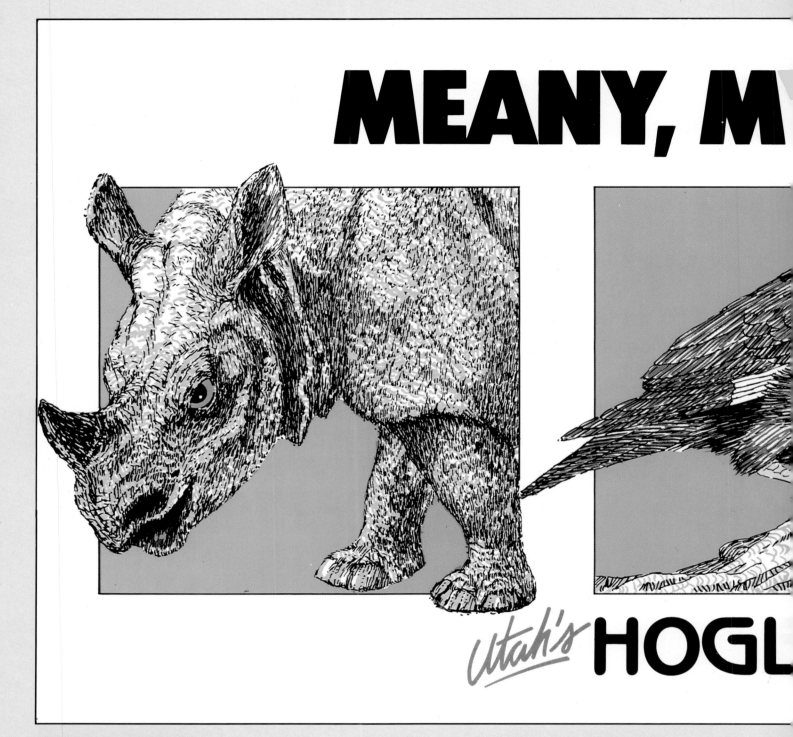

Utah's HOGL

Client: Hogle Zoo, Salt Lake City
Agency: Fotheringham & Associates

A simple but powerful *pro bono* campaign, these two pieces are part of six billboards done for the Hogle Zoo. The charming renderings of the zoo's inhabitants were combined with thirty- and sixty-second television and radio spots to help boost attendance.

WADDLE, WIGGLE, JIGGLE.

Utah's HOGLE ZOO

YNA, MOLE.

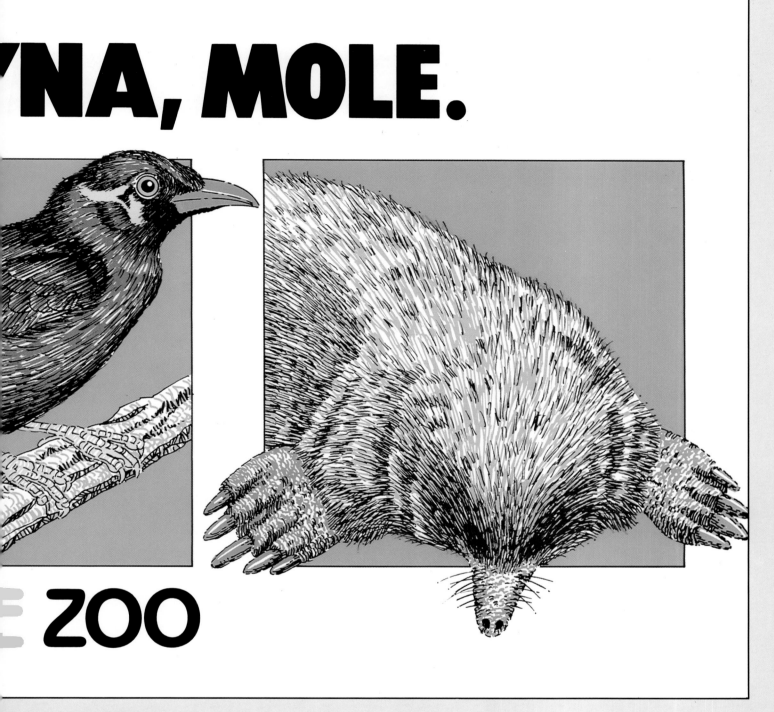

ZOO

Client: Northwest Airlines
Agency: DFS Dorland/Minneapolis

They just don't teach geography in American schools anymore. Do you know the relative positions of Java and New Guinea? Which is closer to Australia: Taiwan or the Philippines? Illustrator John Eggert's masks (overleaf) simplify the matter by appealing directly to the viewer's sense of romance—displaying a wealth of destinations and suggesting their variety. This is a welcome relief from the standard blue-water-sandy-beach school of destination advertising and especially from the oversupply of atlas-style route maps that too frequently turn up in this genre.

Northwest covers

Osaka

Tokyo

Hong Kong

Seoul

Bangkok

Guam

the face of Asia.

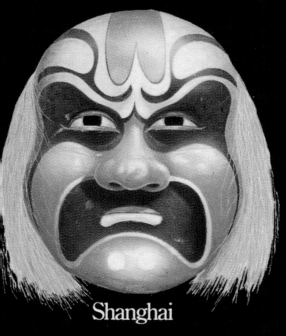

Taipei

Okinawa

Manila

Shanghai

No matter how you look at it, Northwest has Asia covered. With convenient service from over 200 U.S. cities.

Including nonstops from New York, Chicago, Seattle, San Francisco, Los Angeles, Detroit and Honolulu.

And we're the only U.S. airline to give you the comforts of an all-747 transpacific fleet. The luxuries of Regal Imperial service. The experience of 40 years of flying to Asia. And the rewards of our WORLDPERKS℠ frequent flyer program, which gives you the fastest free trip of any major airline.

These are just some of the reasons why we're America's number one choice to Asia.

So if you're looking for a familiar face in the Far East, call your travel agent or call Northwest at (800) 447-4747 for international reservations.

Look to us.

NORTHWEST

Red Cabbage

What turns a tasty dip into "one of life's finer pleasures™?" GREY POUPON® Dijon Mustard, but of course! Of course you can spread it on a ham croissant sandwich, stir it into lentil soup, ladle it over Steak Diane too!

For these and other Grey Poupon recipe suggestions, send your name, address and $1 to: Grey Poupon

Recipe Book, P.O. Box 7120, Clinton, IA 52736.*
Vegetables with Dijon Mayonnaise
Blend 2 egg yolks, 3 Tbsp. Grey Poupon® Dijon Mustard, 1 Tbsp. white wine vinegar and 1 tsp. dill weed in blender for 3 seconds. Slowly add 1 cup oil, blending until smooth. Serve in small red cabbage with assorted vegetables. 1½ cups.

Grey Poupon®

Green Onion

What turns a great appetizer into "one of life's finer pleasures™?" GREY POUPON® Dijon Mustard, but of course! Of course you can spread it on a ham croissant sandwich, stir it into lentil soup, ladle it over Steak Diane too!

We're serving up a whole book of other Grey Poupon recipe suggestions. Send your name, address and

$1 to: Grey Poupon Recipe Book, P.O. Box 7120, Clinton, IA 52736.*
Dijon Green Onion Appetizers
Mix 1 cup mayonnaise, ½ cup grated Parmesan cheese and 2 Tbsp. Grey Poupon® Dijon Mustard. Spread 2 tsp. on slices of French bread. Broil until lightly browned. Garnish with green onion and ripe olives. 40 appetizers.

Grey Poupon®

White Meat

What turns a tender chicken dish into "one of life's finer pleasures™?" GREY POUPON® Dijon Mustard, but of course! Of course you can spread it on a ham croissant sandwich, stir it into lentil soup, ladle it over Steak Diane too!

We're serving up a whole book of other Grey Poupon recipe suggestions. Send your name, address and

$1 to: Grey Poupon Recipe Book, P.O. Box 7120, Clinton, IA 52736.*
Grey Poupon Dijon & Herb Marinade
Combine ¼ cup Grey Poupon® Dijon Mustard, ½ cup white wine vinegar, 2 Tbsp. minced fresh onion, 1 minced garlic clove, ¼ tsp. crushed rosemary. Marinate 45 minutes and grill. ¾ cup.

Grey Poupon®

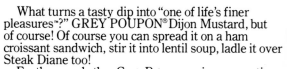

Client: Nabisco Brands, Inc.
Agency: Lowe Marschalk/San Francisco

A splashy print and television campaign have catapulted Grey Poupon to the front ranks of the Dijon mustard category. While mustard sales overall grow less than 5% per year, the Dijon category has been growing in double digits. The campaign began with a series of television executions linking Grey Poupon to well-known symbols of class and distinction: Rolls Royce cars, the Orient Express. The latest, *Gondola* (lower right) features a couple dining in a gondola on the Grand Canal in Venice. Another gondola floats past and the couple in it ask if the diners have any Grey Poupon. "But of course," they reply, repeating the payoff phrase of the video spots.

The agency cleverly leveraged the popularity of nouvelle foods in this series of print executions, stunning in their simplicity. The brilliantly-colored foods and heavy saturation in the photographs make these two-thirds page ads so appetizing they visually dominate whatever is placed next to them, giving the brand the impact of a full-page ad at a much lower cost.

"Well, now that you've drawn my attention..."

MOLSON MAKES IT GOLDEN

Molson Golden beer and ale. The #1 import from Canada. Brewed and bottled by North America's oldest brewery. Martlet Importing Co., Inc., North Hills, N.Y. © 1986.

How to buy a brush.

From head to toe. Use the American Express® Card
for just about everything you want to buy. Whether
you're at a big store or combing through small
boutiques. So next time you're off to shop, pull it
off with style by using the American Express Card.

Don't leave home without it.

This is your brain,

this is drugs,

this is your brain on drugs.

Partnership For A Drug-Free America   N.Y., NY 10017

Client: American Express Corp.
Agency: Ogilvy & Mather

Consumers sometimes "save" their American Express cards
for use only when dining or in expensive retail stores. This
piece (above) was part of a series in which celebrities urge
cardholders to use their plastic for more mundane items,
such as Crystal Gale's hairbrush.

Client: Martlett Importing Co.
Agency: Dancer, Fitzgerald, Sample

When agency DFS was asked to
reproduce its witty sixty-second
radio spots as print ads (opposite),
they were able to distill the essence
of the script to a single headline.
Combined with a dramatic fisheye
view of a deserted beach, it makes
for a striking visual counterpart to the
well-known radio campaign.

Client: Partnership For A Drug Free America
Agency: Keye/Donna/Pearlstein

Another adaptation of a broadcast
spot, this public service piece
inveighs against the use of drugs.
The point is simple and direct. It's
illustrated in a way that even an
adolescent who's partially brain-
damaged from listening to
Whitesnake albums at excessively
high volume can grasp and perhaps
appreciate.

Galileo often contemplated whether Löwenbräu's formula for the best way in the world to brew beer was also the best way in the universe.

In a little known footnote to Galileo's busy career as inventor, physicist, and astronomer, it was also discovered that he was an expert on beer and its relationships to the universe. "The Madman," as Galileo was known to friends, scientifically concluded during in-depth taste tests, that Löwenbräu's Bavarian supervision, plus the richness of Bavarian hops brewed fresh and smooth, was truly the best way in the world to brew beer.

Tragically, Galileo's findings were destroyed in what is now known as the "Big Löwenbräu Bash of 1593" at which his soon-to-be-former girlfriend, Sophie, spilled beer all over the records. Luckily, by conducting your own taste tests with Löwenbräu today, you'll realize what Galileo did hundreds of years ago... it's the best way in the world to brew beer.

This World Calls for Löwenbräu.

Realizing he couldn't imitate Löwenbräu's formula for the best way in the world to brew beer, Leonardo decided to invent stuff.

Little known to most historians is the time Leonardo went into the brewing business with a beer called "Leonbräu." Because he considered Löwenbräu's formula of Bavarian supervision with the richness of Bavarian hops brewed fresh and smooth as the best way in the world to brew beer, he used it as a model. However, the Bavarian supervision would require... Bavarians. And he lived in a predominantly Italian neighborhood.

Sadness besieged him. For a time, all he would do was sit around his parents' basement and wait for Mona to call. Finally he snapped out of it and was heard to say, "Mama, Löwenbräu already invented the best way in the world to brew beer... so I'm goin' to invent stuff and take up painting too." His mother was heard to say, "You can start by painting the garage."

This World Calls for Löwenbräu.

Client: Miller Brewing Co.
Agency: J. Walter Thompson/Chicago

There are no sandlot football players, no volleyball teams, no smoky bars in this series of print executions for Lowenbrau. Celebrity endorsements, of course, are nothing new in beer ads, but what celebrities: Galileo, Leonardo da Vinci, Ludwig von Beethoven and Albert Einstein. Also, being dead, they don't get big royalty checks. The copy is very clever and the ball-point pen style illustrations are just informal enough to let readers know it's all in fun. The details in the illustrations are smashingly funny: Galileo gazing up at a constellation that looks like the Lowenbrau logo; Leonardo with a deskful of Leon-brau imitations; Ludwig playing piano in a singles bar. By far the wittiest is the rebus sketched out on Einstein's blackboard. It's better than most men's room graffiti.

After failing to master Löwenbräu's formula for the best way in the world to brew beer, Ludwig temporarily took a night job.

Like so many before him, Ludwig found that Löwenbräu's formula with rich Bavarian hops and Bavarian supervision was deceivingly simple. Late into the night he would experiment. A handful of hops here, several Bavarians there. But the concoctions never tasted quite like his beloved brew.

Taking a break from his experimentation, he'd climb onto his piano for some twelve bar blues. But finally he realized that he would never outbrew the great brewmasters of Löwenbräu. "I was livin' in fantasy-land, and I was about to be evicted," he later admitted.

After his career as a brewmaster ended on sour note, Ludwig took a job at Fidelio's, a popular Vienna singles bar. And each night, before last call, he'd lament with a swan song to his lost love, "The Brewmaster Blues." And as the lights went down, he'd say softly into the microphone, "Hey baby, it's the best way in the world to brew beer."

This World Calls for Löwenbräu.

INDEX

AGENCIES

PRODUCTS

GENERAL